# MY TRAVELS
# WITH WAGNER

## *Music as Balsam*
## *for the Soul*

CHRIS MCQUAID

Strategic Book Publishing and Rights Co.

Strategic Book Publishing and Rights Co., LLC
USA | Singapore
www.sbpra.net

For information about special discounts for bulk purchases, please contact Strategic Book Publishing and Rights Co., LLC Special Sales, at bookorder@sbpra.net.

ISBN: 978-1-68235-274-8

*Dedicated to the memory of Miriam Murphy, Dramatic Soprano.*
*The world's greatest Isolde.*

Photo credit: Sorcha Carroll

**Books by Chris McQuaid**
*Elegy for a Broken Soldier*
*My Travels with Wagner*

# CONTENTS

# ACKNOWLEDGEMENTS

My sincere thanks to Fergus Sheil for reading this story and writing a beautiful Foreword. Fergus is Director of Irish National Opera, a brilliant initiative which brought *Tristan und Isolde* to the Bord Gáis Energy Theatre in 2012. A miracle! I attended two of the three performances Each one was beautiful. I wish also to express my appreciation to journalist and author Bruce Arnold for reading the manuscript and for his very encouraging appraisal. Finally, this book would not have happened without the invaluable work, dedication and skill contributed by Imelda Conway-Duffy, writer, artist and friend.

# Foreword

It was bittersweet to read this book and write this foreword in the summer of 2020. At the time of writing, opera houses around the world are closed due to the catastrophic effect of the Covid-19 pandemic. A huge international machine of opera production that generates thousands of productions for millions of audience members has completely ground to a halt. The enforced stoppage has triggered some profound questions about the necessity of opera and all of the arts and of our importance or irrelevance for society. For those of us involved in producing opera, it's a moment where we reflect on why we do what we do and what are its deeper meanings and purposes.

In normal times we all enjoy a night out. For some we may go out for dinner or join friends for a drink and then head to the theatre to see an opera. We marvel at the skill of the singers, we are swept away with the power of the chorus, we are driven along by the engine of the orchestra. Occasionally a performance may linger in the mind for days, weeks or even years.

For many, however, opera is more than a night out. It has the power to move you, to challenge you, to reaffirm you, to unsettle you, to raise you to ecstasy or to devastate you beyond words. Most operatic characters are larger than life and they face choices, opportunities and threats that are bigger and more extreme than what we deal with in our day-to-day existence. Yet their choices inform us. Their emotions touch us. Their actions affect us and their fate moves us.

Many enthusiasts have a group of operas that they like to return to again and again, experiencing the same works, but each time looking at them and hearing the music anew. Each experience, even with the same opera, teaches us something fresh. I believe that this constant engagement enriches us as we make sense of our lives and the world around us. The hours spent with each opera give us a door into our own inner thoughts, wishes, fears, ambitions, loves and passions. It can be frightening to confront some of these, but like a bee to a flower we feel compelled to do so, each time experiencing deeper and deeper emotions.

In this book Chris McQuaid gives a disarmingly honest account of his life and how he is drawn again and again to Wagner's operas. Like most of Wagner's own characters, Chris describes himself as a flawed individual, afflicted with challenges in his own physical and mental health. But like the characters in a Wagner drama, he continues his journey forward, dealing with strife, overcoming obstacles, and charting a path forward. He knows both pain and ecstasy. Like Amfortas he has wounds that will not heal, yet he also knows the fulfilment of the holy grail of Wagner's intoxicating works.

Many people find deep meaning and revelation in great works of art. This book is a personal testament by Chris McQuaid giving a first-hand account of salvation through opera.

Fergus Sheil
Artistic Director
Irish National Opera
July 2020

# PREFACE

People adapt differently to traumatic experiences but for most people, trauma creates physical, mental and emotional problems that often remain unresolved; that can cripple a person for life. PTSD – post traumatic stress disorder – is more common than most medical professionals are willing to acknowledge – or even address. However, in the last decade, this condition has surfaced to such an extent that it cannot be ignored any longer. Military servicemen and women are, as usual to the forefront in bringing it to attention; from what was called shellshock that was first seen during World War One to every war since then, military service personnel have borne the brunt of mental illness due to trauma. But in the hundred-plus years since World War One, doctors do not yet make the connection between mental and physical illness resulting from trauma.

In 2014, *New York Times* Magazine published an article about what it called a "revolutionary" treatment for PTSD which includes an interview with a Dutch psychiatrist, Dr Bessel van der Kolk who runs a clinic in the United States for trauma victims. Dr van der Kolk claims that the way to treat psychological trauma was not through the mind but through the body. In so many cases, it was patients' bodies that had been grossly violated, and it was their bodies that had failed them, and it was their bodies that now crumpled under the slightest of stresses – diving for cover with every car alarm or seeing every stranger as an attacker in waiting. How could their minds possibly be healed if they found the bodies that enclosed those minds so intolerable?

"The single most important issue for traumatised people is to find a sense of safety in their own bodies. Unfortunately, most psychiatrists pay no attention whatsoever to sensate experiences. They simply do not agree that it matters."

Dr. Bessel van der Kolk, Boston-based Dutch Psychiatrist

Trauma affects the brain – physically – as well as the individual's thought processes of the mind: perception, emotion, determination, of memory and imagination which eventually affect the body. Even in my studies of psychology, I did not come across any reference to the vast array of effects of trauma on the human system as a whole. At this point – rather late in the day – I am in no doubt that many of my physical health issues arose from stored memories of trauma. Sadly, like Dr Bessel van der Kolk I have found that no medical professionals will explore or acknowledge this fact.

In 1965, I was nineteen years old, a young soldier, on peacekeeping duty overseas when I was sexually assaulted. The perpetrator of the crime was a fellow soldier. From then on living in a body that had failed me became intolerable; there were many times when I wanted to die. Thankfully, it is a tiny few that possess evil tendencies; most are decent human beings, capable of heroic deeds. Most soldiers bond, through shared hardships and through facing challenges together. Most soldiers are greater than themselves, their mutual love, as well as their fear is unspoken yet understood. Our shared brotherhood includes our scars, physical, psychological, neurological and spiritual. Bonding holds it all together, especially in the case of overseas service. and yet, the bonded group can be the loneliest place on earth. I never confided in anyone – inside or outside of the Irish Defence Forces – but some of my fellow soldiers understood and helped me when – and in ways – I least expected. I returned to education and my career advanced despite the all-pervasive depression and mounting anger that I could not manage – nor understand.

In the early 1980s I was visiting a friend in County Waterford and as I approached the house I was met by the sound of the most enchanting music. "It's from one of Wagner's operas," he told me. In 1986 I attended my first opera, *Turandot* at the Gaiety Theatre in Dublin. In 1996 I attended my first performance of *Parsifal* in the magical Festspielhaus in Bayreuth which has been described as "sitting inside a musical instrument". It is only in hindsight that I realise that the Bayreuth experience was the beginning of a healing process that has helped me to survive. In 2013 I began to write about my experience and as I began to read more about mental health in recent years I stumbled upon articles and other material about the effects of sound and light on the human anatomy and physiology and in particular, the healing effects of music. This new knowledge has given me an even greater understanding of the power that draws me again and again to live performances in their proper settings – the opera houses of Europe – and especially Bayreuth.

Thanks to fellow military personnel, to family and friends, my first book, *Elegy for a Broken Soldier* was published in 2019.

Chris McQuaid, Dublin 2020

# CHAPTER 1

# *The Beginning of the Journey*

In 1986, my friend, David Meade and I met for a drink at the Clarence Hotel on the quays in Dublin and then proceeded to our first opera, *Turandot* at the Gaiety Theatre. David had been on the 3rd Potential Officers Course after which he was posted to Cork and eventually moved to Naval HQ in Dublin. We met as mature Leaving Cert. students and later discovered that we both had an interest in opera.

The opera is set in ancient China and Turandot is the name of a beautiful princess, who could be regarded in today's world as a privileged, narcissistic, unfeeling woman who is not very tolerant of men and when it comes to accepting the advances of a suitor, she decides to have a bit of sadistic fun. She comes up with three riddles that prospective suitors must solve before being considered suitable. Failing to solve the riddles will not only mean they lose the princess, but they will also lose their lives! Enter Calaf, an equally cocky prince who solves Turandot's three riddles, but this is just the beginning of a battle of wits between the two. The opera was the final work of the Italian composer, Giacomo Puccini who died before it was completed. The final scenes were written by composer Franco Alfano. The music is breathtakingly beautiful with pieces such as the aria, *Nessun Dorma*, sung by Prince Calaf and immortalised by the late Luciano Pavarotti. *Turandot* premiered on the 25th of April

1926, at La Scala, Milan. La Scala is regarded as one of the leading opera and ballet theatres in the world and is home to the La Scala Theatre Chorus, La Scala Theatre Ballet and La Scala Theatre Orchestra. The theatre also has an associate school, known as the La Scala Theatre Academy.

Dublin's Gaiety Theatre is not La Scala, but the Gaiety still maintains its unmatched presence as the city's premier venue for popular musical shows, ballet, dance, drama and of course, opera. Pavlova, Markova, Krassovska and Dolin; in opera, Salvini, Pavarotti, Joan Sutherland and, in our own time, Veronica Dunne and Bernadette Greev. Popular stars of variety have included Jack Benny, Noel Purcell and Julie Andrews and classic actors included luminaries such as Edwin Booth, Henry Irving, Ellen Terry, Sara Bernhardt, Sybil Thorndyke and more recently, Siobhan McKenna, Peter O'Toole, Ray McAnally and Michael Gambon.

It was under Louis Elliman that the Dublin Grand Opera Society established its two annual seasons, now continued by Opera Ireland. These replaced the regular visits of the celebrated Moody Manners Opera Company, the Carl Rosa Opera, and the O'Mara Opera Company, when operatic touring ceased around mid-century due to prohibitively rising costs. The inspiration behind The Gaiety Theatre came from the Gunn brothers, John and Michael, whose background was a family music business on Grafton Street. They engaged the well-known architect C.J. Phipps, whose original design in the manner of the traditional European opera house has given us the essential Gaiety, with its handsome Venetian façade. Astonishingly, only 25 weeks elapsed between the laying of the foundations and the opening night – the contractors working a 24-hour shift! After twelve years of marked success, the most distinguished theatre architect of the day, Frank Matcham, was brought in to create the spacious parterre and dress-circle bars in the extension to the west of the auditorium, which he then redecorated. Phipps gave the Gaiety its elegant form, and Matcham its attractive baroque adornments.

After the opera, David and I headed back to the Clarence Hotel. The Clarence first opened its doors in 1852. It was refurbished in the 1930's and hosted an eclectic clientele, from visiting clergymen to bawdy musicians. It certainly served as a somewhat entertaining encore to *Turandot* at the Gaiety Theatre. When we arrived, a noisy wedding party occupied the main bar. Hardly had we downed the first gulps of our pints, when we noticed the noise level had escalated. Suddenly, a table was overturned, and a couple of chairs were launched at each other by opposing "combatants." David and I, an army officer and a naval officer, both trained to kill, took refuge behind a group of older women before managing to slink outside to safety. The hotel was bought by U2's Bono and The Edge in 1992 and transformed into a contemporary boutique hotel. It is a rather pleasant place, as I discovered in 2018 when I trundled in on crutches for a pint on my way back from a talk at Smock Alley Theatre by my friend, Declan Power and the legendary film producer/director, John Boorman.

For me, *Turandot* was the beginning of a lifelong love of live performances, some of which I did attend at the famous La Scala. In this rarefied atmosphere I had found something that would help me to distance myself from the evil, lowlife that I found, to my horror, lurking in the ranks of the Irish Defence Forces. Music became my saviour; my enduring comfort in the years that followed a terrifying incident in Jerusalem, when innocence, beauty and *joie de vivre* had been stripped away. Returning home from that that trip, I carried a deep, dark secret of violation and shame, feeling my stomach and chest tightening as the plane approached Dublin. At home, I could hardly speak to anyone. Having served two tours of duty overseas with the Irish UN Peacekeeping Force I had immediately applied for a third. I knew the drill in the army. I could hide from the world in the force and by working hard, I could keep the torment at bay. I had people there with whom I could relate on a light-hearted, superficial level and I now knew how to be on my guard; for much of the time I would have a weapon and I would use it! I also knew that I would never sleep soundly overseas but the only solution to my torment seemed to lie in getting away again.

While I waited for my month's leave to be up, I stayed in my bedroom playing darts and listening to Roy Orbison records. I played 'Only the Lonely' over and over, an apt accompaniment to my own loneliness as I sank deeper and deeper into morbidity. Whenever I ventured out, I avoided public transport, not wanting to be seen. Instead, I took taxis to and from pubs in the city. In one pub I swilled down a glass of beer and gripped the glass so tightly that it broke into pieces in my hand. "Jesus!" the barman exclaimed as blood pumped from the cuts on my palm.

My next tour of duty began in the autumn – again in Cyprus – and I spent my twentieth birthday at a cold, wet and lonely observation post in Limnitis. The camp conditions had improved; the British engineers had built toilets and showers and the accommodation had been upgraded to four-man tents. Even our uniforms were now of a better quality, especially our rain gear. Within easy reach of Jerusalem, I found my thoughts wandering back, fearful yet curious. I decided to pay a return visit, perhaps hoping that by going back to the scene of the crime I could dispel the black dog of depression that lurked just under the surface. Something of the city must have impressed itself during those surreal, doom-laden days following the assault as I wandered aimlessly around the streets. This time I experienced a fleeting sense of the sacred that touched some part of me beneath the damaged shell that I now inhabited. I loved the old city. Some friends and I visited the Dome of the Rock, the second holiest place in the Muslim world. Inside, it was magnificent. Before entering the shrine, we had to remove our shoes and men with camel sticks stood, ready to beat anyone who attempted to enter without being suitably dressed. We stood at the Wailing Wall, walked by the Jordan River, went to visit the tomb of

Lazarus and the Dead Sea and prayed in the Church of the Nativity in Bethlehem, the place where Christ was born.

When I returned from Jerusalem, I found that we were stationed in Kokkina, several kilometres east of the Northern Cyprus mainland, surrounded by mountainous territory, with Morphou Bay on its northern flank. The bay looked inviting, but swimming was deemed to be too dangerous on account of fighting in the area. In August 1964, the Turkish Resistance paramilitary organisation (TMT), had landed arms and provisions from Turkey. The Greek Cypriot Nationalist Guerrilla Organisation (EOKA) retaliated by attacking the town on August the 6th, 1964. Four days later, Turkey sent in fighter jets to strafe and napalm villages and towns, causing heavy casualties. The UN intervened, preventing all-out war. But tensions were still high, and we could not afford to take any chances.

I welcomed the tension because any down time brought no respite from my own internal war; I had to be occupied. I had been drawing and sketching since I was a child. I particularly liked to draw cartoons and I began doodling again, using markers, pencils, pens – whatever was to hand. I was rather chuffed when I was asked to contribute to *McAuley's Roundup*, the A-Company news sheet. Based, as the name suggested on life on a ranch, the *Roundup* was edited by Corporal Michael Lacy, aided and abetted by Signalman, John Durcan, Corporal Benny Molloy and myself. It made fun of all ranks from the CO down. Sending up one's colleagues, including the boss was a risky business so to protect ourselves, we used pseudonyms. Interest grew exponentially when the *Roundup* featured in the third edition of *The Blue Beret,* in February 1966, a magazine that was issued by the information office of the United Nations Force in Cyprus. One man was curious to know who a certain character was based on, probably suspecting that it was based on him! It provided me with a pleasant distraction. Camp duties gave me something to fill working hours. For much of the time I assisted the cook, essentially boiling water for the tea on petrol-powered hydro cookers which were dangerous contraptions, to say the least. Water was not the only thing that boiled; I had broken out in boils and the medics concluded that the cause had been an over-abundance of iron in my blood, from eating too many eggs, supplied by the locals. Then, just prior to repatriation I developed a raging fever and I was taken to the Austrian field hospital where I was diagnosed with pneumonia and pleurisy. I was put in a wheelchair and wrapped in bed sheets that had been soaked in cold water in an effort to reduce my temperature. I shivered and sweated for three or four days with nurses taking my temperature at regular intervals. Finally, a driver showed up. "Get dressed," he said. "You're going home". The Austrian medical team were worried, but they were in no position to protest. I was given a massive shot of Penicillin and handed release papers to sign and I was on my way back to my unit. I could hardly breathe.

Wrapped in an army greatcoat, I arrived in Dublin where I was met by an ambulance and whisked to St. Bricin's Hospital. The course of Penicillin was continued and after a few days my buttocks were raw from needle punctures. An NCO with whom I had served in the Congo was admitted following a heart attack and placed in the next bed. I grew agitated listening to him trying to breathe. The doctor gave me sleeping tablets which had no effect and finally I heard his last breath. Three hours passed before his body was removed. Although I had been in a war zone, this was my first encounter with physical death up close – made all the more shocking by the fact that I knew the man personally, a man in the prime of life. I survived. The medical officer at St. Bricin's told me that I was cured and that if I wished I could return to Cyprus with the next unit. I had become addicted to overseas duty and once again I volunteered. But on the flight to Nicosia I was I was having second thoughts. I wanted to reinvent myself – somehow. I had left school before my sixteenth birthday, a lifetime ago. I had never worked in the world outside the army, apart from part-time stints in a bicycle shop, as a runner in the *Irish Times* and in Cassidy's department store. But I was an innocent and carefree schoolboy then. Now I was half a person, afraid that with one slip, my loathsomeness and defilement would be seen. My qualifications were confined to weaponry and military operations – in the lower ranks. I was a foot soldier, now sullied by the cold, calculating actions of a cowardly degenerate. All I had to show for my trouble was a little extra money and a few medals. The money was my only incentive to return to Cyprus.

Having returned to education and with a college degree under my belt, I was selected for commissioning in 1978 and travelled to the Military College at the Curragh in November to begin the 4th Potential Officers' Course, graduating in 6th place out of twenty-five and I became a commissioned officer on the 1st of November 1979. In April 1980 I was with B Company 47th Battalion, based in As Sultaniyah, Lebanon. The nightmares of Jerusalem persisted but I carried out my duties and as far as I knew, I appeared to be normal – on the surface.

In my first location I was tasked with Company OPS duties – canteen administration and the occasional patrol. Eventually, we were rotated to Barashit where reconnaissance was added to my portfolio. One day I took an armoured vehicle to Tibnin with Cpl. Tagdh Daly, an excellent driver. Then the shit hit the fan. The Israelis said that if the armoured vehicle didn't get off the track, they would blow it off. When we returned to base, everyone was wearing flak jackets. My boss, Freddie Swords came and shook my hand – delighted because the IDF used to say that the Irish did no patrolling! In hindsight it was a stupid thing to do. We could have hit a landmine anywhere along that road. I also took chances going over Hill 880 at At Tiri at night to give the crew a canteen break. Cpl Tagdh Daly could drive up Hill 880, changing the gears from 'Road' to 'Cross-Country' without taking a breath. There was a static AML 90 there, facing the IDF's 'Brown Mound' and we were always in their sights as they watched our every move.

On July the 1st 1980 I was leading a four-man night patrol, with a junior NCO and three privates, along a wadi near Deir Ntar Village. The air was heavy with the scent of trees. Overhead, clouds raced across a bright moon, casting dark shadows one minute, illuminating the landscape the next. The sound of Mullahs, singing prayers – "God is Great" in Arabic – was reassuring. Our patrol was about twenty minutes out from our platoon post, Loc.-622, picking our way through rough terrain when I noticed that two privates were not up with the rest of the party. I posted the remaining private as rear security, and my corporal and I went back to see what had happened to the two missing men. *At Tiri again? Had they been kidnapped?* After about ten minutes I found one of them sitting on a sloping bank under a gnarled tree and asked him if he was hurt. He looked unhurt, but I could feel my legs buckling and I began to think the worst. *Had this soldier been planted under the tree as a ruse to draw someone into a trap?* "Six twenty-three B. Six twenty-three B," he replied. He had a glazed look in his eyes, and I realised that something was wrong. He was incoherent, high on something – probably cannabis.

I slowly removed the magazine from his FN rifle and handed the magazine to my corporal. Then somewhere off to my right I heard the click-clack of a bullet being released up the breech of a rifle. "You're in trouble, Sir," my corporal said. I turned and saw the second soldier stalking out of the shadows with his rifle cocked and pointed in my direction. "Don't take his weapon! Don't take his weapon!" he shouted. My mouth dried up and my throat was tightening. My legs felt like they would go from under me. But some form of survival instinct took over. I gripped my pistol, just to feel and hold onto something solid. "We're all friends here," I said. "Have a drink of water." Ever so slowly he dropped the rifle, barrel pointing to the ground and sat down. Then without being ordered, he said he was going to take out the round from the breech and apply the safety catch. I ordered the rest of the party to sit down and take up security positions and watched as he slowly removed the round. I then checked the other soldier's weapon. Adrenalin was pumping through me, sweat soaking my hair underneath my helmet which felt like a steel vice encircling my head. Immediately, depersonalisation struck, starting with the tingling tremor in my legs – the all too familiar scenario that I had suffered in Jerusalem. I could feel my heart racing and my breathing reduced to short gasps. In seconds, I would be in a crumpled heap on the ground, completely at the mercy of two individuals – two of our own soldiers – who were out of their heads. I could not believe that I had been attacked by my own comrades – first in Jerusalem and now in Lebanon. *Not again*! I thought. "We have reached our objective," I said through dried lips. "We will sit and observe for twenty minutes and then return." I radioed the base to inform them of our plan and waited for things to cool down. After some time, we got to our feet and headed back to the platoon post. The aggressor was holding firmly onto his weapon and clearly had no intention of handing it over to anyone. He then offered to carry the radio set and I allowed him to do this as we made our way back to base. When we arrived at Loc. 6-22, I instructed the party to take off their equipment and relax. All the weapons were put to one side and I asked the guard commander to call for medical help for the two drugged soldiers. "They are both in a bad condition and appear to have heat stroke," I said. I quietly told a guard to lock away their weapons and if either of the two made a false move that he was to shoot them! All I could think of was revenge.

In the years that followed, I struggled to hold myself together. In 1985, at forty years of age, I was promoted to Captain. Some of my Potential Officers' class would be promoted to Commandant when they turned fifty. In 1985, the Quartermaster General considered me suitable for promotion to Commandant, but ten years from then seemed a long time; 1995 seemed a long way off. I was not too good, mentally at this stage and I didn't want to wait. A decision to leave the army was forming in my mind. Turandot, my first opera re-awakened a spark, a small glimmer of recognition from earlier times. The road to fine opera and the opulent theatres of Europe did not begin with attendance at concerts, or exposure to operatic performances. The Christian Brothers at our primary school ruled by the cane. The exception was one young Christian brother who took choir class. He had a liking for opera and taught us "The Huntsman's Chorus", from *Der Freischütz* by Carl Maria von Weber. It was a welcome change from "O'Donnell Abú" and the Gregorian chant of the Latin Mass. Thanks to my mother's love of classical music I heard performers like Mario Lanza and Count John McCormack on the radio. Like my mother, my father's aunt Bridget liked music and the 'finer things in life'. Bridget worked as housekeeper for a canon, first in Malahide, an affluent district in north Dublin and later in the village of Enniskerry in County Wicklow, she was especially kind and generous. The kitchen in the cannon's house was below stairs and led out into a beautifully kept garden. Bridget cooked and baked on a gigantic black range that gave off tremendous heat. I loved visiting her and sitting in the warm and cosy kitchen, made all the more welcoming by Bridget's home baking and home-made jam. Canon Kennedy, for whom she worked was a friend of the family and my father often fished with him. Fr. John Sullivan was a regular visitor to the canon's house. He was known as a healer and a very compassionate man and when he died his remains were brought to St Francis Xavier's church in Gardiner Street. It is now a place where people come to pray and bring their petitions to Fr John, asking him to intercede for them with his prayers. When grand-aunt Bridget died, her coffin was placed beside his coffin at his shrine, on the eve of her burial – a rare privilege. Fr. Sullivan was beatified on May 13th 2017. Someday I may be one handshake away from a saint!

As I look back, I realise the emotional links between the safety and comfort provided by these women who happened to appreciate music, for I always associate music with their presence. On the day that my mother died I sat in my room and played the *Largo* from Beethoven's 9th Symphony (choral) on CD. I had always turned to classical music in times of darkness and I suppose I was trying to reach out to connect with her in some forlorn way, trying to make sense of her passing, trying to keep something of her in the empty place inside, trying to purge the feeling of doom. I wanted to avoid having to accept that she was gone and that nothing and no-one could ever take her place.

One evening as I drove across the snow-covered Curragh Plains under a moonlit sky, I heard Luciano Pavarotti singing the Christmas carol, "O Holy Night", composed by Adolphe Adam. I was overcome with emotion. Something in that magnificent tenor voice touched me deeply. Pavarotti's technique was exceptional. Before I left the Curragh Plains and joined the Naas Dual Carriageway my love affair with classical music had been reignited.

At that time, I had friend who lived in a bungalow on the road to Lismore, a beautiful area adjacent to the Blackwater River in County Waterford. When I visited for the first time, I discovered that he was interested in classical music. As I approached the house, I heard the most glorious sound coming from within. "What is that music?" I asked. "It's a piece from one of Wagner's operas," he replied. "Coffee or a beer?" he asked. I don't remember having either; the music was so powerful that I was suspended in trance. The Prelude to *Lohengrin* was the key to the door of Wagner's music.

Classical music became my reason to live. I am not a musician, simply a man whose soul has yearned for peace and healing and while I have found neither, I have at least been comforted in the presence of the exceedingly fine art of music. The term "exceedingly fine art" was so called by Arthur Schopenhauer, a German philosopher who is best known for his 1818 work *The World as Will and*

*Representation.* In it he said,

*Its effect on man's innermost nature is so powerful, and it is so completely and profoundly understood by him in his innermost being as an entirely universal language, whose distinctness surpasses even that of the world of perception itself.*

Often considered to be a pessimist, Schopenhauer did however recommend ways, via artistic, moral and ascetic forms of awareness – to overcome what he called, 'a frustration-filled and fundamentally painful human condition.' Since his death in 1860, his philosophy has had a special attraction for those engaged in music, literature, and the visual arts. Of these, my one abiding passion is music and the music of one composer in particular: Richard Wagner. I studied music for six years at the Royal Irish Academy and now and then, I play piano – badly. Friends tell me that I am quite an authority on Wagner! I doubt it but having become an ardent Wagner follower, I had become affiliated to the Richard Wagner Verband International, the International Association of Wagner Societies and following advice from Dr James Pritchard of the London society I founded The Wagner Society of Ireland by a notice in *The Irish Times* on the 24th of August 2002. It was during the Limerick Ring, the acclaimed *Ring* Cycle, *Der Ring des Nibelungen* staged in Limerick in June that I made the decision. Many leading Wagnerian singers including Janice Baird, USA and Germany, Suzanne Murphy from Limerick, Frode Olsen from Norway, Cork soprano Cara O'Sullivan, Canadian Alan Woodrow and Robin Legatte from the Royal Opera House, Covent Garden, performed with the National Youth Orchestra of Ireland under the baton of Russian conductor Alexander Anissimov. Held at the Concert Hall in University of Limerick, it was only the second complete performance of the marathon Ring Cycle in Ireland. The first was held at the Theatre Royal, Dublin, in 1913. The vast production, consisting of *Das Rheingold, Die Walküre, Siegfried* and *Götterdämmerung* cost an estimated €530,000 to stage and involved more than fifteen hours of music. Conductor Alexander Anissimov said that he had done some of his most important creative work in Ireland and that to conduct Wagner's *Ring* in Ireland was his dream come true. This spurred me into action. I decided to strike while the iron was hot.

There was a good response to my notice in *The Irish Times* and the society took off. I moved fast, and I co-designed the website with the late Stephen O'Gorman, MSC and Irish Air Corps. He loved all things mythological and of course, *Sibelius* but I couldn't turn his head towards my man, Richard Wagner. As founder and chairman, I attended my first congress in Copenhagen in May 2003. I met Dr Wolfgang Wagner and his wife, Gudrun in Copenhagen. I gave Gudrun my card and followed this up with a letter on gold blocking headed paper with The Wagner Society of Ireland printed in Saint Patrick's Blue with a watermark head of Wagner. Really classy. We applied for tickets for the Bayreuth Festival in 2003 and in 2004 we were allocated forty tickets which was astounding. This practice continued up to 2011 when, after the death of Wolfgang, the system changed and there were no tickets issued to any of the one hundred and thirty-nine affiliated societies. Eventually I was confronted by conflict once again and I stood down from my position of the Wagner Society of Ireland, due to ill health. My retirement from the Irish Defence Forces in 1986 gave me emancipation; I could plan at last to pursue my hobby with vigour. I was now in a civilian position and I could use my annual leave to follow the music.

But even music has been a temporary respite. I probably over-identified with Parsifal, the young man in Wagner's opera who is a "pure fool" – an innocent, a good man who slowly starts to see the evils in the world and who now perceives the world as a place of unending misery. I arrived at the same conclusion.

# CHAPTER 2

# *What the Great Masters Knew*

Apart from music, no other pursuit has brought me as much joy and relief. I really believed that my time on this earth had been an unending struggle – and a requiem for my lost self. The 'shell' that was left was simply a robotic actor playing the dual roles of protagonist and antagonist, reacting to the push of buttons – a non-person. Music had helped to ameliorate the troubled existence that I had come through since I was, like Parsifal in the opera of the same name, a young innocent abroad. As I became less physically active, I found escape – and solace – in music. Part of me was re-born through music. I guess it saved my life. It raised me up to a new level so that even though I have lots of health issues I can be philosophical.

Over the years I escaped to Vienna, to Berlin and other cities to attend opera performances, often for the umpteenth time. I love the music and the visual spectacle on stage and through the music I am transported to a benign sanctuary where I want to remain. I have attended in excess of two hundred operas and at least fifty concerts, mostly composed by Richard Wagner (1813-1883). I attended my twenty first *Tristan und Isolde* at the Staatsoper Vienna on Sunday, 12th of March 2017. The principal singers were the Bayreuther Festspiele Team, the world's best. The staging was beautiful, and I had an excellent seat in the front row of a box on Level One. The concluding "Liebestod" (Love/Death) is the most beautiful vocal piece ever written. It was very emotional, and l shed tears.

Such obsession is not shared by my friends in opera circles, most of whom are a lot more selective. But the music soothes my soul and lifts my spirits. Wagner's *Tristan und Isolde* is a work from another world, way ahead of its time in musical construction. Written when the composer's life was in turmoil, he was inspired to put aside his work on *Der Ring des Nibelungen* and begin work on *Tristan und Isolde*. His marriage eventually broke up and he was living in exile in Zurich, but despite penury and his awful skin condition, he built his own theatre with its sunken pit and introduced other innovations some of which are used in cinema even today. He was a master of choral music, a genius of the highest order. He died in Venice in 1883, aged sixty-nine.

The young Richard Wagner was passionate about *Der Freischütz* by Carl Maria von Weber – whom he met at age nine – and Beethoven, especially the overtures, *Fidelio* and later, *Adelaide*. At age twelve, his mother arranged for him to have piano lessons with Johann N. Hummel (1778-1837) of Weimar. His principal teacher was Christian Theodor Weinlig (1780-1842). Weinlig also taught Clara Schumann. Weinlig's teacher was Stanislao Mattei (1750-1825) who also taught Rossini, Donizetti and others. Finally, Mattei's teacher was Giovanni Battista Martini (1706-1784) who numbered Mozart and Johann Sebastian Bach amongst his pupils.

As a young boy, the youngest of nine children, Wagner was sickly to begin with, but became quite a handful. He was blessed with a caring mother who also encouraged her other children in music – Albert (tenor), Rosalie (soprano), Louisa and Clara (singers). Following the death of his stepfather, Richard's uncle Adolph looked after him, at which time his mother was in Prague with Rosalie, who had secured a good singing post there. Wagner loved Greek and enjoyed translating Homer's poems. He also studied piano and violin. When Wienlig was finished teaching him ("I can teach you no more"), he had the technical mastery. Weinlig knew that Wagner was prepared to complete his education by composition. At sixteen, he wrote two piano sonatas and a string quartet. At seventeen, he arranged *Beethoven's Ninth Symphony* for piano. In 1830 his *Overture in B Flat Major* was performed. He also wrote his first opera, *Die Hochzeit*. He didn't compose music for it but rather transferred some of the ideas to *Die Feen*. In 1833, his brother, Albert arranged for him to take on the post of choirmaster at Würzburg. Wagner was no slouch when it came to writing for chorus. His *Feen* was remarkable by any standards, for a twenty-year-old. Alas, the opera wasn't performed until 1888, in München, five years after his death. He took to choral composition like a duck to water, as exemplified in his later works, especially *Lohengrin* (1850), *Tannhäuser* (1845) and of course the sublime choral conclusion to *Parsifal* (1882).

Johann Sebastian Bach is considered by many to be the father of all music. His *Cantata* 140 and 147 are beyond words. I heard his *St. Matthew Passion* performed live in the Thomaskirche, a number of years ago. It was woundingly beautiful. Three hours, plus. I am very taken by Korngold's *Die tote Stadt* but first and foremost, my man is Richard Wagner. As a youngster his men were Beethoven, Weber and Mozart. I recommend that a beginner listen to *Lohengrin* – and the choral aspects in particular. In this work the power of the umlaut is so important and in his *Tannhäuser*, the choral conclusion, the umlaut causes the shape of the mouth to change and the result is beautiful. This cannot be done in English. I love all of his operas, but *Parsifal* is a favourite.

Wagner was a contemporary of Verdi (1813-1901), who lived for much longer and composed more operas than Wagner – all of a very high standard. I like some but not all. I've been attending the Bayreuther Festspiele now for twenty-five years including a Memorial Service for Dr Wolfgang Wagner (1919-2010). I joined the friends of the Bayreuther Festspiele in 1995. I made contact following the reading of an article in the *Wagner News*,1994, by Eric Adler who said, "There are two types of persons who wish to go to Bayreuth; those who want to go and those who really want to go." He provided a postal address for the 'GDF/Friends'. I was waiting for a ticket for seven years at this time.

Booking ahead was essential. Becoming a Friend – i.e. paying an annual subscription is recommended. All opera houses have Friends to supplement income. My first friendship was with the Royal Opera House, London. I progressed to the Friends of the Wagner Festspiele, where I remain. Getting tickets is a whole different matter. Eric Adler, in the Wagner Society of London Newsletter, advised on how to obtain tickets for the Wagner Festival Bayreuth. He said that there were 'persons who wished to go and persons who really wished to go'. In his article, he gave contact details for the Friends of Bayreuth. I wrote to them and the following week, received a telephone call from Bayreuth. The rest as they say is history. The Festspiele in Bayreuth is unique, opened in 1876 for Wagner's operas and designed with *Parsifal* in mind. It can now seat 1,925 people and is based on the Greek amphitheatre model. Each year, 57,750 seats go on sale. The current waiting period for tickets is seven years.

At this point, I consider music to be a necessary staple in my life. Arthur Schopenhauer, in his *World as Will and Representation* describes the role of music as the highest of all the Arts. I am speaking about classical music – the music of Mozart, Beethoven, Handel, Vivaldi, Verdi, Wagner, Saint-Saëns, Bruckner, Bruch, Korngold, Mahler, Smetana, Richard Strauss, Johann Strauss II, Strauss (Vater) and others. Music has the power to heal, to provide a balsam for one's soul, to cause the intellect to spark, to infuse the whole being with joy.

The 19th-century Danish author, Hans Christian Andersen, wrote "Where words fail, music speaks." In recent decades, science and medicine have come out with information on findings with regard to therapy in both mental and physical health. Music has the power to induce every possible emotion. Science and medicine now acknowledge that music can 'take us to unimaginable heights, calm and comfort us in our grief or loneliness, help us release our anger or frustration in a way that doesn't hurt anyone, get us dancing, and bring peace to our hearts'. Music can:

- boost your immune system by increasing levels of the antibody immunoglobulin A,
- lower your cortisol (stress hormone) levels,
- help decrease depression,
- lower pain levels in some people,
- help with certain neurological conditions by reactivating speech centres of the brain,
- improve the memory of Alzheimer's and dementia patients.

Hospitals throughout the United States are using music therapy to ease the patient's pain, lower blood pressure, and reduce anxiety and depression. A 2007 survey of U.S. health facilities by the Society for the Arts in Healthcare, along with the Joint Commission and Americans for the Arts, found that of 1,923 healthcare facilities, 35 percent offered music, of some type, to patients. In a *USA Today* article (2008), hospitals are becoming more aware of the healing benefits of music therapy. Studies included were:

- Severe stroke patients admitted to a hospital in Helsinki, Finland listened to recorded music for at least an hour a day. They recovered their verbal memory faster and experienced less depression. This compared to those who listened to audiobooks or nothing (Journal Brain, March 2008).
- Premature babies who listened to two hours of Mozart each week had a lower heart rate and slept better, according to researchers at New York-Presbyterian Hospital/Weill Cornell Medical Center in New York.
- Terminally ill patients in Australia had less anxiety, pain, and drowsiness after having a single music therapy session compared

to those who did not listen to music (Journal of Palliative Medicine, May 2008).

Other studies have shown music therapy beneficial for autism, learning disabilities, dementia, and pain management during labour and birth.

When we listen to music we love, it resonates deep inside us. Certain melodies spark our wellbeing, creativity, and sense of adventure. Our problems, worries, and fears lessen when we hear a favourite song. And whatever musical tastes we have, it can help improve our mood. One minute we feel hopeless, then an inspiring tune comes on the radio, and we feel motivated again. When we feel anxious or are having a bad day, a melody or lyric can soothe and revive us. That is the power of music.

Scientists have also found that learning to play an instrument sharpens how the brain processes sound and can improve children's reading and other school skills. To better understand how either listening to or creating music and how the brain processes music, research is now being funded in some states. Now, the National Institutes of Health is bringing together musicians, music therapists and neuroscientists to tap into the brain's circuitry and figure out how. Geneticist and NIH Director Dr. Francis Collins said, "The brain is able to compensate for other deficits sometimes by using music to communicate."

Soprano Renee Fleming sang not from a concert stage but from inside an MRI machine at the NIH campus. The opera star who partnered with Collins to start the Sound Health initiative spent two hours in the scanner to help researchers to work out what brain activity is key for singing. First Renee Fleming spoke the lyrics. Then she sang them. Finally, she *imagined* singing them. "We're trying to understand the brain not just so we can address mental disorders or diseases or injuries, but also so we can understand what happens when a brain's working right and what happens when it's performing at a really high level," said NIH researcher David Jangraw, who shared the MRI data with The Associated Press. To his surprise, several brain regions were more active when Fleming *imagined* singing than when she actually sang, including the brain's emotion centre and areas involved with motion and vision. One theory was that it took more mental effort to keep track of where she was in the song, and to maintain its emotion, without auditory feedback. But Renee Fleming put it more simply when she spoke at a workshop at the John F. Kennedy Center for the Performing Arts, where she is an artistic adviser. "I'm skilled at singing so I didn't have to think about it quite so much." Indeed, Jangraw quotes a saying in neuroscience: "Neurons that fire together, wire together". Brain cells communicate by firing messages to each other through junctions called synapses. Cells that regularly connect – for example, when a musician practices – strengthen bonds into circuitry that forms an efficient network for, in this case, singing. "To turn that ability into a successful therapy, it would be a really good thing to know which parts of the brain are still intact to be called into action. To know the circuits well enough to know the backup plan," Collins added.

Arthur Schopenhauer knew this, the great masters – the composers and musicians – knew this. The physical and emotional effects of music are far-reaching. I also believe that through Wagner's music one becomes more open to spirituality. In this regard, I also view Beethoven's *9th Symphony* as sacred, the slow movement brings great music to its absolute zenith. Pure music.

Wagner requires hard work and dedication, but the rewards are great. After thirty-four years I of attending multiples of Wagner operas and at least thirty others, excluding concerts, I carry music in my whole self – from a cellular level into my life. I wish we had the Festspiele in Ireland. Unfortunately, my hometown of Dublin is the only capital city in Europe that doesn't have an opera house. The National Opera House is situated in Wexford, a regional town on the southeast coast. With its 'niche' and rarely performed operas, Wexford Festival Opera is not for the plain people of Ireland. Fergus Sheil and his Irish National Opera Company is making some progress and maybe I will see a *Parsifal* being performed in Ireland, in my lifetime. I have no interest in the usual "pot-boilers", churned out in the past few years, although *Tristan und Isolde* was very good.

However, who knows what might emerge in the years to come. After the Limerick *Ring*, the late Roger Lee (Wagner Society UK) wrote:

*And so, a great journey of discovery has begun. We ae witnessing the catalytic effect of Richard Wagner's work upon Ireland's musical life as the twenty first Century unfolds. Plans are under discussion for more Limerick Wagner festivals to present the other music dramas over the next few years. As this Wagner dawn takes place in the most westerly part of the British Isles, we may remember the words of the Irish critic, George Bernard Shaw when a similar dawning was taking place in Victorian England: We're all Wagnerians now!*

# CHAPTER 3

# *Light and Sound*

Cinematography is the art of making motion pictures by capturing a story visually on screen. Composition, lighting, equipment selection, camera movement, visual effects and so much more are designed to have the maximum effect on the audience. Aside from operating a camera and setting up the lighting for every scene, it involves controlling what the viewer sees and how the image is presented, by choosing the right shooting techniques that best tell the story.

Richard Wagner was more than a composer and more than a musician; when it came to stage production, Wagner was one of the best. He would be on a par with the best cinematographers of our time as well as notable film directors whose genius made visual storytelling such a powerful medium. He had eye for detail and an innovative mind. All he needed was someone with technical know-how and application.

Adolphe Appia is best known for his many scenic designs for Wagner's operas. Appia was the son of Red Cross co-founder Louis Appia and was a Swiss architect and theorist of stage lighting and décor. Appia critiqued the "inferior" and inadequate contribution of scenographic elements and in rejecting the use of representational painted scenic backdrops, began to articulate a new aspiration for the role of light in the composition of the stage scene.

Inspired principally through the music of Wagner, this first "sceno-graphic" turn presented a radical proposal for determining stage space that would usher in what Baugh terms 'A Century of Light'. As lighting equipment had improved in brightness, performers were able to utilise more of the stage space, upstage of the footlights, but this also emphasised an aesthetic problem: the proximity of the actor's body to the painted scenery created human shadows on the canvas and was therefore in direct conflict with the two-dimen-sional pictorial visual illusion. Two new sources of light – limelight and the electric carbon arc – began to be employed on the stage from the mid-nineteenth century. These connected but significantly different technologies were used to create intense beams of light that were much more powerful than the prevailing methods of lighting the stage. They were therefore able to be employed on top of the general illumination, but a consequence of the new sources of light was the creation of even more incongruous and harsh shad-ows projected onto the painted scenic backdrops.

Appia's idea of "active light" envisaged light as not simply an illuminating agent but as an expressive force that should be modu-lated like music and choreographed and its movement over time as central to the dramatic experience. Active light therefore not only created specific visual effects for the stage – such as a shaft of moon-light – but could also provide a subtle, versatile source with expres-sive potential and could transform the stage environment, reveal three-dimensional form. By varying its intensity, colour and beam quality, for the first time light, when choreographed, could become a co-player in the drama – a poetic and active agent able to animate the stage space and bring the drama to life. He argued that "only simplified staging and the creative use of lighting could rescue Wag-ner's works from the moribund visual aesthetic".

Appia devoted his life to developing ideas and designs which profoundly influenced the subsequent course of Wagner produc-tions – and of theatre as a whole. Appia's ideas were derived from

Wagner's mature belief, underwritten by his admiration for Schopenhauer, that the music is the most important ingredient in opera. Wagner's view of opera as 'deeds of music made visible' and the composer's score as the only reliable guide to what should be seen on the stage strongly influenced Appia's work. Appia held that scenic illusion was absurd because it showed the audience only what they were perfectly capable of imagining for themselves. The settings must therefore be vague and suggestive, capable of seeming to change with time, even as music does.

As with light, sound travels in waves caused by air molecules that vibrate. What is most interesting is that, if a frequency is vibrating fast enough, it is emitted as a sound and if it is vibrating much faster, it is emitted as a colour of light. To convert sound to light requires simply to raise its frequency by forty octaves. Sound travels through the air in the form of vibrations. These vibrations cause particles of air to compress together and this causes the air around them to move in such a way that they are driven in waves away from the source. Everything produces data whether it's sound or smell or vibration. Cymatics is the process of visualising sound by vibrating a medium such as sand or water, but also of exploring nature and trying to find hidden data within nature.

Ernst Florens Friedrich Chladni was a German physicist and musician. His most important work, for which he is sometimes called "the father of acoustics", included research on vibrating plates and the calculation of the speed of sound for different gases. He created an experiment using a metal plate, covering it with sand and then drawing a violin bow down along the edge of the plate to create the "Chladni patterns". Many years later, sound technologists have used a cymatic device: the metal plate connected to a sound driver and being fed by a frequency generator to create an image from a segment of *Beethoven's Ninth Symphony* – "to render the invisible visible".

The history of cymatics began with the observations of *resonance*, by

Da Vinci, Galileo, the English scientist Robert Hook and then Ernst Chladni. The next person to explore this field was a Swiss physicist called Hans Jenny. It was he who coined the term Cymatics. As the frequencies increase, so do the complexities of the patterns that appear on the plate. Devices like the cymascope, have been used to scientifically observe cymatic patterns and the list of scientific applications is growing every day. For example, in oceanography, a lexicon of dolphin language is being created by visualizing the sonar beams that the dolphins emit. Hopefully in the future some deeper understanding will be obtained of how they communicate.

Cymatics is also used as a looking glass into nature. It is possible to recreate the archetypal forms of nature, for example a picture of snowflake as it would appear in nature, alongside a cymatically created snowflake, a starfish alongside a cymatic starfish and so on. Sound does have form. It can affect matter and cause form within matter. Perhaps cymatics had an influence on the formation of the universe itself.

Researchers have harnessed acoustic waves to produce levitating three-dimensional images, create a sensation of touch and even supply a soundtrack. Since the 1940s, scientists have toyed with the concept of acoustic levitation: the use of soundwave vibrations to trap tiny objects in mid-air.

Acoustics is a branch of physics that deals with the study of mechanical sound waves in gases, liquids and solids and includes topics such as vibration, sound, ultrasound and infrasound. Vibration may heal chronic wounds; wounds may heal more quickly if exposed to low-intensity vibration. The human body can generate vibrations at very low frequencies: so-called "infrasonic waves." Such low frequencies are produced by physiological processes like heartbeat, respiratory movements, blood flow through blood vessels etc. (The heart resonance frequency is 1hz). Ultrasound is used to create images of soft tissue structures, such as the gallbladder, liver, kidneys, pancreas, bladder, as well as other organs and parts of the body. Ultrasound can also measure the flow of blood in the arteries to detect blockages. An ultrasound scan, sometimes called a sonogram, is a procedure that uses high-frequency sound waves to create an image of part of the inside of the body. An ultrasound scan can be used to monitor an unborn baby, diagnose a condition, or guide a surgeon during certain procedures.

Meanwhile the digital photos stored in our devices are the result of amazing solid state and optical technology. Our phones, tablets and laptops can carry hundreds of photos and tons of data that can be transformed into exotic melodies via two programmes that transform images into sound. These compositions can range from a basic series of multifrequency notes to complex sequences of various durations complete with adjustable frequencies, variable harmonics and both in- and out –fading and can be added to PowerPoint presentations, blogs and social media sites. What can be deduced by experimenting with them is that they scan the vertical columns of pixels in a photo or drawing from left to right. Each column of pixels is then digitized and transformed into a representative audio tone. As the program sweeps across the adjacent pixel columns, the resultant tones are merged into a melody.

The phenomenon known as synaesthesia often allows people to taste sounds or hear colours. But while less than four percent of the population is estimated to be affected to this degree, far more of us are susceptible to "hearing" what we see in small, everyday ways. According to a new paper published in the *Journal Cortex*, one in five people reported hearing noises that weren't there while they were looking at visual stimuli such as blinking car-indicator signals, flickering neon signs or people walking down the street. In the paper, researchers provide a new name for this pervasive synaesthesia-like phenomenon: a visually evoked, auditory response, or vEAR. "We think that these sensations may sometimes reflect leakage of information from visual parts of the brain into areas that are more usually devoted to hearing," Dr. Elliot Freeman, senior study author and a senior lecturer at City, University of London, said. "In extreme forms of this crosstalk, any abstract visual motion or flashing may be sufficient to trigger the sensation of hearing sounds."

In the new study, researchers recruited more than 4,100 volunteers to complete an online survey, which asked them to rate how much sound they perceived in a series of twenty-four silent film clips. The researchers also asked survey-takers to answer some basic background questions, including, "Do you suffer from tinnitus (ringing in the ears)?", "Do you ever hear music in your head?" and "In everyday life are you ever aware of hearing sounds when you see flashing lights or movement?"

According to the researchers, the prevalence of this synaesthesia-like effect might point to a "relatively direct effect of low-level visual stimulation on auditory processing," suggesting that human audio and visual-processing systems are more intimately linked than previously thought. "We like to listen to music synchronized with flashing lights or dance... and incidental sound effects accompanying action in movies, such as the comic *boing* when a cartoon character slips on a banana skin," the researchers wrote. "These stimuli might reinforce each other via such audio-visual connections."

This comes as no surprise to me. Frequently, I can hear music in my head; sometimes evoked by the sight of a picture like a CD cover and I could quite possibly "conduct" an entire opera – without the aid of a score! For me, all of this is by way of gaining an understanding of – and perhaps gaining a peek into the minds – of some of the great composers and ultimately the power that their music has had – and continues to have on me. Storytellers: writers, film makers, artists, songwriters and musicians have always known how to elicit sympathy, tension, excitement, sadness and joy in an audience. Sounds and pictures have always affected a physiological response in the human body, whether the more obvious like tears or the excited or frightened fluttering of the heart. If an audience is *moved,* the performance is a success.

Albert Einstein said, "Everything in Life is Vibration". The scientific genius, Nikola Tesla said, "If you want to find the secrets of the universe, think in terms of energy, frequency, and vibration." This summarises what the great designers and composers were thinking. Wagner loved to explore the natural landscapes around him. He captured the sounds and atmospheres in music, from Brünnhilde's rocky summit in *Die Walküre*, the twittering woodbird in *Siegfried*, or the shepherd's horn in Act III of *Tristan und Isolde*. He also captured nature at its most tempestuous in the storms that open *Der fliegende Holländer* – inspired by a hasty boat journey from Riga, fleeing from creditors with his first wife Minna and their enormous Newfoundland dog in tow. His Festspielhaus in Bayreuth became the ultimate 'carrier' of these sounds in which I have been completely immersed, drawing me back, time and again.

Physiological and psychological effects of listening to music have been documented illustrating the changes in physiology, cognition and brain chemistry, and "morphology" induced by music has been studied in animal models, providing evidence that music may affect animals similarly to humans. Information about the potential benefits of music to animals suggests that providing music may be used as a means of improving the welfare of laboratory animals, through environmental enrichment, stress relief and behavioural modification. The science of music's effect on animals and even plants reveals something startling: it's not just an art form, it's essentially a force of nature. At dog kennels, researchers found that classical music reduced anxiety in the dogs, helping them sleep more and bark less. The researchers noted the similarities between dogs and people when it comes to classical music. "These results are consistent with human studies, which have suggested that music can reduce agitation, promote sleep, improve mood, and lower stress and anxiety," they wrote.

In a 2012 study published in *The Journal of Veterinary Behaviour*, researchers from Colorado State University monitored the behaviour of 117 kennelled dogs, including their activity levels, vocalisation, and body shaking. The researchers played a few different types of music to the dogs, including classical, heavy metal, and an altered type of classical music. They also observed the dogs' behaviour when no music was playing at all. They found that the dogs slept the most while listening to all kinds of classical music, indicating that it helped them relax. The dogs had the opposite reaction to the heavy metal music, which provoked increased body shaking, a sign of nervousness.

The researchers noted the similarities between dogs and people when it comes to classical music. "These results are consistent with human studies, which have suggested that music can reduce agitation, promote sleep, improve mood, and lower stress and anxiety," they wrote. They also point out that heavy metal music has anxiety-inducing effects on some people.

In 2001, researchers at the University of Leicester played various songs to 1000-strong herds of Friesian dairy cows. Over a period of nine weeks, the researchers alternated between fast music, slow music, and silence for twelve hours each day. They found that calming music, like R.E.M.'s *Everybody Hurts*, Simon & Garfunkel's *Bridge Over Troubled Water*, and Beethoven's *Pastoral Symphony*, actually resulted in the cows producing 3 percent more milk—0.73 litres per cow per day. One of the lead researchers, Dr Adrian North, told the BBC, "Calming music can improve milk yield, probably because it reduces stress." The cows were not so fond of *Space Cowboy* by Jamiroquai or *Size of a Cow* by Wonderstuff!

Elephants are already known for their ability to paint with their trunks, but it turns out that they might be musically inclined as well. In northern Thailand, a conservationist named Richard Lair put together the *Thai Elephant Orchestra*, in which sixteen elephants play specially developed instruments like steel drums and even harmonicas. Neuroscientists who have studied the music of the "Thai Elephant Orchestra" have determined that the animals are able to keep a very stable tempo on a large drum, even more stable than a human can.

Birds are probably the most well-known singers of the animal kingdom. A few years ago, researchers at Emory University set out to learn whether birds are "making" music like humans do. To find out, they examined the brains of both male and female white-tailed sparrows as they listened to the sounds of male birds. When we humans listen to music, our amygdalae often light up in response. It turned out that female white-tailed sparrows had similar brain responses to the bird sounds. The part of their brain that is similar to the amygdala lit up while listening to the male's song. The male birds, on the other hand, had brain reactions similar to humans when they listen to music that they don't like. Sarah Earp, the study's lead researcher, explained, "We found that the same neural reward system is activated in female birds in the breeding state that are listening to male birdsong, and in people listening to music that they like."

Richard Wagner must have been very aware of the significance of sound and vibration, for the secret ingredient in the theatre he designed and built is wood. From floor to ceiling, the interior of the Festspielhaus is wooden, including the pillars of the proscenium. They look like they are made of plaster, but they are made of wood and are hollow inside. Some of the wood was already decades old and cured before it was used in the construction of the Festspielhaus. The stage, the orchestra pit and those notoriously narrow hard and uncomfortable seats in the auditorium are also wooden. All that wood resounds with the music, and the effect has been described as like sitting inside a musical instrument. The sound from the famous orchestra pit deep under the stage is reflected first by a hood onto the stage, where it blends with the singers' voices and then radiates into the auditorium. That unique mix has never been recreated anywhere else and gives a special meaning to hearing Wagner "at the source." Given what I now know about sound and light and especially the effects of the sound of music on the human body, I am sure this repetitive, wrap-around treatment has served as an antidote to past trauma and given a tremendous boost to my compromised immune system and fragile well-being.

# CHAPTER 4

## *The Magic of Bayreuth*

Before going to Lebanon as a young army officer, I was stationed in Fermoy, in County Cork, where I made many friends, both in the defence forces and amongst the civilian population. Thomas Baker was interested in music and as a student at University College, Cork, used to frequent a music library in the city. Having someone who shared a love of music was a godsend. We talked endlessly, we walked and played chess and on Saturdays we would have a few pints at The Hill Hotel or have lunch in Cloyne or at the Garryvoe Hotel, famous in Cork for Sunday lunch. Whenever I caught sight of a Lufthansa aircraft as I waited at Dublin Airport for a flight to London or some other destination, I fantasised about being on board heading to Bayreuth. This sleek giant with a fuselage just under 71 meters long, a wingspan more than 64 meters, two passenger decks and the Lufthansa logo gave me butterflies in my stomach. Each time I saw it take off, I imagined myself sitting in luxury, carried to my dream destination. My fantasy became a reality in 1996 when Thomas and I were on our way to our first performance of *Parsifal*. We took Lufthansa as far as Frankfurt, from where we caught a train to Nuremberg and then another to Bayreuth – a full day's travel. Unfortunately, Thomas became ill during Act 1 and had to leave the theatre. But the following year we managed to get tickets again and this time there were no problems.

Bayreuth in the lush green hills of Upper Franconia has a unique charm. Artists enthuse about it and visitors find the festival a friendly place and despite the hours and hours of opera performances, a place of relaxation, even of spiritual renewal. At festival time, there are none of the distractions of other resorts to take the visitor away from Richard Wagner, which is just as the composer wanted it. The Bayreuth Festival is Germany's oldest festival tradition, and 2016 marked its 105th season. Founded by Richard Wagner in 1876, it continues to present the composer's operas in the very theatre Wagner himself designed for them.

Wagner first mentioned the idea of special music festivals as a showcase for The *Ring* in a letter dated Sept. 14th, 1850 to Ernst Benedikt Kietz (1815-1890).

*I'm seriously considering putting Siegfried to music but I'm not the least inclined to leave the performance realisation to the next best theatre. Quite the contrary: I'm harbouring the most audacious of plans, the implementation of which would cost no less than 10,000 Thalers!! Then I would, as I stand here, build a theatre after my own designs. I would gather the most suitable singers around me and provide all that is necessary for this one special production, so that I am assured of an excellent performance of this opera.*

(Wagner, Complete Letters, Vol. 3, p. 404).

The stage festival plan becomes openly public in the autobiographical *Message to my Friends* (1851):

*I plan to present my myth in three dramas, preceded by a lengthy prelude. Although each drama is in and of itself self-contained, I don't have 'repertoire pieces' in the modern theatre sense in mind, but rather, plan concretely the following for their realisation: At a festival specially created for this one day, to present each drama over the course of three days plus a first evening for the prelude. I will consider the purpose of these performances as fulfilled when my artistic comrades, the true performers, and I manage on these four evenings to artistically convey my*

*intentions of true emotional (not critical) comprehension to those audi-
ence members who gather to become familiar with these intentions.*
(Wagner, Sämtliche Schriften und Dichtungen, Bd. 4, S. 343f.).

But Wagner would not realise his plans until twenty-five years
later in Bayreuth. Immediately after ascending the throne, King
Ludwig II of Bavaria's salvation of Wagner from a deep personal and
financial crisis was crucial. The king's life-long patronage made it
possible for Wagner not only to continue composing; with the
newly won material possibilities the realisation of the stage festival
idea was finally tangible. Plans for a Wagner Theatre in Munich,
however, were foiled when the King's Cabinet ordered Wagner's
deportation. It wasn't until 1870 while living in Tribschen on Lake
Lucerne that Bayreuth captured Wagner's interest and soon after a
first exploratory trip, he made plans to relocate to Bayreuth and
settle down to establish the stage festival enterprise.

The financial costs of building and running the stage festival
were estimated at 300,000 Thalers, to be raised by issuing 1000
so-called 'patronage certificates', costing 300 Thalers apiece. Each
patron was entitled to a seat, leaving 500 seats to be given away free
of charge to less well-endowed friends of the arts. Due to widespread scepticism of the prospects of success for Wagner's plans, the
patronage certificate system was not particularly well-received, and
the sales of certificates were far more sluggish than planned. Thus,
the topping-out ceremony at the festival theatre on August the 2nd
1873 took place under a cloud of gloom. The stage festival originally planned for 1874 had to be postponed first till 1875 and,
finally, until 1876. The Royal Court Secretary's Office in Munich
declined to underwrite a financial guarantee for the stage festival
organisation in early 1874, bringing the enterprise to the brink of
disaster. It took the personal intervention of King Ludwig II, who
wrote to Wagner on January the 25th 1874: "No! No and no again!
It will not end like this! Help must come! We cannot allow our Plan

to fail!", to nonetheless secure a loan which, at least for the moment, afforded relief. Financing however, required ticket-sales, in effect abandoning the idea of free-of-charge access. Construction of the festival theatre was completed in August 1875 and rehearsals began.

As early as 1848, a first draft of a drama, "Siegfried's Death", later to become *Götterdämmerung*, (Twilight of the Gods) and, with that, the last part of the later tetralogy *The Ring of the Nibelung*, detailed Wagner's critique of power politics and capitalism as the antithesis of love and freedom, thus providing expression for his revolutionary convictions. Wagner was convinced that the breadth, content and significance of the tetralogy could hardly be properly performed under the then prevailing conditions of established theatre. Due to this, the "Bühnenfestspiel" (stage festival play) *Der Ring des Nibelungen* (The Ring of the Nibelung) – at the same time a contemporary equivalent to Aeschylus' Oresteia – was intended to be presented as part of a festival performance, thus liberating it from the allegedly complacent routine of the despised repertory theatre practice and also creating a fundamental alternative to current theatre.

The development of the notion of the stage festival was closely linked to the story of the emergence of *The Ring of Nibelung*, the performance of which was intended to create an exclusive artistic space, separated from contemporary society, where politics could be temporarily forgotten. The idea of the theatre festival is a special concept in theatre aesthetics and at the time, set a new benchmark for production, reception and conditions for a definitive oeuvre for a fresh idealised Hellenic style and Wagner's ideal of a theatre festival, cooperatively organised and free of the ruling political command. He presented and epitomized this ideal in *The Mastersingers of Nuremburg*.

Influenced particularly by Schopenhauer's philosophy, as of 1854 Wagner anticipated a renewal of aesthetic consciousness in the public domain no longer as a result of war but, rather, through art. Through the effects of enlightenment, natural science and positivism, religion had lost its previously important function of creating a sense of purpose and now existed only as meaningless ritual. Therefore, according to Wagner in *Religion and Art* (1880), it becomes the responsibility of art to assimilate and transport the meaningful elements of religion. The cult-religious implications of the stage festival idea, as presented by Wagner in the so-called 'regeneration scriptures' surrounding *Parsifal* and within the framework of his later cultural theoretical reflections, likewise arose from his revolutionary, young German critique of religion and its anthropological materialism.

Filled with Schopenhauer's Buddhism-inspired asceticism in overcoming the will, as well as his criticism of classical metaphysics with its aim of human self-redemption, and also as a consequence of his leftist Hegelian roots, Wagner dismissed all Christian denominational-ism and projected this religious function and mission onto art through the term "stage consecration festival opus", which he used to describe *Parsifal*. The underlying assumptions of the stage festival concept include not only a reform-oriented sense of aesthetic conceptualisation with the aim of achieving a high quality, self-confident production and reception form of theatre, whereby the scenes of the "Gesamtkunstwerks" (works of comprehensive arts) unite not only individual art forms to a creative whole, but performers and audience to a creative community as well. The idea equally presupposes a comprehensive integrative concept for politics, society, art, religion and the body politic. This integration is the consequence of an indispensably needed, comprehensive regeneration of culture and society, surmounting differences and separating barriers of nationality, language religious denomination and race.

The Bayreuth Festspiele officially opened with the debut performance of the full cycle of *The Ring of the Nibelungen* from Aug. 13th – 17th, 1876 (the debut premieres of *The Rhinegold* and

*The Valkyrie* having taken place in Munich on Sept. 22nd 1869 and June 26th 1870 respectively). Wagner was dissatisfied with the performances themselves, particularly stage-sets and costumes and promised fundamental changes for the following year. At the same time, these performances were preserved for decades as a sacrosanct, stylised archetype of model performance and staging of Wagner's works. Due to a deficit of 148,000 Thalers, continuation of the Festspiele was cancelled and the festival theatre itself was closed until further notice. The Coinage Act of the 9th of July 1873 set the exchange rate of the Prussian thaler against the Mark at 1 thaler = 3 Mark and the exchange rate for the south German florin at 1 florin = 12/7 Mark. In 1924, the Mark was replaced as the official currency by the Reichsmark. It was primarily the 100,000-Mark payment from Schott Publishing for the *Parsifal* score that financed the second and, in Wagner's lifetime the last, Bayreuth Festspiele.

After Wagner's death, his widow Cosima undertook the management of the Festspiele. With the Bayreuth world premieres of *Tristan and Isolde* (1886), The *Mastersingers of Nuremburg* (1888), *Tannhäuser* (1891), *Lohengrin* (1894) a newly staged *Ring* (1896) and, finally, *The Flying Dutchman* (1901), Cosima built up the Bayreuth repertoire as Wagner had wished (excluding three early works: *The Faeries*, *The Ban on Love*, and *Rienzi*) and developed what initially was a sporadic event into an reputable institution.

Through offsetting the royalties from the Wagner performances in Munich, after a 30-year term, all loans from the State of Bavaria had been paid off by 1906. By the end of Cosima's time, the Festspiel enterprise was free of debt. After Cosima Wagner suffered a stroke she transferred the management of the Festspiele to her son, Siegfried in 1907. Siegfried had first conducted *The Ring* in 1896, along with Hans Richter and Felix Mottl. As stage director and set designer, he was particularly attracted to architecture and undertook tentative modernisation and innovation before the outbreak of WWI in 1914 forced discontinuation of the Festspiele. Due to the economic crisis after the war, the Festspiele could not be continued until ten years later in 1924.

During World War I, the festival remained closed, and subsequent years of hyperinflation impoverished the Wagner family. During the 1920s the Festspiele became increasingly politically charged in terms of extremist German nationalism and its leanings against the Weimar Republic. On October the 1st 1923, Adolf Hitler was a guest at Wahnfried and immediately found an ardent admirer in Siegfried Wagner's wife Winifred. During the Third Reich, Adolf Hitler, a friend of the family, subsidised each new production. Tainted by the association, the festival was nearly abolished forever in the early post-war years.

In 1927 Siegfried Wagner presented *Tristan und Isolde* and *Tannhäuser* under the musical direction of Arturo Toscanini. But during the rehearsal period he suffered a heart attack. A completely new staging, financed by donations of 100,000 Reich Marks organised by Winifred Wagner, resulted in a spectacular new production on the occasion of Siegfried Wagner's 60th birthday. He died on August the 4th 1930, aged sixty-one.

After Siegfried Wagner's death, Winifred took on the management of the Festspiele, assisted by conductor and artistic director of the German Opera Berlin, Heinz Tietjen. After a repeat of the 1930 programme in 1931 and a pause in 1932, *The Ring* as well as *The Mastersingers* were newly staged for the 50th anniversary of Richard Wagner's death. Against a backdrop of the governmental takeover by the NSDAP and the election of Adolf Hitler to Reichs Chancellor. During the entire rule of the Third Reich, the Festspiele remained an expression of cultural identity and propagandist image associated to the Nazi regime. With the regime at the zenith of its power, a first completely newly staged version of *Parsifal* and *Lohengrin* lent extraordinary musical and staged brilliance as well as recognition abroad in the year of the thousand-year celebration of the

Third Reich and the Olympic Games in Berlin.

In 1937 a further re-design of *Parsifal* took place with the set designs of the young Wieland Wagner. In 1938 a new production of *Tristan and Isolde* and in 1939 *The Flying Dutchman*. With the outbreak of WWII, the management of the "War Festspiele" was taken over by the Nazi organisation "Power through Joy". Neither *Tristan*, considered by many Nazis to be decadent, or *Parsifal,* with his idea of redemption through compassionate love, sat well with the propagandist concept and self-identity of the ruling powers and vanished from the repertoire. Hitler himself visited the Festspiele for the last time in 1940, attending a performance of *Twilight of the Gods.*

By 1942, only *The Ring* and *The Flying Dutchman* were presented and in 1943 and 1944 *The Mastersingers of Nuremburg* alone was performed as a folklorist Reich political convention and an opera urging perseverance and staying power. These productions with the sets of the designer, Alfred Roller ran into bitter resistance from the old Wagnerians, for whom the original première staging and sets "where the master's eyes had rested" were sacrosanct. The increasing press and public relations efforts of Winifred Wagner, documented for example, by the addition of a balcony between boxes and balcony for members of the press, were also lamented in these circles.

In order to facilitate a new beginning of the Festspiele after the war, Winifred Wagner had to pass on management of the Festspiele to her two sons, Wieland and Wolfgang. Her political and personal proximity to the Nazi regime, particularly her close personal friendship with Adolf Hitler had become too great a problem.

A reopening of the Festspiele in 1951 featured a new staging of *Parsifal* and the *Ring* directed by Wieland Wagner as well as *Die Meistersinger von Nürnburg* under the direction of Rudolf Otto Hartmann. This was the birth of a "New Bayreuth" illustrated Wieland Wagner's abstractionist, symbolic style of direction and focus on the psychology in drama, which represented a drastic and lasting break with then-traditional staging and ideological history. From that point on, as a matter of principle, one piece each year would be newly staged. The associate management of the Festspiele by Wieland and Wolfgang Wagner was formalised on the 30th of April 1962 with a partnership agreement, lasting until Wieland's untimely death at age 50 on the 17th of October 1966.

From 1967 on, Wolfgang Wagner was solely responsible for managing the Festspiele. In 1969 August Everding became the first external director in the history of the Festspiele, engaged for new staging of *The Flying Dutchman*. The new production of *Tannhäuser* in 1972, directed by Götz Friedrich marked the advent of "Regietheater" (director's theatre) onto the stage of the Festspiele and with that, an openness for stylistic and interpretive pluralism which, under the term "Workshop Bayreuth", made a continuously progressive, multifaceted diversity of perspectives on Wagner's works possible. In 1973, the festival theatre was transferred to the newly founded Richard-Wagner-Stiftung, providing the former family enterprise with a public trust foundation.

The unorthodox idea that the composer might not necessarily have been the ultimate authority on the most effective way to stage his works was argued by Appia in the 1890s but was rejected outright by Wagner's widow, Cosima. Nevertheless, the ideas and designs of Appia and a number of other visionaries would strongly influence the future course of Wagner production and do so to this day. The Bolsheviks were notable for their staging of his works with geometric, abstract stage imagery that would set the greatest departure from the ostentatious romantic opulence favoured by the imperial past. Film director, Sergei Eisenstein brought a cinematic look to Wagner's *Die Walküre* at the Moscow Bolshoi, in keeping with the Bolsheviks' take on Wagner as revolutionary people's hero.

The new staging of the "Ring of the Century" by Patrice Chéreau on the occasion of the 100th anniversary of the Festspiele in 1976 projected the mythological references onto props and costumes of the industrial age and initially created the fiercest uproar in the history of the Festspiele although, by the end of its rotation run, it had found acceptance. Harry Kupfer's staging of *The Flying Dutchman* 1978 presented the drama as a mad dream of Senta's with psychological consistency, nightmarish fantasy and brilliant dynamics. Götz Friedrich's "black" staging of *Lohengrin* in 1979 was followed in 1981 by Jean-Pierre Ponelle's *Tristan* interpretation in which Isolde's love death occurs only in Tristan's feverish madness and Wolfgang Wagner's *Meistersinger* version, where Beckmesser receives a delightful upward revaluation. Friedrich set the anniversary *Parsifal* of 1982 in the war ruins of a toppled fascist building. In the *Ring* of 1983 naturalistic reminiscences under the musical direction of Sir George Solti alternated with the demonstration of elaborate stage machinery.

In his first *Tannhäuser* production Wolfgang Wagner chose the original "Dresden version", faithful to the original with visual references to the 1950's. The film director Werner Herzog staged a neo-romantic *Lohengrin* in 1987 in Henning von Gierke's designs of magical realism. Harry Kupfer's new staging of the *Ring* 1988 under the musical direction of Daniel Barenboim and in a set design from Hans Schavernoch was also controversial, dominated by ladders, lasers and recollections of Chernobyl. In his set and staging of *Parsifal* 1989, Wolfgang Wagner presented the world of the Holy Grail frozen in ritual. The floating upside-down turning house with the spinning room remains a lasting impression from Dieter Dorn's production of *The Flying Dutchman* 1990. Heiner Müller's staging of *Tristan and Isolde* 1993 interpreted the inner plot as intimate theatre with an austerely reduced staging and set, nonetheless expressive and suggestive, creating a focused recollection of the abstract 'New Bayreuth' style of staging. The 1994 *Ring* production by Alfred Kirchner with its focus on aestheticism, the appearance of shape and colour, strove for a playful, myth-debunking perspective of the work, thus forming an interpretive opposite to the ideologically critical *Ring* interpretations of Chéreau and Kupfer; the first year, James Levine conducted the slowest *Ring* in the history of the Festspiele, lasting fifteen hours!

Wolfgang Wagner resigned as a director after his new staging of *Die Meistersinger* in 1996, setting the drama within the context of its social aspects in a time of societal and historical upheaval as well as the conflict between humanity and nature by mixing traditional abstractions of the New Bayreuth style with colourful and stage-technical effects. Keith Warner interpreted *Lohengrin* 1999 resolutely as a dark tragedy in a magical metaphorical-symbolic staging. The new interpretation of *The Ring* by Jürgen Flimm in 2000 viewed the parable of power and love as current events in a world destroyed by politics. Here the myth is grasped in its contemporary subject matter; the tragedy of the characters in this *Ring* is the tragedy of human lovelessness, whose hope lies only in metaphysical-aesthetic realms. Philippe Arlaud was responsible for staging and set for a new production of *Tannhäuser* dominated by light and colour in 2002, the musical direction of Christian Thielemann. A new production of *The Flying Dutchman* by Claus Guth followed in 2003, set the plot in an enigmatic stairwell passage room in an allusion to the Doppelgänger-metaphor of E.T.A. Hoffmann and Strindberg-like ego-fracture as father-trauma for the child Senta. In 2004, the performance artist Christian Schlingensief delivered yet another controversial new production of *Parsifal* under the musical direction of Pierre Boulez) using an associative-additive accumulation of various image and symbolic levels, including the use of video projections, in a consistent referential system alluding to a universal, inter-cultural religiousness, ritualism and iconic-ism.

The first Wagner Festival in 1876 was a financial disaster, followed by six years of nothing. The despondent composer called his festival theatre "a fool's whim". Disappointed by his own stage presentations, he sarcastically remarked that he now wanted to create "invisible theatre". But the second Bayreuth Festival, in 1882, was a success. It consisted of 16 performances of his work *Parsifal*, written with the particulars of the Festspielhaus in mind. Wagner died a year later.

After Wieland Wagner died in 1966 his brother Wolfgang stayed on until 2008 – a remarkable 57 years altogether. He, in turn, was succeeded by his daughters Eva Wagner-Pasquier and Katharina Wagner. Beginning in 2016, Katharina has been the sole festival director. What sounds like a smooth succession has been anything but. Each phase has met with family quarrels and controversy.

As a young man, Adolf Hitler went to every Wagner opera performance he could. He was only one of many who felt personally spoken to by Wagner's music. *Hitler's Bayreuth* by historian Brigitte Hamann documents the fateful mix of the Führer and the Bayreuth Festival, even leading to absurdities such as closed performances for soldiers wounded in World War II on the presumption that they would be healed by Wagner's music. Given what we know today about the power of music in illness and injury recovery, this may not have been as crazy as some might think!

The Bayreuth Festival has always had a certain mystique, which has only been enhanced by the mass media. Even back in the 1920s, the then new medium of radio was employed for shortwave transmissions of Wagner operas – live from Bayreuth. Beginning in the 1950s, the main media partner has been ARD, a German public broadcasting network, which has made performances available for radio broadcasts worldwide by members and associate members of the European Broadcasting Union.

Video, recordings of rehearsals were once compiled into presentations after the fact, preserving milestone productions such as the 1976 *Ring* by director Patrice Chéreau on video cassette and DVD. That is still done, but in recent years, the trend has been towards live transmissions some of which have been relayed directly to outdoor venues in Bayreuth.

The Green Hill overlooking the Franconian city of Bayreuth has been populated by top-tier celebrities in years past including Prince Charles, the Prince of Wales and former Russian President Mikhail Gorbachev. German Chancellor Angela Merkel has been a regular. There is an interesting new publication in two volumes by Oswald Georg Bauer titled *Die Geschichte der Bayreuther Festspiele* (The History of the Bayreuth Festival). As the long-term former spokesman for the Bayreuth Festival, Bauer has an insider's knowledge and was commissioned to compile the book by former festival director Wolfgang Wagner, who specified that it be based "only on original sources". Over a quarter of a century later, Bauer now quips that had he known what he would be getting into, he never would have started the gigantic project. It is not clear whether an English translation is planned but the anthology is a must-have for Wagnerites.

*Wahnfried – The Home of Richard Wagner* is the work of authors Markus Kiesel and Joachim Mildner. Wagner's onetime residence, now a museum, underwent elaborate restoration and was reopened in 2019. This volume provides an inside look for those who have not yet made it to Bayreuth.

# CHAPTER 5

## *Parsifal*

The story of the ignorant and naïve Parzival, who sets out on his adventures without even knowing his own name, uses the classic fairy-tale theme of 'the guileless fool' who, through innocence and artlessness, reaches a goal denied to wiser men and introduced the theme of the Holy Grail into German literature. Wolfram von Eschenbach uses Parzival's remarkable progress from folk-tale dunce to wise and conscientious keeper of the Grail to present a clever metaphor for man's spiritual education and development.

Wagner read von Eschenbach's poem "Parzival" while taking the waters at Marienbad in 1845. Marienbad is still a popular European spa town, still alive with the glamour of a by-gone era with its healing natural resources, architectural splendour and a long list of other famous visitors including Chopin, Goethe and King Edward VII. Then as now, guests wandered among the colonnades, fountains and flower beds, sipping mineral water from drinking cups and blending a desire for good health, with socialising and cultural events.

"Taking the waters" meant bathing in or drinking from thermal springs that drew a regular stream of visitors, bottles and glasses in hand, who believed in their miraculous powers. The Greeks started it with a "Serangeum", a bath cut into the hillside from where hot springs issued. The Romans exported the notion to their colonies, including Britain's Bath, now a town in the southeast of England. The Japanese make annual retreats to their "onsen", or hot springs. The Portuguese, too, boast therapeutic thermal springs. The hot springs in the north originate from a high plateau and trickle down for ten years through layers of granite, picking up minerals as they do so. The Pedras Salgadas mineral water is reckoned to be so effective in treating and preventing arthritis, as well as digestive and skin ailments, that the local government subsidises regular treatments for residents. Centuries later, many doctors advise a stay at a thermal spa to ease stiff shoulders, neck pain and minor sports injuries.

As well as walking and hiking, Wagner attended spas and took them very seriously. He used nature as a remedy for his various illnesses, which included erysipelas (a painful skin infection) and irritable bowel syndrome. It was during these retreats that he conceived several operas – *Das Liebesverbot*, *Tannhäuser* and *Die Meistersinger von Nürnberg*. Even the idea for *Lohengrin* came to him when he was in the bath. Water imagery is important in many of his operas, whether Amfortas's healing bath in *Parsifal* or Lohengrin's mysterious arrival over the water. The entire *Ring* cycle begins with a watery scene at the bottom of the Rhine.

After encountering Arthur Schopenhauer's writings in 1854, Wagner became interested in oriental philosophies, especially Buddhism. Out of this interest came "Die Sieger" (The Victors, 1856), a sketch Wagner wrote for an opera based on a story from the life of Buddha. The themes which were later explored in Parsifal of self-renouncing, reincarnation, compassion. According to his autobiography *Mein Leben*, Wagner conceived *Parsifal* on Good Friday morning, April 1857, in the Asyl (Asylum), the small cottage on Otto Wesendonck's estate in the Zürich suburb of Enge, which Wesendonck – a wealthy silk merchant and generous patron of the arts – had placed at Wagner's disposal, through the good offices of his wife Mathilde Wesendonck. Wegner and his wife Minna had moved into the cottage on the 28th of April. Wagner wrote:

*On Good Friday I awoke to find the sun shining brightly for the first time in this house: the little garden was radiant with green, the birds sang, and at last I could sit on the roof and enjoy the long-yearned-for peace with its message of promise. Full of this sentiment, I suddenly remembered that the day was Good Friday, and I called to mind the significance this omen had already once assumed for me when I was reading Wolfram's Parzival. Since the sojourn in Marienbad, where I had conceived Die Meistersinger and Lohengrin, I had never occupied myself again with that poem; now its noble possibilities struck me with overwhelming force, and out of my thoughts about Good Friday I rapidly conceived a whole drama, of which I made a rough sketch with a few dashes of the pen, dividing the whole into three acts.*

However, as his second wife Cosima Wagner reported on the 22nd of April 1879, this account had been coloured by a certain amount of poetic licence:

*Richard today recalled the impression which inspired his 'Good Friday Music'; he laughs, saying he had thought to himself, In fact it is all as far-fetched as my love affairs, for it was not a Good Friday at all — just a pleasant mood in Nature which made me think, This is how a Good Friday ought to be.*

The work may indeed have been conceived at Wesendonck's cottage in the last week of April 1857, but Good Friday that year fell on the 10th of April, when the Wagners were still living in Zürich.

Wagner did not resume work on *Parsifal* for eight years, during which time he completed *Tristan und Isolde* and began *Die Meistersinger von Nürnberg*. Then, between the 27th and the 30th of August 1865, he took up *Parsifal* again and made a prose draft of the work, containing a brief outline of the plot and a considerable amount of detailed commentary on the characters and themes of the drama. But once again the work was set aside for another eleven and a half years while most of Wagner's creative energy was devoted to the *Ring* cycle. The *Ring* was given its first full performance at Bayreuth in August 1876. Only now that this colossal project had been completed did Wagner find the time to concentrate on *Parsifal.*

On the 12th of November 1880, Wagner conducted a private performance of the prelude to *Parsifal* for his patron, Ludwig II of Bavaria at the Court Theatre in Munich. The premiere of the entire work was given in the Festspielhaus at Bayreuth on the 26th of July 1882 under the baton of the Jewish-German conductor Hermann Levi. Stage designs were by Max Brückner and Paul von Joukowsky who took their directions from Wagner himself. The Grail Hall was based on the interior of Siena Cathedral which Wagner had visited in 1880, while Klingsor's magic garden was modelled on those at the Palazzo Rufolo in Ravello. In July and August 1882 sixteen performances of the work were given in Bayreuth conducted by Levi and Franz Fischer with an orchestra of 107, a chorus of 135 and 23 soloists (with the main parts being double cast). At the last of these performances, Wagner took the baton from Levi and conducted the final scene of Act III from the orchestral interlude to the end.

For the first twenty years of its existence, with the exception of eight private performances for Ludwig II at Munich in 1884 and 1885, the only staged performances of *Parsifal* took place in the Bayreuth Festspielhaus. Wagner had two reasons for wanting to keep *Parsifal* exclusively for the Bayreuth stage: he wanted to prevent it from degenerating into 'mere amusement' for an opera-going public. Only at Bayreuth could this, his last work be presented in the way envisaged by him. Secondly, he thought that the opera would provide an income for his family after his death if Bayreuth had the monopoly on its performance.

The Bayreuth authorities allowed un-staged performances to take place in various countries after Wagner's death (London in 1884, New York City in 1886, and Amsterdam in 1894) but they maintained a ban on stage performances outside Bayreuth. On the 24th of December 1903, after receiving a court ruling that performances in the United States could not be prevented by Bayreuth, the New York Metropolitan Opera staged the complete opera, using many Bayreuth-trained singers. Wagner's wife, Cosima barred anyone involved in the New York production from working at Bayreuth in future performances. Unauthorized stage performances were also undertaken in Amsterdam in 1905, 1906 and 1908. There was a performance in Buenos Aires, in Teatro Coliseo, on June 20, 1913 under Gino Marinuzzi. Finally, Bayreuth lifted its monopoly on *Parsifal* on the 1st of January 1914 in the Teatro Comunale di Bologna in Bologna. Some opera houses began their performances at midnight between the 31st of December 1913 and the 1st of January 1914. The first authorised performance was staged at the Gran Teatre del Liceu in Barcelona: it began at 10:30pm local time, which was an hour behind Bayreuth. Such was the demand for *Parsifal* that it was presented in more than 50 European opera houses between the 1st of January and the 1st of August 1914.

At Bayreuth performances audiences do not applaud at the end of the first act. The tradition of Bayreuth audiences not applauding at the end of the first act is the result of a misunderstanding arising from Wagner's desire at the premiere to maintain the serious mood of the opera. After much applause following the first and second acts, Wagner spoke to the audience and said that the cast would take no curtain calls until the end of the performance. This confused the audience, who remained silent at the end of the opera until Wagner addressed them again, saying that he did not mean that they could not applaud. After the performance Wagner grumbled that he didn't know what to do and wondered if the audience liked it or not. At subsequent performances some believed that Wagner had wanted no applause until the very end, and there was silence after the first two acts. In fact, during the first Bayreuth performances, Wagner himself cried "Bravo!" as the Flower maidens made their exit in the second act, only to be hissed by other members of the audience! At some theatres other than Bayreuth, applause and curtain calls are normal practice after every act.

Among the more significant post-war productions was that directed in 1951 by Wieland Wagner, the composer's grandson. At the first Bayreuth Festival after World War II he moved away from literal representation of the Hall of the Grail or the Flower maiden's bower. Instead, this production was heavily influenced by the ideas of the Swiss stage designer Adolphe Appia: lighting effects and the bare minimum of scenery were used to complement Wagner's music. The reaction to this production was extreme: Ernest Newman, Richard Wagner's biographer described it as 'not only the best *Parsifal* I have ever seen and heard, but one of the three or four most moving spiritual experiences of my life'. Others were appalled that Wagner's stage directions were being flouted. The conductor of the 1951 production, Hans Knappertsbusch, on being asked how he could conduct such a disgraceful travesty, declared that right up until the dress rehearsal he imagined that the stage decorations were still to come. Knappertsbusch was particularly upset by the omission of the dove which appears over Parsifal's head at the end of the opera, which he claimed inspired him to give better performances. To placate his conductor Wieland arranged to reinstate the dove, which descended on a string. What Knappertsbusch did not realise was that Wieland had made the length of the string long enough for the conductor to see the dove, but not for the audience. Wieland continued to modify and refine his Bayreuth production of *Parsifal* until his death in 1966. My friend, the late Fr. Richard McLoughlin said it was "The Real Presence". There is no doubt in my mind that it has immense power to move people. Intoxicating in the best possible sense.

The more recent performances of *Parsifal* have failed to live up to the Wolfgang Wagner production. The production directed by Christoph Schlingenseif in 2004 was laden with social and political interests and included film clips and costumes that focused the action on the conflict between Christianity and Islam. The decor was full of religious symbolism. In the revolving set, amid nomads' dwellings and multifunctional projection screens, Kundry, who accompanies the hero on his quest for the Holy Grail was a black-clad, Islamic fundamentalist fighter. The Grail was presented with allusions to the contrast between the opulence of Catholic ritual in South America and the squalid social conditions in the slums. Much of it was beyond me; none of it to my liking. Sadly, Christoph Schlingenseif died from lung cancer at the age of forty-nine. Too young.

Stefan Herheim, born in Oslo is regarded as one of opera's most innovative directors. As a young boy he sat at the side of his father, a violist, in the pit at the Norwegian National Opera. At about age six, he started putting on his own productions at home, using puppets. His production of *Parsifal* in 2008 was almost like a film: a plot and a sub-plot, the latter the story of the Bayreuth Festival intertwined with Germany's tormented history. I was not too impressed. Many subsequent performances left a lot to be desired, yet, paradoxically, each time I return, I come away yearning for more.

Montsalvat, in the northern mountains of Gothic Spain is the place where the action in *Parsifal*, Wagner's final work, is set. "Montsalvat is inaccessible to your steps" (Lohengrin, In Fernam Land), which is, I like to think, a parallel universe, under the protection of the Holy Spirit, as manifested by a dove that comes each year to strengthen the Grail, the vessel into which Christ's blood flowed at the foot of the cross. In earlier times, after the Flood, the dove presented Noah with a sprig from an olive tree. Then again, after Christ's baptism in the River Jordan, the dove is present. To gain access to the Kingdom of the Grail, one has to be chosen. To be chosen, one has to be pure of heart, or have the potential to so become, like Amfortas and Kundry. Access is therefore granted through a portal, if you like. Access is controlled by a spiritual power. Gurnemanz, in an earlier long narrative brings the story up to date. We meet him and some boys and knights and learn of the king's distress; he awaits "a pure fool, made wise by compassion". Parsifal is chasing a sacred swan and blunders into the Kingdom of the Grail in pursuit of his victim.

The prelude to Act I, is just sublime. It is played with the curtain closed, hence eyes closed, so that we open our minds to listen to the music and contemplate what is to follow. A tone poem or symphonic introduction, perhaps? Gurnemanz describes how the Grail and Spear were brought down to earth by angels and presented to Titruel. In Act I then we meet Gurnemanz, Amfortas, Parsifal and Kundry. We hear Titruel and not "the Grail shines more brightly today". Yes! Parsifal is present and the Grail recognises his presence. Parsifal does not partake in the Love Feast; had he done so, he would have marched off the stage with the knights, singing his head off! In order for Act II to work, Parsifal must be a witness to the Love Feast and to be affected by it. The action in the third part of Act II is pivotal, so care must be taken here to be alert in order to hear it. Productions that are too slow or too fast can lead to either boredom or absence of concentration, which can lead to failure to understand – and/or to sleep! Act I can come in at 1:45, 1:50, 1:55, or, God help us, two hours. At Bayreuth, two hours would be roundly booed.

In Act II we meet Klingsor, Parsifal and Kundry. Kundry is a witch; she can fly through the air with her horse. She saw the gaze of Christ as she mocked Him on the Via Dolorosa. He saw her essence and was compassionate, even though He was in great pain and anguish. She is 1,937 years old when she confronts Parsifal, a youth of eighteen years of age. She was present at his birth and at his mother's death. She saw his father slain. She knew him when he was in the womb. She has waited for him over the years. Her interest in him is sexual and not pure love. She is under the spell of Klingsor, a powerful and evil magician. He has the Holy Spear which he gained with the fall of Amfortas. Amfortas fell under Kundry's charm and was seduced by her. The wielding of the Holy Spear in battle was a profane act. Parsifal, we learn, does not repeat this error. In Act II, Kundry's attempted seduction of Parsifal fails, despite her using every trick available to woman – even his love of his mother.

After the Kiss, Parsifal is metamorphosed: he is Amfortas and the Grail. He feels the pain of the Saviour running through his veins. He feels emptiness and despair and the desolation of same. We understand what 'Erlösung dem Erlöser' means (The Redeemer redeemed) – if alert to it. Parsifal regains the Holy Spear, through the intercession of the Holy Spirit. He destroys Klingsor and his Magic Garden. Kundry curses him and he leaves the stage – to return twenty-five years later, perhaps.

Act III is set on Good Friday. Gurnemanz is aged, yet still vigorous. Kundry is in a death-like sleep. She is awakened by Gurnemanz and hears that she is repentant. Parsifal arrives, armed as a knight and is greeted by Gurnemanz who recognises him and the Holy Spear. Parsifal is anointed King by Gurnemanz and Kundry is baptised. She dries Parsifal's feet with her hair. The obsequies for Titruel lead to the appearance of Parsifal, as Amfortas cries out in his terrible pain and anguish, pleading to be slain by the knights, demanding that he perform his office. Amfortas is cured of his wound by the Holy Spear. Parsifal, the newly anointed king performs the ritual of the Love Feast. The Grail glows in ever-brightening light. Kundry is granted eternal rest while the dove returns and shines its light of approval on the ceremony. The chorus of knights give benediction to all assembled – on stage and in the audience: redemption to the Redeemer; redemption to all. "Erlösung dem Erlöser".

The experience of my first *Parsifal* was immensely profound. Like Ernest Newman, Richard Wagner's biographer's experience, mine was one of the 'most moving spiritual experiences of my life' – and

I was hooked for life. Not all productions or performances of the work have matched my first, but I still need at least one performance a year. To date I have attended thirty-three performances of *Parsifal.*

One of my preferred performances was the Wolfgang Wagner production in 2001. I attended with the late Fr. Richard McLoughlin O.P. Richard was spiritual director of the local Pioneer Total Abstinence Association of which my father was president. When I met him, he told me he loved rugby and was a huge fan of Wagner. I wrote to the Friends of Bayreuth and asked for two tickets to *Parsifal.* They very kindly responded with tickets and I gave one to Fr. McLoughlin. He was overjoyed. Our journey to Bayreuth was not without its challenges: the flight was delayed and then cancelled. We eventually made it although I can't remember how! After we settled in at our hotel, I phoned his room. "I'm so tired I could die!" he told me. Although in his middle seventies at the time, Fr. Richard had been a rugby player and a keen hill-walker and the next day, I observed him foraging in the dining room after breakfast and later, walking briskly around the town, full of vigour and no doubt eager to see as much of Wagner Territory as possible. I hoped the performance that evening would live up to expectations. He loved it. I have a card that he sent me afterwards in which he referred to the trip as "a treasured memory". I treasure his card and remember him with great fondness. I spent a short time with him just days before he died – St Stephen's day, 2005 – at Tallaght Hospital. A very humble, spiritual man who, to me, was a saint.

# CHAPTER 6

# *My Hunger for Culture and Joy*

When I founded the Wagner Society of Ireland in 2002, I was a member of the London Wagner Society and the Wagner Society of Scotland and I had attended all thirteen of Wagner's operas, including *Die Feen* in Paris and *Das Liebesverbot* in the old opera house in Wexford. Dr. Jim Pritchard, Chair of the London Society advised me to affiliate with the Richard Wagner Verband International in order to get tickets for the Bayreuth Festival. The International Association of Wagner Societies (RWVI) unites regional Wagner Societies around the world. Founded in 1865 to create interest in and deepen the understanding of Richard Wagner's works, to provide support for the next generation of artists, to support the Richard Wagner Scholarship Foundation, which was founded at the behest of Richard Wagner, to ensure the continuing success of the Bayreuth Festival and to promote international co-operation. An international Wagner congress is held every year. The congresses offer over several days a full programme of musical performances, lectures, discussions, social events and light entertainment.

In my capacity as Chairman of the society, I attended the Richard Wagner Verband International Congress in Copenhagen in May 2003. As first Chair of our society, I considered it a great honour to represent the society at this prestigious event. From my room at The Admiral Hotel, I could see Copenhagen's new opera house under construction. It would take another two years to complete and would have a seating capacity of 1,400, with a rehearsal room thirteen meters below sea level! Over the next three days I attended *Die Walküre*, *Salome* and *Tristan und Isolde* at the Royal Theatre as well as two concerts, one was the opening event of the Congress, held at the Det NY Theater and the other at the Tivoli Concert Hall. At dinner, I was seated at table with Gudrun Wagner, wife of Wolfgang Wagner, Danish opera singer, Poul Elming and a former bomber pilot whose name I have forgotten. I took the liberty of giving my card to Gudrun Wagner and asked her if she could help our fledgling society in any way. She seemed very receptive and delighted to have a new society 'in the fold'. I later followed up with a letter, asking for tickets to the Bayreuth Festival in 2004 and was amazed to receive forty tickets. The meeting of the chairpersons was held the Royal Danish Conservatory of Music where I was warmly greeted President, Josef Lienhart, chairman of the Richard Wagner Verband International, Derek Watson and Andrew Medlicott. The meeting last three hours and was conducted throughout in German. Derek Watson was very helpful in translating the important points before a vote was taken. A proposal to hold the Congress every two years, for reasons of cost was defeated, much to the delight of all present. The weather was glorious, and I found the city beautiful. I even had time to visit The Little Mermaid and purchase a small watercolour painting of her. More importantly, our society had been accepted with joy, warmth and friendship into the family of Richard Wagner Societies, worldwide. On Sunday, the first of June, a farewell concert was held, followed by a meal. Then we said our goodbyes and took taxis to the airport. For me, it was an outstanding experience.

Bright skies in Munich gave way to cold and rain in Augsburg on the opening day of the 14th Richard Wagner Verband International Congress, held in the Dorint Hotel in May 2004. In excess of 160 delegates gathered with undampened enthusiasm for the fare to follow, a programme commencing at 9.00 a.m., concluding at midnight.

The meeting of chairpersons was opened by esteemed president, Josef Lienhart, now head of 138 societies, worldwide, with in excess of 38,000 members. Chairs of new societies, Delhi, Halle, Perth and Zagreb were introduced and welcomed, as were new Chairpersons of existing societies. The agenda included the singing competition for Wagner voices in Bayreuth 2003, and the competition planned for stage design to be held in Graz, Austria in 2005, the registration deadline for which was August 9th, 2004. Reports on activities of RWVI were presented by Herr Lienhart and the Treasurer. Payment of the annual subscription using IBAN was explained in French, English and German, via overhead projection. There were lots of speeches from the top table and from the floor and in a very good-natured and friendly atmosphere. Help, as ever, was readily available for delegates with little German.

A very pleasant lunch followed the meeting, after which VIP buses were laid on to take delegates to places like Füssen, Hohenschwangeu Castle, Linder Hof Castle and Kirchheim. For those who took the excursion to Kirchheim, the highlight of the day was a concert by Stefan Mickish, pianist in the beautiful surroundings of the Zedersaal of the Fugger Castle at Kirchheim. Stefan played his own adaptations and arrangements from *Tristan und Isolde* on the grand piano, which would have impressed both Franz Liszt and Richard Wagner.

On Saturday morning, May 22nd the delegates re-assembled in the Goldenersaal of the city hall for a speech of welcome by the mayor, Dr. Paul Wengert. At 2 p.m. a seminar was held on "Richard Wagner, his life and work". A question posed was "Did Richard Wagner write primarily for men?". The consensus was that he wrote for women and men. Later in the evening a festival performance of Tannhäuser was performed at Augsburg Theatre – Dresden version. I can well imagine that the great master, Richard Wagner would take issue with this description, given what was to happen after the prelude! Poor Venus was strangled by a manic Tannhäuser in Act I, then removed like a sack of potatoes by the ensemble, not to appear again in Act III in any shape – i.e. flesh, spirit or voice. I missed her screams as a cue to the choral finale. This aside, the production was musically and vocally fine. Tannhäuser's treatment by the virtuous in Act II was cruel; led by a rope around his neck, then branded with a red-hot iron before being sent out into a snowstorm – very modern! The virtuous then toasted their night's work as the curtain was pulled across the stage by Wolfram von Eschenbach. Act III, like the preceding acts was out of the modern film version of *Romeo and Juliet*. Some distinguished Wagnerians were in the audience including Frau Verena Wagner Lafferentz. Whilst overall the evening was enjoyable the absence of Venus from the third act spoiled it somewhat.

On Sunday morning we revisited Augsburg Theatre for speeches by the Mayor of Bayreuth and the Mayor of Augsburg. The Philharmonikor Choir, Augsburg sang the choral from *Meistersinger* and pieces by J. Brahms and Robert Schumann. Josef Lienhart, President of the RWVI presented gold RWV insignias to the organisers of the 14th RWVI Congress. Dr Martha Schad and Frau Hilde Lutz, Augsburg. The morning concluded with pieces from Ludwig Von Beethoven and Richard Strauss.

The afternoon commenced with a festival dinner in the congress hall foyer. Over 800 persons were in attendance, i.e. delegates and guests. I was seated at a table with representatives from Florida, Edinburgh, New York, Copenhagen and Venezuela. During the meal 'Historic Women of Augsburg' displayed traditional costumes, from over the centuries.

The congress concluded with a festival concert by the Swabian Youth Orchestra. The programme included Richard Wagner's *Overture in D Minor*, Franz Liszt's Concerto for Piano and Orchestra in E Sharp Major and Anton Bruckner's *Symphony No. 3 in D Minor*, dedicated to Richard Wagner. As in Copenhagen farewells were exchanged as we prepared to return home from a very well organised and successful congress.

Anthony Linehan attended the Congress in Tallin, Helsinki in 2006, on behalf of the Wagner Society of Ireland and had written an excellent report. My next Congress was in May 2007. The town of Weimar was bathed in sunlight for the duration of a culturally outstanding congress, of which all aspects were at the highest level, which is only to be expected in a city steeped in a thousand years of history and art, the home of Goethe, Schiller and Liszt. It was in Weimar on August 28th, 1850 that Franz Liszt conducted *Lohengrin*, its composer being in exile.

On Day One, we had an interesting production of *Das Rheingold*, conducted by Carl St. Clair and produced by Michael Schultz, in the National Theatre. Elements of Bayreuth and Baden-Baden in this production. The musicianship was of a very high standard. Guided tours of Weimer in English and French – great eras of Weimer – Classical Weimar on Day Two was followed in the evening by an organ recital of J.S. Bach's music, opening concert at the State chapel: Franz Liszt Piano Concerto No. 1; Hector Berlioz and Richard Strauss. Day Three was a very busy day for delegates – a symposium covering: Liszt and Wagner, Piano Transcriptions; Wagner and Liszt as authors; Johan Wolfgang Von Goethe. The day ended with a German classic play (in German). There was also a tour to Naumburger Dom and the house of Friedrich Nietzsche. Day Four consisted of the meeting of the chairmen of the societies in the RWV and RWVI in Weimar Castle, Weisser Saal. The meeting opened with an introduction to the thirteen new chairmen, all of whom said a few words. Reports from the President, the International Commission, Foundation of Bursaries, Treasurer and Auditor, other business and finally, 'The Strategic Paper'. The meeting lasted four and a half hours. Lots of speeches. The annual subs are increased for German societies from €2 to €3 per member. The proposal caused quite a degree of heated debate. Non-German societies are charged a single levy depending on ability to bear, and membership. As regards the Strategic Paper, this generated a great deal of debate – e.g. one organisation or two? – and getting younger people interested. The subject of tickets for the Bayreuther Festspiele raised its head. Delegates were allowed every opportunity to speak and more than once they wished to amplify a point. Whilst no translators were present, I was attended to by Frau Ingrid Budde of the International Commission, on the instruction of the president. Both were marvellous company at the meeting and later, at the National Theatre.

Having survived the meeting of Chairs we prepared to attend *Die Walküre* at the National Theatre. The singing and general musicianship were excellent, the production odd in that it had a prologue, which was really strange. The storm music commenced and Acts I and II went quite well. But in Act III we had bunk beds and the Von Trapp Family *Walküries*. They really had fun. The audience initially booed – shock and horror at the bunk beds – but all became calm and it was fine. Brünnhilde wore a beautiful wedding dress at the conclusion and went Elsa-like up the stage into a very bright light. Wotan handed his spear to Loge and as the stage darkened the spear went on fire – a fine interpretation of the drama. No boos at the end. Lots of encores. Frau Verena Wagner Lafferentz stood and applauded the artistes and if she was satisfied, then surely it was a successful production? And it was a successful production, overall.

The final day commenced with a concert in Weimar Hall with the Youth Symphony Orchestra from the Liszt School of Music. They were wonderful. *Lohengrin*, Prelude Acts I and III, *Der fliegende Holländer* Overture and finally *Die Meistersinger von Nürnberg* in Prelude to Acts III and I. Back to the Dorint Hotel for a festival dinner. The day ended with a performance at the National Theatre of Verdi's *Don Carlos*, at which time I was en route back to Dublin.

The Richard Wagner Verband International Congress in Dresden from May 14th to the 17th, 2009 was a special congress, special because it was the Verband's 100th Birthday, having been born in Leipzig in 1909. Special also because the Richard Wagner Verband International and the Richard Wagner Verband had merged. All societies now had a vote. There was also a new Constitution which would issue with the report of the Congress in due course, written in the three principal languages: German, French and English. The President of the new body, Professor Eva Märtson (Hannover) replaced esteemed past President Josef Lienhart the previous year in Geneva. There are four vice-presidents and twelve working members, half of which are German and half non-German. This was a major change and welcome step forward for non-German societies.

As ever, the congress had a prestigious set of events, including Verdi's *Aida* at the Semperoper. The high point for me was the concert in the restored Frauenkirche with the Champs-Élysées Orchestra directed by Phillippe Herreweghe. They played the overture to the oratorio *Paul* by Felix Mendelssohn Bartholdy, *Concert for Violin, Cello and Orchestra* by Robert Schumann and *the Scottish Symphony* by Mendelssohn. The soloist was Steven Isserlis.

The restored Frauenkirche stands in pride of place in the cobblestoned, hexagonal pedestrian area with its modern hotels and massive statue of Martin Luther. The area is delightful. The interior of the Frauenkirche is beautiful with gold-laden altar decorations. It is a monument to the resolve of the people of Dresden who contributed to its restoration after the devastation of the city during the second world war and it exemplifies the will and resolve of the human spirit. It was impossible not to be overcome with emotion as this beautiful place was filled with the music of Mendelssohn in his 200th anniversary.

The final event was on Sunday morning in the Schauspielhaus and was interspersed with speeches by Professor Märtson and Josef Lienhart, the latter giving the history of the Verband and its foundation in Leipzig in 1909. Its mentors included Cosima, Siegfried and Winifred Wagner. There was a wonderful musical programme with the Staatskapelle Halle directed by Karl-Heinz Steffens, *Symphony Nr. 2 C-Dur Op 19* by Carl Maria von Weber, *Four Last Songs* by Richard Strauss with Soprano, Carola Höhn. The programme concluded with the prelude to *Parsifal* by Richard Wagner.

The concert was followed by a long walk over the Elbe to the opposite side, to the festival meal on what was a glorious morning. The guests of honour were Frau Verena Wagner- Lafferenz and her niece, Eva (daughter of Wolfgang), co-director of the Bayreuther Festspiele. There were two informal speeches from the centre of the room by the president and by Eva Pasquier-Wagner.

At table, I had a very agreeable banter with French delegates; the French are very supportive of congresses. The room was filled to capacity. Prof. Märtson's final exhortation was for all societies to continue their support for excellence in music and the works of Richard Wagner. Again, I observed that the Richard Wagner Verband International is a marvellous organisation. Whenever this body meets in Congress, beauty, joy and friendship are close by.

On behalf of the Wagner Society of Ireland, the Wagner Society of Scotland and on my own behalf, I attended a commemoration service for Dr. Wolfgang Wagner in April 2010. It was a very digni-fied event (over 1,500 attended) with speeches interspersed with music. Artistes came from all over the world. I saw Peter Schneider and Sir John Tomlinson in the Bayerischer Hof. Waltraud Meier was there as was Siegfried Jerusalem. I met members of the Richard Wagner Verband including Hon President, Josef Lienhart. The co-directors of the Bayreuther Festspiele, Katharina and Eva Wagner-Pasquier, daughters of Wolfgang were there. In attendance was the German Chancellor, Dr. Angela Merkel who attended in a private capacity. Speeches were given by Bavarian Minister-President, Horst Seehofer, Christian Thielemann and Professor Joachim Thiery,

Dean of the Faculty of Medicine, Leipzig, a life-long friend. The music was conducted by Christian Thielemann with members of the Festspiele orchestra and choir, with chorus master, Eberhard Friedrich. The music programme was the prelude from Act I of *Lohengrin*, Siegfried's Rhine Journey from *Götterdämmerung*, the motet, *Denn er hat seinen Engeln befohlen* (Psalm 91) by Felix Mendelssohn-Bartholdy, concluding with the prelude to Die Meistersinger with chorale. Wolfgang Wagner was deeply loved by all staff, artistes and those who love what is the miracle of Bayreuth. He devoted his whole working life (57 years) to the work of his grandfather. I was privileged to meet him in Venice, 2006 at the RWVI competition for Wagner Voices and grateful to be invited to attend his service of farewell.

The City of Stralsund, Germany would be my final Congress destination in May 2010. The congress formally commenced on May 13th but was preceded by cultural events in Stralsund Theatre: small but intimate. *Der Rosenkavalier* on May 12th was followed by *Der fliegende Holländer* the next day. There was a Wagner Gala with overtures from *Rienzi*, *Tannhäuser* and *Lohengrin*, and a concert performance of Act I of *Die Walküre*. Present at the Gala was the Mayor of Bayreuth, Dr. Hanl and Frau Verrena Wagner-Lafferentz, last surviving granddaughter of Richard Wagner. On Sunday, May 16th the usual closing event with a symphonic concert by a young persons' orchestra from Northern Germany. Finalists from the 6th Wagner Voices Competition were present. The usual farewell dinner ended the congress. *Turandot* was performed that evening in Stralsund Theatre – a hectic week! On this occasion, the meeting of delegates took place on Friday May 14th, 2010 at 9 a.m. in Stralsund Theatre. I was seated in the front row with Maureen McIntosh (London) and Derek Watson and Will Scott (Edinburgh), all of whom I knew from previous events. We were given translation radios, so we heard every word.

Professor Eva Märtson, President, RWVI welcomed all present, especially those from abroad. She spoke about deceased members since the last congress: Paris, Amsterdam, Saarland and Venice. Werner Herzog was remembered as was beloved Dr. Wolfgang Wagner ("the freeing of a great soul who did so much for music in Germany"). She spoke also of the new production of *Lohengrin* and referred to Richard Wagner's "artwork of the future".

The president advised that a questionnaire was sent to all societies six months ago, seeking feedback. A hundred and twenty-two of one hundred and thirty-nine were returned which was very high. The Verband has 9% French speakers, 44% English speakers and 47% German speakers. Communication by the Worldwide Web was now the principal means used by the Verband. The website has been modernised. It was receiving about two thousand hits each month which could be analysed by country. Ireland had eight hits last month. Professor Märtson said that while the importance of this was now well-known, "nothing beats meeting people in person."

One person cannot run the organisation, therefore the RWVI has an Executive Committee with four Vice Presidents, a Treasurer, a Secretary and eight others. The four Vice Presidents have been assigned a number of societies to form links with. In our case – Dublin, London and Edinburgh – our Vice President was Prof. Dr. Hans-Michael Schneider of Karlsruhe, a very friendly gentleman whom I met in Copenhagen in 2003. The Annual Report still issues each year, but the main communication medium is the Internet. Indeed, pictures from the congress were posted to the website. Much can be sourced by going to Ireland's society website where a link to "International Congresses" can be found on the main page.

We received an excellent briefing by the Treasurer in an oral and visual presentation of the Verband's financial position. Now that we were one organisation, equal treatment was desired as regards members' subscriptions. Following a proposal from the Treasurer, supported by a majority of the Executive Committee and several speeches from the floor, the meeting voted for a per capita criteria whereby all societies should pay €2 per member subject to a ceiling at high membership levels – c. 1,200 – 2,500.

The Executive Committee was progressing matters in the following areas: Stage design competition, annual scholarships – 247, Networking, the RWVI Archive, Bayreuth and continuous development of the Website. By now, the RWVI had 139 societies with a membership of 26,000. From 2011 to 2013 congresses would be held in Wraclaw, Praha and Leipzig. Reaching out to youth remains a principal goal of the Verband and associations with Cambridge University, Singapore, Baltimore, Oxford University, Bodrum and Normandy were in formation.

The Mayor of Bayreuth, Dr. Hohl encouraged members to visit the city. He recognises the beautiful work being done by the RWVI. He spoke of the restoration of the Baroque synagogue in Bayreuth, the only synagogue in Germany which wasn't destroyed during 'Kristallnacht'. While he acknowledged cruelty and barbarism, he also emphasised that Bayreuth was a city of culture and joy. I hungered for culture and joy. The Verband, the novelty of visiting new cities plus the performances during the rest of the year helped feed the hunger. The Wagner Society of Ireland gave me focus but within a very short time unease started to creep in. Some of the members were beginning to get up my nose and I was feeling disrespected, unappreciated and let down. Some members of the society began to die off, among them four of my supporters whose presence had been a comfort to me. They liked me. I simply wasn't liked by the rest of them and I reacted to their dislike by rudeness. I didn't care. My perception was one of 'me against the world'. I stood down as Chair of the Wagner Society in 2007, due to ill health. I asked Professor Stephen Mennell to take the Chair which he did and in November 2007, he wrote to the members:

Dear Member

I am writing to all members to attend the Society's Annual General

Meeting, which will be held on Wednesday 12 December at 8.00 pm in the United Arts Club. The agenda has already been circulated.

The occasion is especially noteworthy and important, because it follows upon the retirement from the chair of our Founding Chairman, Chris McQuaid.

Although, following my return from a sabbatical year in Cambridge, I formally took over the chair from Chris after the dinner for Veronica Dunne on 17 October. He has continued to carry the burden of the administration of the Society. I want to pay tribute to Chris for all that he has done since the Society was formed in the wake of the NYOI/Anissimov Ring Cycle in Limerick and Birmingham in 2002, right up to the present. Members may not appreciate the extent to which he has been responsible for organising so many of our activities here in Ireland and for liaising with the Richard Wagner Verband International.

I believe it is now vital that we spread the work and responsibility more widely – and not just because I personally am not in a position to take on everything that Chris has done hitherto. We need a strong and active committee.

For that reason, I urge you not only to attend the AGM, but also consider offering yourself for election either as one of the officers or as a committee member. I will accept nominations (by post or email) in advance, although the constitution also permits nominations to be made at the AGM itself.

With best wishes

Yours sincerely

Professor Stephen Mennell, Chairman


Professor Mennell arranged for me to be elected Life Honorary Vice President. Then, at the AGM of the society I was asked to represent the current Chair, Anthony Linehan at the Verband International Congress in Stralsund, Germany because he was unable to attend. I agreed and was given a voter's letter. On my return, having departed for home, I was stranded in Frankfurt due to the "ash cloud", volcanic events at Eyjafjallajökull in Iceland which, although relatively small for volcanic eruptions, caused enormous disruption to air travel across western and northern Europe over an initial period of six days in April 2010. Seismic activity had started at the end of 2009 and gradually increased in intensity until on the 20th of March 2010 when a small eruption began, rated as a 1 on the volcanic explosivity index. From 14–20 April, ash from the volcanic eruption covered large areas of Northern Europe. Additional localised disruption continued into May 2010. About twenty countries closed their airspace to commercial jet traffic and it affected approximately ten million travellers. Consequently, a very high proportion of flights within, to, and from Europe were cancelled, creating the highest level of air travel disruption since the Second World War.

Travelling alone I decided that having a heart issue, and rather than endure the discomfort of the airport terminal, now stuffed with angry, weary passengers, that I would take a flight to Paris. I overnighted in Paris, took a taxi to the train station and took a train to Cherbourg. There, I boarded a ferry to Rosslare. I felt I hadn't breathed until I was sitting on the train from Rosslare to Dublin. The total cost of my elongated journey was €1,322.22. I invoiced the society, but a refund – even part-payment – was refused. I was livid, particularly as another member of the society had attended an EGM of the Richard Wagner Verband International in Frankfurt, representing not the Wagner Society of Ireland, but the Wagner Society of Scotland – and was refunded travel expenses. My persistence in trying to recover at least some of my expenses eventually led to my expulsion from the society. My name has been airbrushed from the history and all my reports and images have been deleted from the society website.

Now dealing with serious health problems – prostate cancer,

Type 2 diabetes, and recurring heart arrythmia. I took risks travelling to mainland Europe to attend Wagner operas. I needed the music and adrift without my beloved Wagner society, I needed something to do. I had grown into the persona that I thought I was presenting to the world. I tried to ignore the gnawing yearning for the person I once was when I was nineteen – happy and carefree, although in truth, I had no clue as to who I was.

I had joined the Association of Retired Commissioned Officers but had fallen foul of the organisation. In 2016 I joined Óglaigh Náisiúnta na hÉireann Teoranta (ONET), a support organisation for ex-service personnel of the Irish Defence Services. The organisation began sometime around 1950 and was formed as an amalgam of a number of ex-servicemen's organisations which had sprung up after soldiers, sailors and airmen had been demobbed following service during the "Emergency", known to the rest of the western world as World War Two. The old house, Brú na bhFiann in Smithfield in Dublin's north inner city was demolished during the redevelopment of Smithfield Market area and replaced with a state-of-the-art forty-bedroom complex which was officially opened by the then President of Ireland and Patron of ONET, Mrs. Mary McAleese. The new home contains a reception area, a bar, a kitchen, and a dining room capable of seating up to ninety people as well as a laundry and administration offices. The other two houses are Beechwood House in Letterkenny, Donegal and Custume House in Athlone, County Westmeath. The organisation's patron is the current President of Ireland, Michael D. Higgins. Most of the members of ONET have served overseas, many of them recipients of awards for bravery and distinguished service. Others who have no living family or who have fallen on hard times avail of the services and will see out their days in the care of the only family they know – army comrades. Ceremonial parades and wreath-laying ceremonies as well as outings and social events are features of the organisation's activities.

I complained about accounts and the issue of 1916 commemorative medals. Having once again assumed that with membership came an entitlement to take them to task, I complained to the Board about spending. But all I have succeeded in doing is dirtying my bib. Friends insist that the money is well spent; homeless men are finding shelter and solace, medical care is also provided, and their needs taken care of. I laud the work, but I had always been of the opinion that those in charge should be doing this work on a voluntary basis. Friends tell me this is naïve; that large charitable organisations around the world have salaried boards of management and staff. On reflection, I am beginning to understand that I cannot see the bigger picture. I suppose my philosophy would be "rob the rich and help the poor".

At times I thought I was making progress, that I was slowly rising above the need to concern myself with matters that had little relevance to my personal life. But then, something else would irritate me and I'd be off again – digging up whatever evidence of some misdemeanour or a remark made that didn't sit well with me. One minute I was jovial, the next minute I was swamped in venom.

I had been trained to fight as part of an army; to kill an enemy on behalf of the group. At the same time, with the exception of short periods throughout my military career, I seldom felt part of a group and with the exception of my trips to opera performances, my social life had been deficient, to say the least. Groups scared me and yet it was in groups that I tried to find social connection and a sense of fraternity. I continued to be deeply depressed. At times I fought the urge to kill myself to rid my family of the "moody one" and to rid myself of pain, all the while traipsing in and out of hospitals and doctors' consulting rooms as my physical health deteriorated. All I could do was follow the music. My travels with Wagner have taken me to the more cultured and beautiful parts of many European cities, rubbing shoulders with people of 'cultured' tastes – a long way from army life in Ireland and the war zones of the

Congo, Cyprus and Lebanon. I would return from performances in Europe physically exhausted but mentally and spiritually refreshed.

# CHAPTER 7

# *Making Opera Accessible*

Wagnerians like to follow the steps of the Great Master. The starting point is Bayreuth and Haus Wahnfried, a palatial residence built with monies given by King Ludwig II before the Festspielhaus was built. At the rear of the house Wagner had his grave built. It is in a large green area shaded by trees. Cosima is interred here too. Wagner had lots of visitors at Wahnfried – Liszt, Nietzsche, Ludwig II, Rubinstein. The house had a very large library, which housed hundreds of books. Wagner devoured books. He was very well informed. Of course, his piano was here. Wreaths are laid annually on his grave by the town and Verband.

Our next journey is by train to Zurich to the Wesendonck Villa – two homes facing each other. It is here that Wagner and Mathilde Wesendonck developed an intellectual relationship. She was his Muse especially for *Tristan und Isolde*. Wagner put four of her poems to music one was *Traume* (dreams). Wagner scored them for soprano voice but some years ago Jonas Kaufmann took the plunge and sang them, followed quickly by Klaus Florian Vogt, both first class. Not Heldentenors, e.g. Rene Kollo, but both are very good. My particular favourite is Vogt (my sister says he is handsome), his long melodic phrases as 'Walther' in *Meistersinger* are beautiful, and he has vocal stamina. He has five children, rides a motor bike and can fly a small aeroplane. His principal roles at present are Walther,

*Lohengrin*, *Tannhäuser*, and Paul, (*Die tote Stadt*). Kaufmann's repertoire is similar, but he also sings Italian. Jonas Kaufmann sang *Lohengrin* at Bayreuth in May 2010, after that he was ill. I was fortunate to hear him. He is a very good Lohengrin. He is dark and handsome. Vogt is blonde and handsome.

Around the corner is the Liszt Museum. Liszt was very helpful to Wagner during his exile period, gave him funds and conducted the premiere of *Lohengrin* in Weimar on 28th August,1850. Our next stop is Magdeburg, where his *Das Liebeversbot* was premiered on 29th March 1836. Wagner was conductor here and it was here that he married Minna Planter, his first wife.

Wilhelm Richard Wagner, about whom more has been written than about anyone else in history, came from a middle-class family. He was not royalty; his father, Carl Friedrich Wagner, was a police actuary; his mother, Johanna Rosine Pätz-Wagner was a baker's daughter. He was interested in theatre from early childhood. Initially he wanted to be a poet and playwright. But after seeing Beethoven's opera *Fidelio* at age sixteen he decided to be a composer. As early as 1831, as a student of music, he planned his first opera, for which he penned the text himself – an approach he was to take for the rest of his life.

The Wagners lived in Paris in dire circumstances, yet Richard was able to complete his early operas *Rienzi* and *The Flying Dutchman* there. By age twenty Wagner was directing the Theatre in Magdeburg and fell in love with the actress Minna Planer. They married in 1836 but had no children. Riga and Paris were the next destinations for the itinerant artist, who was plagued by financial worries and pursued by creditors.

In 1842, Wagner moved to Dresden, where he became court composer. A musical breakthrough came in October of that year with the premiere of Rienzi. Always working on various works simultaneously, he began to develop the vision of a new blend of words, music and action into "a total work of art" to achieve 'the unconditional, immediate depiction of human nature in a state of completion.

While living in Paris, he developed leftist revolutionary ideas. In May 1849, he participated in a grass-roots rebellion in Dresden, after which he became a wanted man and was forced to leave Germany. Wagner fled to Zurich, having narrowly avoided arrest for his political involvement in the May uprising in Dresden. His arrival in Zurich marked the beginning of a transformation during which the thirty-six-year-old composer re-conceived his ideas of art and introduced new artistic models.

Then in 1864 – back in Germany and in dire financial straits – he was close to suicide when a letter from the new King of Bavaria, eighteen-year-old Ludwig II., arrived. The king offered his full support for Wagner and his work and continued to do so for the rest of Wagner's life.

After many affairs before and after the death of his wife Minna, Wagner lived in Tribschen, near Lucerne, with Cosima von Bülow, daughter of Franz Liszt and wife of the conductor Hans von Bülow, one of his friends and promoters. Three children were born before the couple finally married.

In the little Franconian town of Bayreuth, Wagner eventually found the location for his vision. In August 1876, far from the bustle of big-city life, in a self-designed festival theatre, audiences were able to come together to enjoy the combination of music, stage action and scenery at the premiere of Wagner's four-opera cycle, *The Ring of the Nibelung.*

Wagner fled to Zurich in 1849, at the age of thirty-six, having narrowly avoided arrest for his political involvement in the May uprising in Dresden, where he had been living. His arrival marked the beginning of a transformation during which the young composer redefined his ideas of art and introduced new artistic concepts.

More than two hundred years after his birth, Richard Wagner is a much-discussed subject. Some see him as the genius who created the "total work of art". Others reject him for his anti-Semitic writings. In any event, his operas are performed today more often than ever before.

His great-granddaughter Katharina Wagner said, "In Wagner's works in particular, it's all about the basic elements of human existence and of basic qualities like jealousy, power, love, and hate. Those are of course things that will always be timely and move us as long as humanity exists." No stranger to adversity, perhaps it is the emotionally stimulating quality of the basic elements of human existence in the music that I relate to?

Although Oscar Wilde was not considered an aficionado of music in his day, yet his opinion that "Music is the art which is most nigh to tears and memory" reveals an inner musical consciousness that was reflected in the rich symbolic imagery that characterised some of his most powerful writings. Had Wilde lived a few years more, he would have witnessed the unprecedented musical revolution his *Tragedy of Salome* would have when Richard Strauss adapted it for his opera *Salome* in 1905. Subsequently he would have seen how *A Florentine Tragedy* and *The Birthday of the Infanta* influenced the Austrian composer, Alexander von Zemlinsky who adapted them for his challengingly inventive operas *Eine Florentinische Tragödie* in 1917 and *Der Zwerg* in 1922.

Unfortunately, the perception of opera as an inherently elitist art form still persists because it was originally an art form exclusively for the very rich. Wealthy nobles would commission new works, pay all of the costs of production and then present the opera, with food and drinks laid on, to their court. This put opera above other forms of music and later became something the new middle classes were happy to latch onto as a way of raising their own status. Opera moved out of the courts and into public theatres and specially designed opera houses, and touring opera companies were in great demand.

The mid-to-late nineteenth century was a golden age of opera, led and dominated by Wagner in Germany and Verdi in Italy. During the nineteenth century, similar operatic traditions emerged in central and eastern Europe, particularly in Russia and Bohemia. The twentieth century saw many experiments with modern styles, such as atonality and serialism (Schoenberg and Berg), Neoclassicism (Stravinsky), and Minimalism (Philip Glass and John Adams). The popularity of opera continued through the verismo era in Italy and contemporary French opera through to Puccini and Strauss in the early twentieth century. Eventually, opera came to reflect the stories and musical styles of each of these countries. The Italians have always been famous for their love of singing, and so in Italian opera there has always been great emphasis placed on the singer and the beautiful sounds of the human voice. It wasn't until the late 19th century and early 20th century with the later works of Verdi and the operas of Puccini was a balance achieved between the role of the orchestra and that of the singer, and the combining of these two forces, to give a more effective presentation of the story.

Opera is an art form in which singers and musicians perform a dramatic work combining text (libretto) and musical score, usually in a theatrical setting. Opera incorporates many of the elements of spoken theatre, such as acting, scenery, and costumes and sometimes includes dance. The performance is typically given in an opera house, accompanied by an orchestra or smaller musical ensemble.

The word opera comes from the Latin and, later, from the Italian, a noun formed from the word operari, (to work). The style evolved in Italy around 1600 and was initially a chance for soloists to show off. In the mid-18th Century the emphasis shifted to both strong story and exquisite singing. But the concept of opera was developing many years before the first opera was written. Its beginning can be traced to the ancient Greeks who blended poetry and music, creating plays that incorporated song, spoken language and dance, accompanied by string or wind instruments. In the 1100s, the early Christian church set religious stories to music known as "liturgical drama".

Opera is a dramatic story told through song. It is considered by many to be the most complete art form, combining all of the elements of art, words, music, drama and dance. The earliest Italian operas were called several things, such as "favola in musica" (fable in music) and "dramma per musica" (drama by means of music). Emotion is an important quality, a trait carried over to 'soap operas' which have no singing but plenty of dramatic action and false tears! Opera is unique because it uses music to deliver an entire story or plot. Opera takes any type of dramatic story and tries to make it more exciting and more believable with the help of music. This is based on the belief that music can communicate people's reactions and emotions better than words or pictures. Many famous stories have been made into operas, including *Cinderella*, *Hansel and Gretel*, and *Romeo and Juliet*.

The French have favoured the pictorial side of drama, and this has led to a continuing emphasis on the visual spectacle, especially with dancing. An example of this: the Paris opera in the 19th century would not accept a work for performance if it did not contain a major ballet. Verdi, an Italian composer, had to add ballets to all of his works to get them performed in Paris. Today the most renowned figure of late-eighteenth-century opera is Mozart, who began with opera "seria" but is most famous for his Italian comic operas, especially *The Marriage of Figaro* (Le Nozze di Figaro), *Don Giovanni*, and *Così fan tutte*, as well as *The Magic Flute* (Die Zauberflöte), a landmark in the German tradition.

Germany has the most performances of opera than any other country. This is in large part to the country's publicly funded art initiatives. In Germany, opera is lavish and in the metropolitan areas, a quarter of the population see at least one opera each year. The Germans have always sought to extract from both the Italian and French traditions and go beyond both traditions to present more than just a story. Richard Wagner chose legends or myths for most of his opera plots so that he could communicate philosophy as well as just a story.

In recent years singers and musicians have begun to go into schools, thus bringing the music to young children. This can be very effective, as cultural taste is formed at an early age. Filmmakers have done a lot for the art, using pieces from the great composers to lend drama and atmosphere to their stories, putting opera in a more familiar place.

Fergus Shiel has done more than anyone for opera in Ireland, not least through establishing the trailblazing Irish National Opera. When still a teenager, he played violin and viola with any orchestra that would have him. He then got an opportunity to conduct in Trinity College Dublin, where he started the Trinity Orchestra in 1989. While consciously avoiding the limelight, Fergus is passionate about getting people interested and generally prefers to put forward the artists involved for media coverage. He considers it an honour to introduce children to this music. "You can see it in their faces when they start to get it. They get as excited as I am, it's an amazing feeling." He reminds us that in the 19th century we had a large number of opera composers like Balfe, Wallace, O'Dwyer. "Lots of opera happened in Ireland in the 17th-19th centuries and it's fallen away, it's become more of a French, Italian and German sport, but we have every right to claim our patch in the operatic world." Of the company, he says, "We're at a starting block in the whole business of running an opera company in this country. We're so passionate about championing Irish artists and developing the relationship with our artistic partners. We've done lots of international launches and we're planning some in the United States. It's all about telling the story wider and further around the world – and in Ireland."

The Bord Gáis Energy Theatre is a new performing arts venue located in the docklands area of Dublin. Designed by Daniel

Libeskind for the Dublin Dockland Development Authority, built by Joe O'Reilly at a reported cost of 80 million Euro, and opened by Harry Crosbie on the 18th of March 2010, it is Ireland's largest fixed-seat theatre. It would rank alongside the fourth largest London West-End theatre and exceeds the capacity of all New York Broadway theatres.

On September the 30th of October and the 3rd and 6th of November 2012 Richard Wagner's *Tristan und Isolde* was performed in the Bord Gáis Energy Theatre, the first performance in Ireland since 1912 when it was staged in the Theatre Royal on Hawkins Street, since demolished. The new Irish Opera company Wide Open Opera deserves credit for even attempting this gargantuan work. Directed by Yannis Kokkos, and originating from a production by Welsh national Opera, I couldn't wait to see it.

Conductor Fergus Sheil, along with the RTÉ National Symphony Orchestra, opened Act I with a very impressive prelude. Isolde was sung by our own Miriam Murphy. Tristan, by Lars Cleveman who, like Ms Murphy has a remarkable back catalogue, having appeared in Wagner's home of Bayreuth to sing the title role of Tannhäuser. Miriam Murphy proved her worth vocally as Isolde, as did Imelda Drumm in the role of Brangäne, providing some of the most convincing acting of the evening. This production of *Tristan und Isolde* although showing some cracks in Acts Two and Three, is hopefully the beginning of a new era of Opera in Ireland.

# CHAPTER 8

# *When Two Worlds Collide*

In May 1989, *Stars of the Kirov and Bolshoi Opera* took me to Cork City Hall and in December, I was back in London's Barbican Centre for The Chamber Orchestra of Europe with Claudio Schiff, piano and Maria Ewing, a leading soprano/mezzo-soprano singing Mozart's *Requiem*. In January 1990, I travelled to The Royal Opera House, London to see *Othello*, conducted by Carlos Klieber. My next opera was *Götterdämmerung*, the last in Richard Wagner's cycle of four music dramas titled *Der Ring das Nibelungen* (The Ring of the Nibelung). *Götterdämmerung* (Twilight of the Gods) premiered on the final evening of *Der Ring das Nibelungen* at the Bayreuth Festival on the 17th of August 1876, conducted by Hans Richter.

I attended the opera for the first time on the 2nd of March 1996 at The Royal Opera House in London. This is a very long opera – just under five hours! Despite the intervals, I was almost locked in a sitting position when it ended! But it was worth it. I was overwhelmed with emotion. I immediately booked a ticket for the next performance on the 19th of October 1996, again at The Royal Opera House and then a ticket for the 11th of August 1998, in the famous theatre in Bayreuth a hundred-and-twenty-one years from the date of the premiere, almost to the day.

The opera begins with a prologue in which the three Norns: daughters of Erda the Earth Goddess, are spinning the rope of destiny. This rope is a symbol of what has to happen in the end. They take it in turns to tell the story of the past, spinning as they sing and pass on the rope to the next one. The first Norn tells how Wotan went to drink from the Well of Wisdom for which he lost an eye. He then cut a spear from a tree which then died. The second Norn tells how a young hero broke Wotan's spear and how the gods were sent from Valhalla to chop down the World Ash. The third Norn tells how the logs from the ash tree have been piled around Valhalla ready for a fire that will burn everything. The Norns have visions of the future. The rope breaks. The Norns disappear into the earth. The story continues from the end of the third opera which was called *Siegfried*.

Brünnhilde and Siegfried come out of a cave by the rock where they were left at the end of the third opera. Siegfried has to go off to do heroic deeds. He gives Brünnhilde the ring as a token of his love for her. She gives him her horse which is called Grane. And Siegfried travels down the river Rhine.

Act One takes place in the Hall of the Gibichung palace. Gunther is the chief of the Gibichungs. His half-brother Hagen tells him he would look more important if he got married. He also says that Gunther's sister Gutrune ought to get married. He tells him about Brünnhilde who, he thinks, is still asleep on the rock surrounded by fire that no one except Siegfried would be able to get through. He says that if they manage to get Siegfried to marry Gutrune, then she could persuade him to go and catch Brünnhilde for Gunther. He says that they could give Siegfried a potion which would make him forget that he loved Brünnhilde.

They hear Siegfried's horn outside, and the great hero arrives. Siegfried asks Hagen whether he knows him. Of course, Hagen does. Siegfried is carrying the magic tarnhelm (helmet) which allows a person to change their shape or become invisible. Siegfried, however, does not know what the tarnhelm can do, and Hagen has to explain it to him. Gutrune appears and offers Siegfried a drink.

It is the potion which is going to make him forget any other woman. He drinks to the health of Brünnhilde. As soon as he has drunk it he looks at Gutrune and is in love with her. He agrees to marry her, and he agrees to get a wife for Gunther. Hagen tells him about Brünnhilde on the rock. Siegfried has forgotten about her. He agrees to put on the tarn helmet and disguise himself as Gunther and to go and get Brünnhilde. He goes off, leaving Brünnhilde and Hagen guarding the palace.

The next scene takes place on the top of the Valkyrie rock. Her sister Waltraute arrives on a flying horse. She says that Wotan (their father, the chief God) returned to Valhalla with his spear broken. She says he told the gods to pile up the logs from the World Ash for a fire which will burn everything. Wotan desperately wants the ring to be given back to the Rhine Maidens (who were guardians of the, from which the ring was forged, in the first opera). Brünnhilde refuses to give her the ring that Siegfried had given her as a token of their love. Waltraute disappears.

After the weather calms the flames flicker again. Siegfried arrives, disguised as Gunther. Brünnhilde is horrified to see a person she thinks is a stranger. Siegfried says she is his bride and forces the ring from her finger and drags her into a cave for the night, although he has placed the sword between them.

In Act Two we are back at the palace Alberich tries to persuade his son Hagen to get the ring. Hagen wants to get the ring, but only for himself. Siegfried arrives. He no longer wears the tarnhelm, so he looks like himself. Hagen blows his horn to call his vassals (soldiers) for a celebration. Gunther is to marry Brünnhilde and Siegfried is to marry Gutrune. Brünnhilde cannot understand why Siegfried is doing this. She sees the ring on his finger and asks him how he got it, as she thinks Gunther snatched it from her. Siegfried says that he won it by killing a dragon. He tells people how he tricked Brünnhilde and swears that a sword lay between them during the night, although Brünnhilde tries to make people think otherwise.

Brünnhilde is left alone with Gunther and Hagen. She tells them
that, although Siegfried is so strong and impossible to kill in battle,
he has one weak spot on his back. Gunther does not like the idea
of having Siegfried killed, but Hagen promises him that he can then
have the ring. They decide to kill Siegfried and to tell Gutrune that
he was killed by a wild boar.

The last act takes place in a wild forest. Siegfried's hunting horn
is heard, and then the hunting horn of the Gibichungs. By the river
Siegfried happens to meet the Rhine Maidens and teases them by
showing them the ring but does not let them have it. They tell him
about the curse on the ring, but Siegfried does not believe them.
He meets Hagen. They drink together. Siegfried tells the men all
about his life, how he was brought up by Mime, about the sword,
the dragon and the bird singing. Then he cannot remember any
more. Hagen gives him another drugged drink which makes him
start to remember what actually happened. He remembers
Brünnhilde and how he found her surrounded by fire. He gradually
realizes how he has been tricked and feels unbearable sadness. Two
ravens fly overhead, and Hagen plunges his spear into Siegfried's
back. He dies while speaking the name of Brünnhilde. His body is
carried off to a funeral march. The story and the music still bring
tears to my eyes.

Back at the palace his body is brought in. Gutrune accuses Gunther of murdering him, but Gunther says Hagen did it. Hagen says
he did it because Siegfried, when disguised as Gunther, had slept
with Brünnhilde. He tries to snatch the ring from the dead Siegfried's finger, Gunther tries to stop him but is murdered by Hagen.
He tries again to snatch the ring but to everybody's horror the arm
of the dead hero rises in the air.

In Act Three, Brünnhilde enters and tells everyone how she
promised Siegfried her love. Gutrune curses Hagen and falls onto
her brother's dead body. Brünnhilde orders a funeral pyre (a fire) to
be prepared. She sings to Wotan that Siegfried is now at peace in

death and that she understands more now. She takes the ring and promises to return it to the Rhine Maidens. She lights the fire which flares up and she rides on her horse Grane into the flames. The whole building catches fire, the Rhine breaks its banks and floods. Hagen jumps into the water trying to get the ring from the Rhine Maidens who drown him. The flood dies down and Valhalla (the gods' palace) is lit up by the fire. The gods and the heroes die in the flames. The Twilight of the Gods has now happened.

I was carried by every note of music, beautifully complementing the drama. The ultimate musical experience. Several pieces from this opera have been woven into film scores; *Siegfried's Funeral March* is used in John Boorman's film, *Excalibur,* when King Arthur dies, and Sir Percival throws the sword Excalibur back to the Lady of the Lake.

Just a few weeks after I returned from London, the real world was plunged into mourning by the dramatic death of Diana Princess of Wales in a mysterious car crash in Paris. Elton John's tribute to Diana, *Candle in the Wind,* or *Goodbye England's Rose,* became the biggest-selling single of all time. The film *Titanic,* about the sinking of the liner that was 'unsinkable' was released in November as the shock and sadness of Diana's death lingered. Diana's ill-fated love affair with Dodi al Fayad, another story fused by love and tragedy: one ending in a car crash, the other at sea. The song, *My Heart Will Go On,* from the film's score became, for a time, the soundtrack to all our lives and the film score was the bestselling classical album of the previous twenty-five years.

# CHAPTER 9

# *Death and Destruction at Home and Abroad*

The new year began on a positive note, politically: The Good Friday Agreement, or Belfast Agreement was signed on the 10th of April 1998 that ended most of the violence of The Troubles, a political conflict in Northern Ireland that had been ongoing since the 1960s. The Good Friday Agreement was a major development in the Northern Ireland peace process of the 1990s and also created a number of institutions between Northern Ireland and the Republic of Ireland, and between the Republic of Ireland and the United Kingdom. The Agreement was approved by voters across the island of Ireland in two referendums held on the 22nd of May 1998. In Northern Ireland, voters were asked in the 1998 Northern Ireland Good Friday Agreement referendum whether they supported the multi-party agreement. In the Republic of Ireland, voters were asked whether they would allow the state to sign the agreement and allow necessary constitutional changes (Nineteenth Amendment of the Constitution of Ireland) to facilitate it. The people of both jurisdictions needed to approve the agreement in order to give effect to it. The British–Irish Agreement came into force on the 2nd of December 1999.

During the Troubles, Irish troops and Reserves were deployed along the border with Northern Ireland to provide assistance and protection to An Gárda Síochána – the unarmed civil police force in the Republic – as well as protection for the hundreds of refugees from Northern Ireland who were flooding into the border counties. Three new infantry battalions, the 27th the 28th and the 29th were established and the 4th Cavalry Squadron was redeployed to the border. The Irish Defence Forces purchased a new transport fleet, equipped soldiers with modern weapons and recruitment was stepped up.

Having left the defence forces after six tours of duty overseas I found temporary work with the Postal Service and later with Aer Lingus. With the escalation of the 'Troubles' I decided to re-enlist. I wanted to go to Artillery but was told that I would have to re-train as a recruit. Although I considered this a stupid policy, I went to the Curragh. It looked even more like a kip than I remembered! I suddenly got cold feet and immediately went AWOL but the recruiting NCO telephoned me. "Go back to the Curragh, they'll be generous with you," he said. I followed his advice and returned the next day and was introduced to Sergeant O'Shea who was indeed generous and a rock of sense, a beacon of light in a dark place. He gave me a travel warrant and instructed me to go to Collins Barracks, Dublin. But on arrival there, I immediately applied for a "Discharge by Purchase". The Adjutant sent for me and gave me a severe bollocking; I had wanted to re-enlist, then I ran away, I went back and now I wanted to leave. I was an administrative pain in the backside.

My desire to re-enlist eventually won out and I was armed with a sub-machine gun and given a job on guard duty on the back gate. After a few weeks, Commandant Andy Maguire came ambling up the hill and spoke to me. He was on full-time service, having been called up due to the Northern crisis. He had heard about the enlist/re-enlist shenanigans and he had something to tell me. "There's an education course pilot scheme commencing. I think you should apply", he said. "You can be studying for the Leaving Certificate examination at night while carrying out your army duties by day." I took his advice and went for it because I would be busy, with no time to ruminate. Shortly after this conversation I was asked if I would do border duty. I was delighted as it meant I would be occupied during the long, summer school holidays. My company commander said that the border posting would also bring a promotion to Acting Sergeant.

I was posted to Dundalk, an old garrison town close to the border and the last stop on the Republic side of the border on the Dublin-to-Belfast railway line. Nicknamed "El Paso", after the Texan town on the border with Mexico, the town of Dundalk's position close to the border with Northern Ireland was rumoured to harbour a "nest" of IRA activists during the Troubles. I found it dull and dreary with a gloomy atmosphere that seemed to weigh me down. The company commander in Dundalk knew me from my time training recruits in Cathal Brugha Barracks. He said that he couldn't promote me because I was not a 'specialist', meaning that I was not qualified to instruct in mortars or machine guns. I was however wont to dispense advice to others as to how to work on their career trajectories. One young soldier found himself at the receiving end of a treatise on promotion while occupying a top bunk bed in Dundalk Barracks. I am not sure if it was my advice or his ambition that worked for him, but he went on to become the youngest sergeant major in the Irish Defence Forces.

The commanding officer, a gruff Antrim man and a real soldier, suggested that I transfer to Castleblayney. I agreed, knowing that some of my friends from Collins Barracks were already stationed there. Duties consisted mainly of patrols and guard duty. I had taken up running and the countryside around Castleblayney provided some pleasant and varied terrain for an early morning run. The forces of the British Crown that were north of the border seemed to have matters under control and there were no terrorist incidences in our neck of the woods. We mixed with the locals and if there were any IRA or Loyalist sympathisers among them, they didn't make themselves known – overtly or covertly. The Ponderosa

Public House, with Country and Western music on offer became our watering hole. The only threat to our well-being was the possibility of an ambush on our way back to base by local lads who took exception to local girls taking up with soldiers whose spending power was viewed as a lethal attraction! I missed out on promotion, but I had some good fun.

Back in Dublin, I applied myself to study with gusto and passed my Leaving Cert. exams and was then encouraged to attend university. In 1973 I registered in the Faculty of Commerce at University College Dublin for a four-year degree course, again studying at night, taking a bus into the centre of the city and another bus out to the university campus in Donnybrook on the south side. I graduated in 1977 and was selected to undergo a one-year course in the Curragh for a Commission. This was a big surprise as I had never sought a commission. It was also a great boost to my morale.

With a college degree under my belt, I was selected for commissioning in 1978 and travelled to the Military College at the Curragh in November to begin the 4th Potential Officers' Course. I was met by the smell of turf smoke and the twenty-four others who would be in my class. Training and classes began the following day – in Recruit Training, Junior Leader training, and NCO training. We had square training, drilled by a corporal. The tactics were enjoyable: Offence, Defence and Retrograde Operations. We did a night shoot and attack during two weeks' training back in the Glen of Imaal, high in the Wicklow Mountains, where I had trained as a young recruit in 1963. We did a course in the Army School of Administration on Quarter-mastering and Adjunting as well as a sub-catering course at the Army School of Catering. We studied Transportation, did Syndicates on Geophysical Studies and studied history and military symbols. Later on, we had sword drill. Extra-curricular activities included soccer which we played indoors in bad weather. I had inherited a liking for the game from my father but although I was nifty and fast, I never excelled at it and got into trouble many a time. I almost had my leg broken during an indoor soccer game by a fellow who must have thought we were playing in a World Cup game.

I finished the course in 6th place out of twenty-five and I became a commissioned officer on the 1st of November 1979. In February 1980, my report from the colonel of the Military College stated that I was an excellent student, with highly commendable work, that I had a pleasant and modest personality, good powers of reasoning, great resilience in field exercises, a shrewd, tactical brain and that I should make an excellent officer. But I did not see the report. Class reports are passed on to the office of the Chief of Staff where they remain on file, gathering dust. I never knew until many years later what my report contained. I considered myself very fortunate to have made it to the college because in those days the process involved a recommendation from one's commanding officer followed by two interviews. Looking back, I wonder if my report would have made any difference to my self-esteem. I wonder too how I could possibly have had "a pleasant and modest personality" and a "shrewd, tactical brain" while trying to keep depression at bay. I can only conclude that I was so engrossed in the packed curriculum that I had no time to ponder.

At the end of November, I was posted to the far end of the country, to the 1st Motor Squadron in Fitzgerald Camp, Fermoy in County Cork. The barracks was a former British army base that had been used for training troops for service in India. The town of Fermoy expanded around these facilities and retained its British military facilities until 1922 when the Irish Free State was first established. During the War of Independence, Fermoy was the scene of the first attack by the IRA against British troops and following the Treaty of 1921 and the subsequent Irish Civil War, the town had suffered badly, and most buildings were dilapidated. A nearby aerodrome which had been owned by Britain's Royal Flying Corps (RFC) was handed over to the Irish Air Corps in 1923.

My fellow officers were all Dubliners, like myself, with the exception of the officer commanding and three captains who hailed from Cork, Cobh, Blackpool and Glanworth, respectively. The officer commanding was Commandant Tom Stapleton, a gentle giant. He was standing in for another commandant who was on overseas duty. I was Quartermaster in charge of Ordnance, Food Bedding, Clothing, Fuel, Light, Accommodation, Lands, Cooks, Dining, Rations and Staff. On arrival, I had to do a full audit of all accounts. The ordnance account was in order, but I found deficiencies in Rations and Clothing. When I reported this to Comdt. Stapleton, he ordered two senior quartermasters from the 13th Battalion to do a re-check and two NCO quartermasters confirmed my findings.

Other issues arose with my boss, now returned from overseas. I wanted to run a tightly organised and transparent accounting system and his nonchalance annoyed me intensely. One evening, I wanted to check the contents of a freezer storeroom. The corporal on duty informed me that the keys were locked away. "Get them or I'll shoot the lock off!" I told him. The keys were produced.

It is only in retrospect that I can see the beginnings of my downward spiral in the army. I was inflexible and unreasonable, hung up on scruples, obsessive about the letter of the law and on rules and regulations, without the ability to deal with anyone unless they were on my wavelength. I was prone to knee-jerk reactions, always on the alert for anything out of place and unrelenting in the pursuit of wrongdoing, as I saw it. If I found wrongdoing, I wanted heads to roll. Although I didn't see it at the time, it was thanks to the Northern Ireland Troubles, and the intervention of some astute, observant and helpful senior officers that my military career had taken off. I should have been grateful. Instead I was a bomb waiting to explode.

In the period between 1978 and 2001 Ireland undertook the most significant operational tasking in its history on behalf of the United Nations, when it sent almost 40,000 troops to participate in the UNIFIL operation in Lebanon. This campaign added to an already prestigious standing by Irish peacekeepers, begun in 1960 in the Congo and later in Cyprus but it also had an adverse effect on bilateral diplomatic and political relations between Ireland and Israel due to clashes and tensions between Irish UNIFIL peacekeepers and Israeli troops and their south Lebanese Christian allies.

One of those events took place in July 1980, while I was serving in Lebanon. One evening a couple of high-end cars drove into our Post, flags flying. The second in command to Major Hadaad of the South Lebanese Army (SLA) had come to tell us calmly that the town of Ayta Az Zutt was about to be shelled. I was aware that the SLA referred to their commanding officer as "Major". I asked him if he would like to speak with our 'Major'. If I had said 'commanding officer' he would not have understood. He agreed and produced a box of Dutch cigars and offered it to me. "Would you like a coffee?" I asked. "Yes," he said. While we waited in the tent for the "major" to arrive, he told me that "Forty-Six Battalion, LA Battery. Forty-Seven Battalion, Mingy Battery". Mingy was a word that we acquired from our time in the Congo. It means "many" or "much". He was clearly not impressed by the 46th Battalion but he was in no doubt that the SLA were not to mess with the 47th! When Freddie Swords, our 'major' arrived, the two talked for a few minutes and then our visitors left. Forty minutes later the shelling of Ayta Az Zutt began. All we could do was stand by and listen to the noise of the shelling, trying not to think about the carnage that was being deliberately and callously created amid the smoke and the fire – under our noses – a sickening, bloody mess that ambulance personnel and UN troops would have to clean up, to the accompaniment of sirens, the wailing survivors, the pitiful cries of orphaned children and the stench of charred and burning human and animal flesh. When it was all over, I smoked cigar after cigar until the box was empty and I slept with my pistol within easy reach. Already traumatised by having been threatened at gunpoint by one of the soldiers under my command, the attack on Ayta Az Zutt was yet another of many incidents that led to what I would later discover was Post Traumatic Stress Disorder (PTSD).

I eventually left Fermoy in 1982 because of the differences of opinion with my boss and I headed for the Curragh with a heavy heart. The latest news from Lebanon seemed to match my gloom. Israel had attacked Lebanon on June the 6th 1982, stating that that it wanted to put a stop on the raids aimed at Israeli territory from Southern Lebanon. By the end of the first week of fighting, the International Red Cross and Lebanese police figures claimed that almost ten thousand people had died and almost seventeen thousand had been injured. By the end of the second week, the numbers had increased to fourteen thousand deaths and twenty thousand injured, mostly civilians. As the war dragged on UN peacekeepers were caught in the middle. Forty-seven Irish soldiers would lose their lives in this troubled Middle Eastern country.

But the war in Lebanon seemed very far away as the first snow of winter blanketed the open ground and the hollows across the Curragh. Every evening I drove home to Dublin, listening to the car radio. One evening as I drove across the snow-covered Curragh Plains under a moonlit sky, I heard Luciano Pavarotti singing the Christmas carol, 'O Holy Night', composed by Adolphe Adam. Overcome with emotion, I had to stop the car and wait until I could gather myself together before continuing my journey home. I left the army in 1986.

# CHAPTER 10

# *Internal War*

The Troubles in Northern Ireland had never really gone away. Dissident paramilitary groups still lurked on the perimeters of a fractured society – on both sides of the political divide. On the 15th of August 1998 a bomb went off in the town of Omagh, County Tyrone. The bombing was carried out by a group calling themselves 'The Real Irish Republican Army', a Provisional Irish Republican Army (IRA) splinter group who opposed the IRA's ceasefire and the Good Friday Agreement. The attack, which came four months after the signing of the Agreement, was the single deadliest atrocity in the history of the Troubles.

It reminded me of Cyprus where I had served as a peacekeeper, where a vicious hatred existed between the Greek and Turkish Cypriots and these people could, at any moment begin killing each other without mercy – and killing us in the process. The capital, Nicosia was divided by a 'Green Line' with the deployment of UNFICYP troops, the Irish among them. The mission in Cyprus had three main aims: to prevent the recurrence of fighting; to help maintain law and order and to contribute to the restoration of normal life for the Cypriot people.

We were stationed in Kokkina, several kilometres east of the Northern Cyprus mainland, surrounded by mountainous territory, with Morphou Bay on its northern flank. The bay looked inviting, but swimming was deemed to be too dangerous on account of fighting in the area. In August 1964, the Turkish Resistance paramilitary organisation (TMT), had landed arms and provisions from Turkey. The Greek Cypriot Nationalist Guerrilla Organisation (EOKA) retaliated by attacking the town on August the 6th 1964. Four days later, Turkey sent in fighter jets to strafe and napalm villages and towns, causing heavy casualties. All-out war was prevented by UN intervention, but tensions were still high, and we could not afford to take any chances. I welcomed the tension because any down time brought no respite from my own internal war.

After each tour of duty in Cyprus I returned to my shattered life, becoming more exhausted, unable to get a decent night's sleep and having to lie down several times during the day. My room, with curtains drawn at all times, became my hermit's cave, shunning the light. The world outside my window became more distant – and the more distant the better. Sleep brought escape from memories, from guilt, from anger from having to talk to friends. Dreams turned to nightmares; scenes of havoc, battles, gunfire, screams would wake me up in a lather of sweat. Sometimes, I wished I wouldn't wake up.

Because I couldn't divulge my secret to anyone, I muddled through close to twenty-three years in the army untreated. When I found music, I was miraculously transported to a place of wonder: a world where love and redemption was driven by exquisite orchestral music and singing in the opulent, rarefied atmosphere of opera houses and theatres. The parts of my being lost through trauma seemed to come back, restoring a connection that gave me some semblance of balance. Eventually, help came along in the form of a work colleague who was astute enough to see that I was in need of medical intervention. I began treatment with anti-depressants, and I was attending a psychiatrist, having weekly sessions of Cognitive Behavioural Therapy that had begun to have a positive effect on my mental health. But it was music I wanted – music and more music.

After three performances of *Götterdämmerung*, each just under five hours, in 1996 and 1997 and Strauss's *Elektra*, also at London's Royal Opera House, with Christian Thielemann conducting, I felt I had done my 'training' for the marathon that is *Der Ring des Nibelungen* booked for August 1998 at the epicentre of Wagner's music – the Festspielhaus at Bayreuth. I could not account for the feeling of gloom as I prepared for the eight days in Bayreuth but as the flight got under way, I began to relax.

*Parsifal* gently gathered me into the first night of August the 4th. A splendid performance. The next day, I could feel my legs turn to jelly and my breathing coming in short, shallow gasps. I had been taking Frisium as prescribed by my doctor, but I soon began to realise I was in crisis, heading for a full-blown panic attack. I telephoned my pharmacist and my doctor; both advised me to increase the dose to three tablets a day. A couple of hours before that evening's performance of *Rheingold*, I also had a glass of whiskey. I made it through the performance – and through the night. *Die Walküre* and *Siegfried* on the 7th and 9th were simply magnificent but I stressed myself by worrying about how to occupy myself on the free day coming up on the 10th. Reading some brochures at the hotel, I found that I could visit Wahnfried, Wagner's house in Bayreuth (paid for by Ludwig of Bavaria), which is a living memorial to Richard and Cosima Wagner. The excitement of being in his house with his music playing in the background was immense. The modern museum consists of three buildings that house photographs, manuscripts, personal items and costumes. The garden and the grounds where Wagner is buried and a bust of Ludwig in front of the house are beautiful.

In the afternoon, I took a train to Prague to see the opera house. Built in 1888, the Prague State Opera (Státní opera Praha) presents opera and ballet by Verdi, Tchaikovsky, Puccini, Rossini, Donizetti, Prokofiev and other well-known composers. Formerly the New German Theatre (Das Neue Deutsche Theater) built for Prague's German-speaking people by Fellner & Helmer and opened with *Die Meistersinger aus Nürnberg* on January the 5th 1888, where great musicians of the world music history such as Gustav Mahler, Alexander Zemlinsky, Georg Szell, Richard Strauss, Enrico Caruso, Beniamino Gigli, Lilly Lehmann, Emy Destinn and others performed.

Apart from the opera house, all I knew about Prague was the name – from a small wax statue of the Christ Child, dressed in elaborate red and gold robes. During the 1940s and 50s, millions of reproductions of this statue were to be found in Catholic homes around Ireland. It was a custom to call upon "The Child of Prague" to help ensure good weather for family occasions such as wedding, communions and confirmations. The night before the big day, the little statue of the "Child of Prague", normally kept in the house, was carried outdoors and placed under a hedge. The original, medieval statue is housed in the Carmelite Church of Our Lady Victorious in Malá Strana, Prague. I returned to Prague for opera, some years later. I was never inclined to visit the "Child of Prague".

In Bayreuth, my daily custom was – and still is – breakfast, followed by "duties" left over from my army days – shoe-polishing, getting out shirt and evening wear – followed by bed rest until lunchtime. Sometimes, more bed rest after lunch, then shower, change, dinner and then opera taking up the afternoon and evening. I always needed routine, order: one thing followed immediately by another, to fill the waking hours. Sleep – the few hours here and there – filled the rest of the time.

On the 11th of August, *Götterdämmerung* concluded the *Ring*. I had survived! I had been lifted up by the music and I was very glad I had stayed. I had been so close to coming home when I was in the throes of panic and if it hadn't been for the advice of my doctor and pharmacist to increase the medication, I would have missed the most wonderful experience.

Many years later, while in Karlsruhe, I suffered another panic attack, due in part to an underlying chest infection. I was prescribed antibiotics and was on the verge of coming home, but Professor Eva Märtson, president of the Richard Wagner Verband International asked to meet me – on "Walküre Day". My only discomfort was a rash that had broken out on my knees, hands and feet, which I put down to swallowing antibiotics on an empty stomach.

In retrospect, I can see that even though it was under the surface of my awareness, the prospect of eight days away from home had been frightening. However, I cannot deny that I have suffered for my passion; each time I travel overseas, I have to take pills in order to function at all! It is a far cry from my carefree days as a young soldier of eighteen, patrolling the Angolan Border in the war-torn Congo, in central Africa. Yes, I was homesick at first, but homesickness soon wore off, in the company of fellow youths, officers looking out for us, days filled with activity, falling into blessed exhaustion to the song of crickets and sounds of the jungle.

Thankfully, I managed to travel to Bayerischer Staatsoper in Munich to see *Lohengrin* in January 1999. In my diary I wrote, 'Abend in Himmel'. I was obviously floating! In July and August, I attended the Bayreuth Festival with *Lohengrin*, *Der fliegende Holländer*, *Die Meistersinger von Nürnberg*, *Parsifal* and *Tristan und Isolde* on the menu. Sublime.

But back in real life, anger, borne of a fractured persona and memories deeply buried, led me into to an alcohol phase that was like climbing a greasy pole. I had recovered from an eating disorder through re-education from 1969 to 1977. But as time passed, I was plagued by obsessional behaviour, manifesting in failure to let go of an argument, writing irate, complaining letters, having arguments with employers and learning to hate. Hate became an indulgence and yet I craved acceptance and union with someone – someone who would personify the whole and stable human being that I had lost. Like the fabled Humpty Dumpty I was beyond repair.

No-one seemed to notice; at least, no-one said anything – until October 1992, not long after I began working at Baldonnel, when a friend of mine, a fellow army officer said that I had "changed drastically"! I clammed up and didn't press him to elaborate any further, perhaps afraid that he, or someone else would have me committed to a mental institution. My biggest fear was that I would lose my job. Although I was still in my forties and still physically fit, I gathered from my friend's observation of my demeanour that I was unfit for work. Astute that he was, he advised me to apply for a disability pension. "I have no knowledge of the application procedure," I said, lamely. He scribbled a number on a piece of paper and handed it to me. "Ring Eileen," he said.

Eileen sent me an application form. The application for a disability pension seemed like a straightforward procedure. I outlined the circumstances of the assault in Jerusalem, resulting in post-traumatic stress disorder, respiratory issues that had lasted since I had pneumonia and pleurisy in Cyprus as well as a hearing problem that had manifested at an early stage when, as a young soldier, training on the Vickers machine gun, I was lying in the lowest position underneath the weapon, rolling my head from side to side, trying to ease the pain in my head from the deafening explosions. I was not alone as regards hearing problems; hundreds of army men paid a high price, their hearing damaged for life. Captain Cathal O'Neill was the first officer that I had seen wearing ear protection during an all-army competition at the Curragh and I witnessed an officer from Operations ordering Cathal to remove it!

With the application form completed, I signed it and sent it off, expecting to be called for a medical examination and an interview or a discussion before being granted my pension. Having been examined by the Pensions Board doctor in 1993, I was sent to an Army Medical Corps psychiatrist, then in a training post at St Patrick's Hospital, who found some evidence of Post-Traumatic Stress but reported that I 'failed to fulfil the criteria for the complete PTSD' whose report stated that I was 'immature'. A GP I had seen in Fermoy then arranged for me to see an eminent psychiatrist in

Cork who only saw private patients after hours. The psychiatrist in Cork found that I was suffering from PTSD "in a profound way".

I submitted this report to the Army Pensions Board. I was deemed eighty percent disabled – attributable to service. But nothing happened. It would be many years later before I discovered, under the Freedom of Information Act that the Pensions Policy Section of the Board, the section responsible for the formulation and review of pension policy, legislation and schemes had criticised the board for the award and questioned the incident in Jerusalem in 1965, where my troubles began.. They said that because I was "on holiday" in Jerusalem in 1965 it didn't count. The life-threatening incident in Lebanon in 1980 was of little interest to them.

Between November 1994 and March 1995, a number of representations were made by public representatives on my behalf to find out what was the cause of the delay – to no avail. As I awaited the Board's determination, my disability had been downgraded to fifty percent then to zero percent, then altered to a fifteen percent, then back to thirty percent. I knew none of this this. Finally, I received a letter signed by the Administrator of the Pensions Board informing me that my case had not succeeded. It was then that I went, under the Freedom of Information Act, to the APB and to the army for my service record. I received a letter from Pensions Administration rejecting my claim and stating that I was thirty percent disabled but this was likely "due to a pre-existing condition prior to enlistment". I eventually instructed my legal advisor and in due course, my application was granted for a judicial review. Following this, I received a phone call from the Pensions Board Administrator bluntly telling me that if I lost the case the State would pursue me for costs and I would, in all likelihood be sent to prison! At this time, I was being pursued for legal costs by my solicitor. I sought a bank loan but was refused. I also wrote to the Association of Retired Commissioned Officers for help. Three months later I received a refusal, but they wished me well.

Once the case was listed for a full hearing in the High Court the State entered into secret talks with my Senior Counsel and I was requested to present myself to yet another army psychiatrist at St. Bricin's Hospital. I was reluctant to do this but following legal advice, I eventually agreed. The outcome was an acknowledgement of fifty percent disability attributable to service and an award of a disability pension in accordance with the findings. At the time, I couldn't come to any conclusion other than that this was a sinister move to reduce the impact of my complaint and the cost to the State.

The cumulative effects of the stress induced by the lengthy legal wrangle, the financial burden of legal and other costs and the injustice suffered at the hands of those in power had served to bring me close to total destruction. My health issues worsened, necessitating frequent visits to doctors. Eventually, having obtained some compensation and costs, I began attending psychiatric services, as a private patient. This was getting me nowhere and again, I sought out some way to occupy my mind.

The sense of team spirit, fraternity, and common purpose had sustained me in the army and still appealed to me enormously and I joined the Cavalry Club, an officers' club, founded in 1944 and authorised by the military authorities in 1946. Membership is open to all serving and retired commissioned cavalry officers of the Permanent Defence Force and the Army Reserve and members pay an annual subscription of twenty-five Euro. Members of the committee are elected at the Club's Annual General Meeting. The current tenure of office is for one year and the club's president presents a report at the Annual General Meeting, which takes place during the month of December. Under the chair of the club's president the committee arranges functions and activities it deems appropriate to the achievement of the club's objectives.

As well as the need for social activity and comradeship, I was also drawn to the ethos of the club which was originally established to provide a refuge for officers who were being demobbed after the

"Emergency" (1939-1945). St Brigid was selected as Patron because the club was formed in the Curragh in County Kildare where St. Brigid founded her first monastery. A St. Brigid's Cross features on the president's chain of office. Brigid is renowned for her hospitality and hard work and her cheerful, generous giving of food and shelter. As a woman of God and a woman of the people, a powerful personality who appealed to all – from those in high places to the humble beggar – she was the most appropriate symbol that would set the standard for the hospitality of a place where individuals were made welcome.

It was around this time that I suffered my first heart attack. But I continued working, I continued running the Wagner Society of Ireland – which I had also founded – and I was helping my sister to look after my father. The work at Baldonnel filled the week and the Wagner Society gave me focus. My heart problems worsened and following a Cather ablation in 2013, I awoke from the anaesthetic bursting with so much energy that I thought my body would explode. For two weeks I wanted to climb walls. No longer able to run like I did in the past, I became more and more agitated. Unable to contain this gut-wrenching agitation, I opened my laptop that was sitting on top of the piano and started writing – spilling my guts, rambling through the hellish highlights of fifty years of a broken life which began in Jerusalem in 1965. As I wrote, the injustices that I had suffered at the hands of the defence forces and the Irish State began to take on even bigger proportions. My feeling that it had been me against the world grew into ferocious rage and became so profoundly embedded in my mind that I couldn't see the wood for the trees. I didn't even read what I had written. Each time I was gripped by anger I just kept adding more. Eventually I was led to a ghost-writer who helped turn it into a book. *Elegy for a Broken Soldier* was published in January 2019.

Through writing I learned many things, one of which being that at this point – rather late in the day – I am in no doubt that many of my physical problems arose from stored memories of trauma. The human body cannot lie. According to Dr Bessel van der Kolk, an Austrian psychiatrist, the human body "keeps the score". Sadly, few medical professionals in this country were willing to explore or acknowledge this, one exception being Dr Ivor Brown who was viewed by some of his peers as "nuts".

I also gained some understanding of the extent of my dependability on music: music had become a drug. Listening to music can change my mood. But, according to some experts in the field of music therapy, music does more than just put us in a good mood. It is a wonder drug that sets a lot of things right. It energises the mind, eases stress, evokes emotions and soothes the soul. Scientists claim that it has the power to heal us. In trials, they found "swelling crescendos increased the listener's blood pressure and heart and respiration rates, while relaxing passages of music did the opposite". However, other factors also affect perceptions and emotions. The psychology of music is a very deep study. Musicians claim that music is a universal language. They say that with music you can communicate across cultural and linguistic boundaries in ways that you can't with ordinary languages like English or French. Weaving a story and at the same time, composing music to tell it is a fine art.

Studies have found that music is universal because it exists in every society and music does have the power to evoke deep primal feelings at the core of the shared human experience. It not only crosses cultures, it also reaches deep into our evolutionary past. I now realise that I do easily respond to music – perhaps too easily. Maybe even the *thought* of an upcoming opera, coupled with being away from home can lead to a panic attack! Music is cleverly used to heighten the drama or elicit feelings of sadness or fear – or their opposites: joy and happiness; to use a well-worn phrase, to "lighten the mood". And of course, some music can elicit too much emotion; I can become over excited, a condition that can produce fight-or-flight hormones. I need to be more vigilant.

# CHAPTER 11

# *Lohengrin*

The Holy Grail is a metaphor for all that is treasured, mysterious and elusive. Once a popular subject of Pre-Raphaelite painters and writers such as Malory and Tennyson, in the latter half of the 20th century it has been the subject of films like *The Da Vinci Code* and *Indiana Jones*.

In the late 12th century, according to poet and knight, Robert de Boron and his sources, the Grail as the cup of the Last Supper and after Christ's crucifixion, Joseph of Arimathea carried the body of Christ to the tomb where it was washed and the divine blood from His wounds was caught in the cup.

The Holy Grail first appears in a written text in Chrétien de Troyes's Old French verse romance, *Le Conte du Graal* (Story of the Grail), or *Perceval*, of c.1180. During the next 50 years several works, both in verse and prose, were written although the story, and the principal character, vary from one work to another. In France these stories culminated in a cycle of five prose romances telling the history of the Grail from the Crucifixion to the death of King Arthur. The Old French romances were translated into other European languages. Among these other versions two stand out: Wolfram von Eschenbach's Parzifal (early 13th century) and Sir Thomas Malory's *Le Morte D'Arthur*.

By the 15th century, the Grail or cup had become the Sangrail, an object of knightly romance. In Malory's *Le Morte D'Arthur* arduous quests are undertaken by Knights of the Round Table to find the Sangrail, In his poem *Merlin,* French poet, Robert de Boron maintains that the wizard, Merlin, through his magical powers, knows the history of the Grail. Continuing the Joseph theme in the first poem, he says that Merlin instructed Uther Pendragon to set up the Round Table and to base it on the Grail Table.

The search for the vessel became the primary quest of the knights of King Arthur. It was believed to be kept in a mysterious castle surrounded by a wasteland and guarded by a custodian called the "Fisher King", who suffered from a wound that would not heal. This is the story of Wagner's opera, *Parsifal* in which the character of the same name stumbles upon the castle. Amfortas is the king whose wound will not heal. In *Le Morte D'Arthur*, the Fisher King's recovery and the renewal of the blighted lands depended upon the successful completion of the quest. Equally, the self-realisation of the questing knight was guaranteed by finding the Grail. The magical properties attributed to the Holy Grail are said to have satisfied the tastes and needs of all who drank from them.

Like *Parsifal,* Wagner's opera *Lohengrin* is based on the legend of the Holy Grail. Lohengrin is the son of Parzival (Percival), he is a knight of the Holy Grail sent in a boat pulled by swans to rescue a maiden who can never ask his identity. It is also like a fairy tale. It was first performed in Weimar, Germany on 28 August 1850 with Franz Liszt conducting, and it immediately became very popular.

Wagner said, "It is no mere outcome of Christian meditation, but one of man's earliest poetic ideals." Just as the composer traced the myth of the *Flying Dutchman* to the Hellenic Odyssey, "so do we already meet in the Grecian mythos, the outlines of the myth of Lohengrin". Zeus and Semele, Eros, and Psyche, Elsa and Lohengrin – all, Wagner insists, stand for the same old story: the necessity of love. All heroes yearned for woman, for the human heart. "Music is a woman," Richard Wagner wrote in *Opera and Drama.* Her organism is a vessel merely for bearing, not for begetting; that force of creation lies beyond it." Wagner believed that only once fertilised by a poet's thoughts can music bring forth "true, vibrant melody."

According to the tradition followed by Wagner, The Holy Grail is the fountain of an even higher form of love – divine love. Its knights (Lohengrin and the others) are sent to bring some of that love to earth by rectifying wrongs and promoting righteousness. But they may dwell only where there is purity of heart and perfect faith in their power. "Lohengrin," he says, "sought a woman who should trust in him, who should not ask how he was or whence he came, but love him as he was, and because he was "whate'er she deemed him". In other words, he sought the woman who would not call for explanation or defence, but one who should love him with an unconditioned love. Therefore, he must hide his higher nature, for only in hiding this higher essence could he be certain that he was not adored because of it alone, or humbly worshipped as a god. His longing was not for worship nor for adoration, but for the only things sufficient to redeem him from his loneliness, to still his deep desire for love, for being loved; for being understood through love." The character Elsa, at first innocent and trustful, begins to harbour suspicious of Lohengrin, and therefore loses him. It is the usual idea that as soon as we begin to distrust, we are undone. In the keeping of Parsifal as the lord of the sacred palace of Montsalvat, whose son Lohengrin is one of the earthly champions of the Grail, the tradition has a prominent place in Wagner's drama.

Richard Wagner was probably one of the great dramatists. Wagner's *Lohengrin*, conceived, as Liszt said, "on a grandiose scale" represents a drama that is most complete, a work that is unapproachable. The old Celtic legend of King Arthur and his knights and the story of the Holy Grail are mixed up with the German myth of the knight, Lohengrin who arrives in a boat drawn by a swan. Throughout the ages and all over the world, stories have always been told of heroes and heroines embarking on hazardous quests in search of lost loves, the secret of immortality or great riches. Many of these stories have clashes with monsters, battles with the elements, interventions by the gods and tests of moral character, mental cunning and physical strength. The symbol of the Grail as a mysterious object of quest and as the source of the ultimate mystical, or even physical, experience has endured into the into the 20th century in the novels of Charles Williams, C.S. Lewis and John Cowper Powys. Similar themes: the quest for true love, everlasting glory and spiritual enlightenment are still being told, under many guises, in books, comic strips, interactive games and action films.

*Lohengrin* and *Tannhäuser* were staples of the touring opera companies that visited Dublin theatres in the 1890s and early 1900s, where James Joyce is certain to have seen them. Joyce, like his father, was both an excellent singer (with a sweet tenor voice) and an accomplished pianist with an encyclopaedic mastery of music of every type and genre. As a writer, he incorporated music into all his works in increasingly complex ways. If he had not become a writer, he may well have made a name for himself as a vocal performer. Wagner's influence on Joyce shines through in details throughout *Ulysses* and *Finnegan's Wake*. The character, Siegfried in Wagner's opera of the same name is a parallel for Stephen Dedalus in *Portrait of an Artist* as a Young Man and *Ulysses*. Joyce found an excellent counterpart to Siegfried in the hero of *The Flying Dutchman* and Joyce's use of the literary leitmotif and his attention to the music was emblematic of the universality provided by this combination of music and myth in his work. As well as having a fine tenor voice James Joyce was a talented musician, who played piano and guitar. In 1909 Joyce performed the famous quintet from *Die Meistersinger* in a concert in Trieste. While writing Ulysses, he reported:

*I finished the Sirens chapter during the last few days. A big job. I wrote this chapter with the technical resources of music. It is a fugue with all musical notations: piano, forte, rallentando, and so on. A quintet occurs in it, too, as in Die Meistersinger, my favourite Wagnerian opera.*

Although asserting that the musical effects of his own 'Sirens' episode in Ulysses were "better than *Die Walküre*", Joyce later fully embraced Wagner's concept of "a total work of art".

Joyce empathised with a man whose career paralleled his so closely. Like Wagner, Joyce set out for Paris in his youth on the slimmest of prospects, in part, at least, to establish himself as an artist. Like Wagner, he met indifference and grinding poverty. Both artists would spend much of their lives in exile from their homelands, supported by loyal women whose endurance would be put to the most severe of tests. During his residence in Zurich Joyce must have been aware of the mark Wagner had left on that city during his own exile two generations earlier.

The prelude to *Lohengrin* never fails to take me back to my friend's house on the road to Lismore in Waterford, where I first heard the music that would be the key to the door of Wagner music. At my very first live performance of the opera at The Royal Opera House, London the music was otherworldly, the chorus producing immense power in its moments of fear and jubilation, the trumpet fanfares resounding from the boxes on either side, and the orchestra demonstrating the utter magnificence of the score left me almost afraid to breathe; I didn't want it to end.

What Wagner did with the violins in the Prelude to *Lohengrin* was years ahead of his contemporaries. Four sections. The choral singing is sublime, especially at Bayreuth where the Chorus is comprised of c.120 singers. Wagner didn't hear it performed for years because he was in exile when it was premiered in Weimar, conducted by Franz Liszt.

# CHAPTER 12

# *Wagner*

Not all music appeals; tastes in music are as varied as pebbles on a beach. Wagner's music does not appeal to everyone. To me, a dyed-in-the-wool worshipper of all things Wagner, this is incomprehensible! I do have to accept that some people don't like his operas, but he has a really dedicated cohort of fans, across the world. Most major cities have a Wagner Society and as far as I know, there is only one other composer, Korngold, with a society named after him.

American humourist Bill Nye said, "Wagner's music is better than it sounds", a line frequently wrongly attributed to Mark Twain, a Wagner enthusiast, who enjoyed quoting it. There are some who are born Wagner-lovers. For others he is an acquired taste. Wagner music is not "nice tunes"; many people find Wagner's music unattractive because it is mainly discordant. I had a friend who told me the music "had no melody". I was so incensed I didn't speak to him for months! I have another friend who detests Wagner. "I like about three pieces of his music," she says, "but the rest is bleak – a bit like heavy metal: odious noise. It was probably the punk rock of its day." We are still friends because I let her away with a great deal!

Wagner was a niche composer in his day, but the popularity of his music has grown and has lasted for centuries. In Wagner's day German nationalism was respectable. After World War Two that kind of nationalism was no longer fashionable and the way in which Wagner's operas were used by the Nazis made certain passages very uncomfortable for many to experience. During the Nazi era Wagner was one of Adolf Hitler's favourite composers. Historical perceptions of Wagner have been contaminated by this association ever since, and there is even debate over how Wagner's writings and operas might have influenced the creation of Nazi Germany. Based on perceptions that arise from Wagner's published opinions he is associated by many with Nazism and his operas are often thought to exalt German nationalism.

Wagner was a prolific writer who published essays and pamphlets on a wide range of subjects throughout his life. His writing style has been described as 'verbose, unclear and turgid', which has added to the confusion about his opinions. Several of his writings have achieved some notoriety, in particular his essay *Das Judenthum in der Musik* (Jewishness in Music), a critical view on the influence of Jews in German culture and society at that time. The essays he wrote in his final years were also controversial, with many readers perceiving them as an endorsement of racist beliefs. Some commentators also believe that some of Wagner's operas contain adverse caricatures of Jews. Many also believe that the women in his life are not given credit for having played a more significant role in his work. Later generations have viewed both Wagner's female stage figures as well as the real women in his life as his self-sacrificing servants.

Minna Planer, Wagner's first wife seems to have been a practical, down-to-earth, woman who took care of him, but she is not considered to have been of equal intellectual calibre. Later in life, Wagner referred to his marriage to Minna as "youthful folly", yet he had once said that he "could not live without her". Indeed, with the exception of *Parsifal*, they both worked on all of his operas together. But their relationship had many ups and downs, fraught by Wagner's affairs and their persistent poverty, worsened by Wagner's extravagant lifestyle. After their wedding in Königsberg in 1836, Minna followed her husband to Riga, Latvia. Three years later they were forced to flee from creditors to London and then to Paris. Flagrantly disregarding his wife's need for material security and stability, he became involved in the May Uprising of 1849 in Dresden and lost his lucrative position as the Saxon court's Kapellmeister and ultimately found himself on wanted posters.

In Mathilde Wesendonck, the wife of a wealthy patron, Wagner found a soul mate who inspired his work. "Wagner's muse had a dramatic impact on the creation of *Rheingold*," said Detlef Giese, dramaturg at Berlin's State Opera. "In addition," he noted, "people are familiar with Wagner's musical scores of five of her poems – the *Wesendonck-Lieder*, as they are known today". The relationship between Mathilde and Wagner was presumably platonic, but it seemed to have been intimate enough to lead to conflict with both their spouses. The composer dedicated the prelude to *die Walküre* to Mathilde, and the love triangle between him, Minna and Mathilde is said to have inspired *Tristan und Isolde*. After Minna intercepted a gushing letter from Wagner to Mathilde, the composer fled to Venice. In spite of it all, Mathilde's husband, Otto Wesendonck, remained a loyal patron of Wagner's and supported the composer's project of the building of a festival hall in Bayreuth.

Following the demise of his relationships with Minna and Mathilde, Wagner turned his attentions to Cosima von Bülow, the illegitimate daughter of Franz Liszt and French countess Marie d'Agoult. Cosima was still married to conductor Hans von Bülow when she became Wagner's lover. Wagner was doing well financially during that time, receiving generous support from Bavarian King Ludwig II. Wagner and Cosima ultimately married in 1870. They already had three children together: Isolde, Eva and Siegfried, with whom, Cosima later founded the Bayreuth dynasty.

Cosima was the only one of these three women in Wagner's life who made clear the impact she had on his work. Following his death in 1883, Cosima took over direction of the Bayreuth Festival until 1906, turning it into a huge attraction for high society. Though Wagner did not leave a Will or instructions for the future of the festival, Cosima transformed what was originally an experiment into an institution. Despite being aware of her power and autonomy, Cosima ultimately sacrificed her own identity to preserve public remembrance of Wagner's creative genius, laying the foundation for the "cult" of Wagner and completely devoting her life to the composer's works.

The women in Wagner's life may not have seen themselves as self-sacrificing in any way but may have simply and quietly put up with his extravagance and propensity for extra-marital affairs because they were in love with him. His female stage figures are a lot more audacious: substantially endowed figures from Germanic legend and myth that heave and pulsate in boiling romances.

Charles Baudelaire was an ardent Wagnerian. Hearing *Tristan und Isolde* elicited from him breathlessness, sighs, joys, torments, and finally, he wrote, "The mightiest blast, the most violent effort to find the rupture which unlocks for the boundlessly craving heart the path into the sea of unending sexual bliss." If *Tristan und Isolde* was based on the love triangle between Wagner, Minna and Mathilde, this makes for very interesting speculation!

"Wagner's devotion to depictions of sexual desire was exceedingly unconventional, indeed unprecedented in the history of art," writes Laurence Dreyfus, a professor of music at the University of Oxford. He attributes to Wagner a vast musical palette, profound psychological insight, and an aesthetic sensibility of stunning refinement. "Wagner's many champions would nod, his many detractors scoff. Those gifts allowed the composer to generate extended representations of erotic stimulation, passionate ecstasy, and the torment of love – erotic far advanced on anything that preceded him in music." He proposes that people in the audience imagine that their own personal desires are somehow getting played out there in a very specific way but more in the music than in the heaving about on stage.

Translating carnal desires into music was a gargantuan task. And yet, according to Dreyfus, "Wagner summoned up intertwining bodies through melodic combinations and invertible counterpoint, suggested gender or bodily position through high and low instruments and their tessituras, and enacted sexual climaxes through tonal closure and percussive explosions." No wonder audiences emerged from his operas exhausted!

Not all 19th-century Europeans acknowledged the merits of so much arousal. Friedrich Nietzsche called it "Wagner's sickness" while other critics considered him a "diseased decadent". Yet, Nietzsche found in *Parsifal* "a synthesis of emotional states, with such acuity and insight that it slices into the soul as with a knife". He said that *Tristan und Isolde* was "the real opus metaphysicum of all art". Were Wagner's critics as controversial and contradictory as himself? In *Death-Devoted Heart: Sex and the Sacred in Wagner's Tristan and Isolde* (Oxford University Press, 2003), Roger Scruton acclaims the "re-sacralising of a de-sacralised world" that Wagner attempted in *Tristan's* evocation of a consuming but redeeming erotic passion.

The summoning up of intertwining bodies through melodic combinations and invertible counterpoint may have been helped by Wagner's unusual practices in private. The first exposé of Wagner's predilections for cross-dressing, and his fetish for ladies' pink satin undergarments and rose-scented perfumes, came in 1877. Certain schools of recent Wagner scholarship have focused on the composer's "erotics". Joachim Köchler, author of *Richard Wagner: The Last of the Titans*, conveys, according to author, Stewart Spencer, "a lively portrait of a cross-dressing composer who needed an aura of femininity to stimulate his senses". In the mid-1870s he had an intense friendship, which may or may not have been consummated as a sexual relationship, with a woman named Judith Gautier, who supplied him with the silks and perfumes with which he so adored to surround himself.

The origins for Wagner's penchant for silks may go back to his childhood when "his heart used to beat wildly while touching his sister's theatrical wardrobe", as he reveals in *Mein Leben*. Later in life, the evidence for his satin fetish is omnipresent. Between 1869 and 1874, Wagner wrote some twelve letters to a Milanese tailor named Gaetano Ghezzi, who worked with his wife, a couturiere, Charlotte Chaillon, from whom he ordered women's clothing, claiming that a garment was for Cosima when in fact it was for himself; the clue being the colour; there is no evidence that Cosima ever dressed in pink. In a letter to a French seamstress he writes: "We need two underdresses to go with the jacket, one in pink satin, the other in white satin".

When there were revelations in the Press in 1877, Wagner considered emigrating to America. On the day she discovered the press coverage, Cosima was too weary to persuade him against the idea of another exile. The storm blew over and only a few months later, Wagner was again placing regular orders with Judith Gautier for pink satin, lilac satin, silk undergarments rose water, scented bath oils, and aromatic powders. The letters to Gautier, with precise details, are a good indication of how very important these garments, oils and scents were to Wagner's compositional process. Writing to Judith in December 1877, he begins by dismissing out of hand her Jewish composer friend, Louis Benedictus, who "has fallen substantially in my affection". Wagner then turns "to more serious matters" such as the identification of his very own personal shade of pink: "very pale and delicate":

*First of all, the two chests which have not arrived. Well! They will arrive and I shall immerse myself in your generous soul. Cancel the pink satin entirely; there would be too much of it and it would be good for nothing. Can I expect the two remnants which I mentioned in my last letter? – The brocade can be reserved; I'm inclined to order 30 meters, but perhaps the colours can be changed to flatter my taste even better; in other words the fawn striped material would be silver-grey and blue, my pink, very pale and delicate... You frighten me with your oils. I shall make mistakes with them. In general, I prefer powders, since they cling more gently to fabrics etc. But, once again, be prodigal, above all in the quantity of oils to put in the bath, such as the 'ambergris' etc. I have my bathtub below my 'studio', as I like to smell the perfumes rising.*

Enveloping his body in soft fabrics and feminine perfumes seems to have heightened his senses in order to compose sensuous and erotic scenes. The erotic nature of operas such as *Parsifal*, apparently required the creation of a very specific environment to provoke the composer's inspiration. *Parsifal* is a work that grapples with carnality and the pain caused by sexual desire. The second act involves the hero striving to overcome the sexual allure of the Flower Maidens who try to seduce him in a magical, scent-filled garden. Scholars have also connected his taste for embroidered dressing gowns and floral perfumes with the fragrances described in the Venusberg in the opera *Tannhäuser* – a grotto where sirens, naiads, nymphs and bacchantes indulge in orgiastic pleasures, and with the flowery banks described in the great love duet in *Tristan und Isolde*. His letter to Judith goes on:

*For the rest, do not think ill of me! I am old enough to indulge in childish pursuits! I have three years of Parsifal ahead of me and nothing must tear me away from the peaceful tranquillity of creative seclusion.*

But, anxious to prevent any further scandal, Wagner had Judith's parcels sent to him secretly – care of his local barber, Bernhard Schnappauf in Bayreuth. He had to source his perfumes elsewhere.

In 2012 I took issue with Barry Millington, Chief Music Critic for the *London Evening Standard* and founder/editor of *The Wagner Journal* after he had delivered a talk to the Wagner Society of Ireland, during which he showed a picture of Wagner's pantaloons on a screen. At the time, I thought that his rattling on about Wagner's underwear left a lot to be desired. I personally found it tasteless and

unsavoury. Personally, I couldn't care less what Wagner wore. I felt
Millington was ridiculing Wagner. However, Millington is a
staunch Wagnerite. In an article, by author, Della Couling writes:
"Millington's unquestioning adoration of his subject is moving; he
reminds me of Donna Elvira, in love with Don Giovanni to the
end, desperately forgiving in the face of unforgivable evidence, but
never losing sight of the man's unique genius".

To add to his list of controversies, Wagner was said to have surrounded himself later in life with homophilic if not homosexual
young men, whom he welcomed as 'idolaters' rather than as active
sexual partners. Perfume, cross-dressing, and homophilia also
appear in Wagner's works.

Sometime in the 1990s an article, under the heading, *Sex 'n'
Drugs 'n' Wagner*, by art historian, writer and journalist Peter Bloch
(1921-2008) in *The New York Times* carried a stark warning about
the "evils" portrayed in Wagner's operas. Bloch wrote:

"Now that the major record companies have agreed to stamp
warning labels on offensive rock albums, the public should be
alerted to an even greater danger that has not been acted upon.

Richard Wagner's 16-hour, four-opera *Ring of the Nibelungen*,
one of history's most pernicious works of art, can be found in any
large record store. Perused even briefly, it reveals itself to be more
objectionable than any rock 'n' roll song at the centre of the label-
ling controversy.

The *Ring*, now being performed at the Metropolitan Opera in
New York City, violates just about every modern taboo imaginable.
Moreover, history proves it dangerous.

Consider a warning label that was once proposed:

'Warning!: Contains lyrics or matter which describes or advo-
cates one or more of the following: suicide; explicit sexual acts
including but not limited to rape; sodomy; incest; bestiality and
sadomasochism; murder; morbid violence; or the use of illegal
drugs.'

Take three egregious examples: the incest of Sigmund and his sister Sieglinde is obviously presented as a virtue; Siegfried betrays his true love, Brünnhilde, while under the influence of a drugged potion, and the entire cycle ends when Brünnhilde redeems mankind by burning herself and her horse alive. Furthermore, the operas grossly insult 'little people" (dwarfs), advocate violence to animals and contain almost continuous sexist references. The *Ring's* history and that of its composer leave no doubt in any thoughtful person's mind of the dangers these operas pose. Wagner's epic manages to include almost all of these offenses, often cloaked in seductive, heart-pounding music whose rhythms all too often can move an incautious listener to be carried away by – even identify with – the evils being acted out on stage. Wagner was a notorious anti-Semite who campaigned viciously against Jews during his lifetime, and his widow was one of Hitler's most fervent admirers. The Führer loved Wagner's music; it was under the spell of these super-nationalistic Teutonic harmonies that the conquest of Europe and the destruction of the Jews was plotted. Surely, there is thus more evidence of the direct evils of the *Ring* than anything alleged against Ozzy Osbourne, Motley Crue or Twisted Sister. Any offense committed by these relatively innocuous heavy metal bands pales by comparison with the demonstrated outrages contained in Wagner's masterwork. And unlike the music of most heavy metal groups, these objectionable operas will be shown on prime-time television, paid for in part by taxpayers' dollars. In June, four consecutive evenings will be set aside on public TV channels for the Ring, with subtitles that guarantee that not one offensive nuance will escape any viewer. Senator Jesse Helms, the Rev. Donald Wildmon, Tipper Gore and Terry Rikolta have their work cut out for them. The public deserves no less than their eternal vigilance."

As far as I am aware, Mr. Bloch's recommendations were never applied and to date, no recording of Wagner's music carries a 'warning' of any description.

Few of the afore-mentioned "offenses" are unique to Wagner. In Act One of *Der Rosenkavalier* by Richard Strauss, a mature woman of thirty-two years is having sex with a seventeen-year-old boy. However, all commentators acknowledge the part of Wagner's life that taints all aspects of his work: his odious anti-Semitism. Like many Wagnerians, I have disagreed with this. Wagner was no worse or no better than any of his contemporaries. He, however, provided a hook for the likes of Millington to hang their hats upon.

I met Professor John Davidson in 2016, just after his book of poems about Wagner was published. Professor Davidson was at the Bayreuth Festival in August 2016. John Davidson had recently published a book of 57 poems in an illustrated collection entitled *Visions of Valhalla*: A poetic tribute to Richard Wagner. We met at the Bayerische Hof, just beside the station. In the Foreword to the book, Barry Millington wrote: "Richard Wagner referred to himself repeatedly as a poet rather than as a composer and would surely have been delighted to find himself the subject of a volume of poetry. John Davidson's poems evince a deep love and knowledge of Wagner and his works: avoiding both hagiography and sentimentality, he makes the reader think about the subject in new ways – the mark of a true poet. This volume will doubtless appeal to committed Wagnerians but deserves to find an audience beyond them too".

Although Davidson describes himself as "obsessed with his subject matter", he tries to maintain a balance. In the introduction to his book he explains: "The poems are a mix of the serious and not-so-serious. Most are concerned with aspects of Wagner's life, with individual works or series of works, with his ongoing influence, and with reactions and responses to the man himself and his musical/dramatic legacy". He goes on to say: "Wagner is nothing if not a polarising figure, and his musical compositions are likewise objects of ongoing controversy. There seems to be no let-up in the fascination Wagner has exerted on so many minds and hearts".

There is no doubt that Richard Wagner promoted himself better than anyone else. In a self-promotional effort that began around 1840 in Paris and lasted for the remainder of his career, Wagner maintained that he was the "most German" composer ever and the "true successor" of Beethoven. He was an opera composer who declared that he was not composing operas but mapping out a new direction, creating works that would break with tradition and be brand new. Wagner made himself a celebrity, promoting himself using every means available – through autobiography, journal articles, short stories, newspaper announcements and letters and created a distinctive niche for his works in the crowded opera market of his day.

Wagner seemed destined for a life of controversy – even from the beginning. It is suggested that he was the son of Ludwig Geyer, rather than his legal father Carl Friedrich Wagner, and some of his biographers have proposed that Wagner himself believed that Geyer was Jewish. A belief also exists that at the end of his life, his fatal heart attack followed an argument with his wife Cosima over the singer Carrie Pringle, with whom some claim he had an amorous relationship. Whatever about the validity of some of the material that has been written about Richard Wagner, I would have given anything to have met him. Today, I am grateful to him for the music that has undoubtedly saved my life. I too may be "desperately forgiving in the face of unforgivable evidence, but never losing sight of the man's unique genius".

# CHAPTER 13

# *Giving Thanks to Ludwig*

It was one of those magnificent sunny days, rare enough in an Irish summer. A friend and I had finished a wonderful lunch at a well-known restaurant, surrounded by mountains, near Glendalough, in County Wicklow. We decided to sit outside to have coffee and continue our chat. "I suspect that in another lifetime, you might have been a spy!" she said. "Why do you say that?" I asked. "Well, while attending performances across Europe you slip into and out of cities 'under the radar', rarely engaging with people and talking to no-one other than taxi drivers and hotel staff. From what I gather, you get off a plane, get in a taxi, straight to your hotel, stay in your room, only coming out to eat. You go to the opera, then back to the hotel, sleep, eat, taxi, airport. A clandestine operation. You'd be a great spy!"

Maybe I would. I have become a loner – almost a recluse. Since I left the army in 1986, my circle has considerably shrunk, leaving a tiny, select few friends. I usually travel alone and have been to Vienna, Berlin, Rome, London, Bayreuth and Munich more often than I can remember; if I didn't keep diaries, I certainly would not remember, but after the first or second visit, I have no wish to wander about or take in the sights of any city, with one exception: Munich. Even in Munich, I like to visit just one place – the grave of King Ludwig II of Bavaria, Wagner's champion.

118

Born in Nymphenburg Castle, Munich, in 1845, Ludwig II was a member of the Wittelsbach dynasty, and became king of Bavaria at the early age of eighteen after the sudden death of his father Maximilian II. The young Ludwig was totally unprepared to reign and after a lost war against Prussia, he had no interest in politics. He loved art and music and soon found his vocation in helping to further the arts. He was intensely interested in the operas of Richard Wagner. This interest began when Ludwig first saw *Lohengrin* at the impressionable age of fifteen, and *Tannhäuser* ten months later. These operas appealed to the king's fantasy-filled imagination.

By now, Wagner had a notorious reputation as a political radical and philanderer who had been on the run from the authorities in Dresden after a political uprising and he was constantly on the run from creditors. However, on the 4th of May 1864, the fifty-one-year-old Wagner was given an unprecedented lengthy audience with Ludwig in the Royal Palace in Munich. Later, the composer wrote: "Alas, he is so handsome and wise, soulful and lovely, that I fear that his life must melt away in this vulgar world like a fleeting dream of the gods".

A year after meeting the King, Wagner presented his latest work, *Tristan und Isolde*, in Munich to great acclaim. However, the composer's perceived extravagant and scandalous behaviour in the capital was unsettling for the conservative people of Bavaria, and the King was forced to ask Wagner to leave the city six months later, in December 1865. Ludwig considered abdicating to follow Wagner, but Wagner persuaded him to stay. Ludwig provided the Tribschen residence for Wagner in Switzerland. Wagner completed *Die Meistersinger* there; it was premiered in Munich in 1868. When Wagner returned to work on his "Ring Cycle", Ludwig demanded special previews of the first two works, *Das Rheingold* and *Die Walküre* at Munich in 1869 and 1870.

Wagner was now planning his great personal opera house at Bayreuth. Ludwig initially refused to support the grandiose project.

However, when Wagner exhausted all other sources, he appealed to Ludwig, who loaned him 100,000 thalers to complete the work. Ludwig also paid for the Wahnfried villa for Wagner and his family to reside in, constructed between 1872 and 1874. In 1876, Ludwig attended the dress rehearsal and third public performance of the complete *Ring* Cycle at the newly completed Festspielhaus. Ludwig was the saviour of Wagner's career. Without Ludwig, it is doubtful that Wagner's later operas would have been composed, much less premiered at the prestigious Munich Royal Court Theatre (now the Bavarian State Opera).

Ludwig's interest in theatre was not confined to Wagner. In 1867, he appointed Karl von Perfall as Director of his new court theatre and under Ludwig's supervision, introduced theatregoers to Shakespeare, Calderón, Mozart, Gluck, Ibsen, Weber, and many others. He also raised the standard of interpretation of Schiller, Molière, and Corneille. Over the next thirteen years, the King had 209 separate private performances given for himself alone or with a guest, in the two court theatres. He attended forty-four private operas including twenty-eight by Wagner, with eight performances of *Parsifal*), eleven ballets, and one hundred-and fifty-four plays at a cost of 97,300 Marks. These private performances were due to his disdain for anything that would spoil the experience of escape into fantasy. He complained to the theatre actor-manager Ernst von Possart: "I can get no sense of illusion in the theatre so long as people keep staring at me and follow my every expression through their opera-glasses. I want to look myself, not to be a spectacle for the masses".

Ludwig's own life was probably in itself a tragic opera. The greatest stress of Ludwig's early reign was pressure to produce an heir. In 1867 Ludwig became engaged to Duchess Sophie Charlotte in Bavaria, his cousin and the youngest sister of his dear friend, Empress Elisabeth of Austria. They shared a deep interest in the works of Wagner. A few days before their engagement was announced Ludwig wrote to Sophie:

*The main substance of our relationship has always been Richard Wagner's remarkable and deeply moving destiny.*

However, Ludwig repeatedly postponed the wedding date, and finally cancelled the engagement in October. After the engagement was broken off, Ludwig wrote to his former fiancée, *My beloved Elsa! Your cruel father has torn us apart. Eternally yours, Heinrich.* (Elsa and Heinrich were names they used, taken from characters in Wagner's opera *Lohengrin.*) Sophie later married Prince Ferdinand, Duke of Alençon.

Ludwig never married. It is known from his diary which began in the 1860s, his private letters, and other surviving personal documents that he had strong homosexual desires. He struggled all his life to suppress those desires and remain true to the teachings of the Catholic Church. Homosexuality had not been punishable in Bavaria since 1813, but after the Unification of Germany in 1871, homosexual acts between males were criminalised. In intensely Catholic and socially conservative 19th-century Bavaria, the scandal of a homosexual monarch would have been intolerable. However, throughout his reign, Ludwig had a succession of close friendships with men, including his chief equerry and Master of the Horse, Richard Hornig, the Bavarian prince Paul von Thurn und Taxis, the Hungarian theatre actor Josef Kainz, and his courtier Alfons Weber.

Louis XIV of France became Ludwig's inspiration. In his letters, Ludwig admired the French architecture, art, and music and was saddened by how miserably lacking Bavaria was in comparison. It became his dream to accomplish the same for Bavaria. In 1867, he visited Eugène the Palace of Versailles in France, as well as the Wartburg near Eisenach in Thuringia, which largely influenced the style of his construction. He built three castles: Linderhof, Neuschwanstein and Herrenchiemsee, for which he personally approved every detail of the architecture, decoration, and furnishing at enormous expense. These projects provided employment for many hundreds of local labourers and artisans and brought a considerable flow of money to the relatively poor regions where his castles were built.

His extravagance and spending sprees soon began to stir opposition. Although the king had paid for his pet projects out of his own funds and not the state coffers, that did not necessarily spare Bavaria from the financial result. By 1885, the king was 14 million marks in debt, had borrowed heavily from his family, and rather than economising, as his financial ministers advised him, he planned further opulent designs. He demanded that loans be sought from all of Europe's royalty, and remained aloof from matters of state. Feeling harassed and irritated by his ministers, he considered dismissing the entire cabinet and replacing them with fresh faces. The cabinet decided to act first.

Seeking a cause to depose Ludwig by constitutional means, the rebelling ministers decided on the reasoning that he was mentally ill, and unable to rule. They asked Ludwig's uncle, Prince Luitpold to step into the position. Luitpold agreed, on condition the conspirators produced reliable proof that the king was in fact helplessly insane. Between January and March 1886, the conspirators drew up a medical report, on Ludwig's fitness to rule. Most of the details in the report were compiled by Maximilian Count von Holnstein, who used bribery and his high rank to extract a long list of complaints and gossip about Ludwig from among the king's servants. The litany of supposed bizarre behaviour included sloppy and childish table manners, his pathological shyness, his avoidance of state business, his complex and expensive flights of fancy, dining out of doors in cold weather and wearing heavy overcoats in summer, dispatching servants on lengthy and expensive voyages to research architectural details in foreign lands; and abusive, violent threats to his servants.

In early June, the report was signed by a panel of four psychiatrists: Dr. Bernhard von Gudden, chief of the Munich Asylum, Dr Hubert von Grashey (who was Gudden's son-in-law), and their colleagues, Dr Friedrich Wilhelm Hagen and Dr Max Hubrich. The report declared in its final sentences that the king suffered from paranoia, and concluded, "Suffering from such a disorder, freedom of action can no longer be allowed and Your Majesty is declared incapable of ruling, which incapacity will be not only for a year's duration, but for the length of Your Majesty's life". The men had never met the king, except for Gudden, wo had met him only once, twelve years earlier, and none had ever examined him.

Ludwig was certified insane by a government commission in his bedroom at Neuschwanstein and taken to castle Berg. A few days later, on June the 13th he went out for a walk around Lake Starnberg with his physician Professor von Gudden but neither of them returned. A few hours later he was found floating face down in knee-deep water, the dead body of the doctor next to him. Today, Ludwig's behaviour would probably be interpreted as a schizotypal personality disorder and he may also have suffered from Pick's disease during his last years, an assumption supported by a frontotemporal lobar degeneration mentioned in the post-mortem report. Shortly after his death, Ludwig's younger only brother and successor, Otto, was also considered insane, providing a convenient basis for the claim of hereditary insanity.

His cousin and friend, Empress Elisabeth held that, "The King was not mad; he was just an eccentric living in a world of dreams. They might have treated him more gently, and thus perhaps spared him so terrible an end." One of Ludwig's most quoted sayings was "I wish to remain an eternal enigma to myself and to others."

An iron cross marks the spot in Lake Starnberg where he was found. The so-called "Swan King" is also said to have inspired the story behind the classical ballet *Swan Lake* by Russian composer Tchaikovsky. This could be referenced to the days of his childhood when he spent much of his youth in a castle named Hohenschwangau (High region of the swan) in the Bavarian Alps. Ludwig grew up there among swan images and icons, and the nearby

Schwansee (Swan Lake).

Ironically, the castles which were causing the king's financial ruin have today become extremely profitable tourist attractions for the Bavarian state. The palaces, given to Bavaria by Ludwig III's son Crown Prince Rupprecht in 1923, have paid for themselves many times over and attract millions of tourists from all over the world to Germany each year.

To my mind, the treatment of this young man at the hands of the government of the time, and the lack of support by his family and the so-called medical profession, was cruel and inhumane, a conspiracy of a most foul nature. Sadly, almost a hundred-and-twenty years later things had not changed in medical – specifically mental health – fields anywhere in Europe. In Ireland, I – and a number of other Irish army personnel – had fallen into a system where the need for self-preservation was alive and well among the shrinks in the army pensions board who could not understand the actual role of *trauma* in post-traumatic stress disorder (PTSD)! Back then, I'd love to have been a spy – surreptitiously listening to their excuses and concocting their so-called conclusions in order to preserve the status quo and save their own skins. Since then however, thankfully things have changed, and better support systems are in place for soldiers returning from war zones.

But it is not the conspirators who are remembered; it is Ludwig's great legacy that lives on and the contribution he made to Bavaria's culture will never be forgotten. His body is interred in the crypt of the church of St. Michael in the heart of Munich. Today visitors pay tribute to him by visiting his grave as well as his castles. I have been to the lake where Ludwig died, and each time I "slip into" Munich "under the radar" I visit his tomb. Had Ludwig not sponsored the premieres of *Tristan und Isolde*, *Die Meistersinger von Nürnberg*, and, through his financial support of the Bayreuth Festival, those of *Der Ring des Nibelungen* and *Parsifal* I would not be here. It was music that became my lifeline.

# CHAPTER 14

## *Tristan und Isolde*

After the Anglo-Irish Treaty in December 1921, Ireland was a country divided. In 1922, fighting broke out between "Free-Staters" (Free State Army) and anti-Treaty forces. The ensuing Irish Civil War in the south of the island lasted less than a year but left permanent bitterness between political parties and families south of the border and between Catholics and Protestants in the north where Catholic Nationalists wished to see the whole island of Ireland united under the Irish flag whilst Protestant Unionists were supporters of the link with Britain. By and large, Catholics in Northern Ireland were the underclass, suffering discrimination in almost every area of life. I had served in war zones overseas, but I was not expecting to be immersed in a battle just a hundred miles up the road from home.

A merciless bombing campaign began throughout Northern Ireland as well as on the British mainland. The Provisionals also targeted policemen and they became more and more involved in civilian demonstrations and riots. In retaliation, the loyalist Ulster Volunteer Force (UVF) began to use violence to protect the Protestant community from the Provisional IRA and launched their own offensives against Catholics – and against the Irish Republic. By August 1971, Internment (to arrest and hold people without charge) was introduced but internment intensified support for terrorism on both sides. As the situation in Northern Ireland began to look like it was descending into civil war, the Taoiseach, Jack Lynch said that the Irish government would not stand by and see innocent people injured. With the escalation of the Troubles, Irish troops and Reserves were deployed along the border to provide assistance and protection to An Gárda Síochána – the unarmed civil police force in the Republic – as well as protection for the hundreds of refugees from Northern Ireland who were flooding into the border counties. Three new infantry battalions, the 27th the 28th and the 29th were established and the 4th Cavalry Squadron was redeployed to the border. The Irish Defence Forces purchased a new transport fleet, equipped soldiers with modern weapons and recruitment was stepped up. Now a young corporal and studying for the Leaving Certificate examination at night I was on secondment from the 5th Battalion helping to turn a hundred and fifty civilians into soldiers at Collins Barracks. It was hard work. However, there was great camaraderie among the young NCOs and the next six months training the new recruits were immensely gratifying.

Over forty years later, at the end of January 2015, defence co-operation between the Irish and British armies was formalised when the Irish Minister for Defence and the British Secretary of State for Defence, Michael Fallon signed a historic memorandum of under-standing at a ceremony in Dublin. New developments would now include the Irish Army training British soldiers in peacekeeping operations. Irish Minister for Defence, Alan Shatter described the initiative as historic, saying it was yet another indication of the normalisation of relations between Ireland and the United King-dom. "In that sense it is a historic step and provides a tangible manifestation of the very positive relations and mutual respect that now exists between our two countries," he said. One of the motivat-ing factors behind the Agreement was to provide the British with access to the peacekeeping expertise of the Irish Defence Forces. One newspaper article stated, "While the British Army is regarded as one of the best equipped and most experienced in the world in combat operations, it did not have the Irish Army's experience in peacekeeping". We had come a long way since the Troubles in Northern Ireland. Had I been younger I might very well have been interested in training soldiers from across the 'pond'. "Once a soldier, always a soldier", as the saying goes. It was news like this that often brought home the fact that I was one of the elderlies – an elderly army veteran, actually – missing army life. I know there are thousands like me, from defence forces all over the world listening to military matters, wishing they were still answering a bugle call, still marching to fifes and drums. But as joints stiffen and creak, the marching ceases and the bugles and the fifes and the drums and the war pipes fade. Over the years I had been drawn to music of a very different kind, although an old marching tune might, on occasion, trigger a memory or two from my army days.

The 18th of August 2015 would be my seventeenth *Tristan*, the origins of which may have come from a more distant relationship between Ireland and England. Departing Dublin on the 17th, taxi, plane, train, bus, train, I was exhausted on arrival at Bayreuth but delighted to be there. This time, I would be joined by a friend from Istanbul. We had met here in Bayreuth some years earlier and he had become a member of the Gesellschaft der Freunde von Bayreuth (Friends of Bayreuth) of which I had been a member since 1995. He was travelling from Paro Airport, Bhutan to New Delhi and then to Frankfurt. By 11 p.m. there was still no sign of him. Next morning, he appeared after breakfast, looking a bit the worse for wear. He had missed the train to Nürnberg and hadn't arrived at Bayreuth until 2 a.m. At the evening's performance he had a seat in Row 13. I was in Row 26. We swapped tickets for Act III. Seated in Row 13 I had a better view of the stage and could see everything clearly.

*Tristan und Iseult* is a tragedy about the adulterous love between the Cornish knight Tristan and the Irish princess Iseult (Isolde/Yseult). The narrative predates and most likely inspired the Arthurian romance of Lancelot and Guinevere and has had a substantial influence on Western art and literature. There are two main traditions of the *Tristan* legend. The early tradition comprised the French romances of Thomas of Britain and Béroul – two poets from the second half of the 12th century. Beroul's version is the oldest known version of the *Tristan* romances and is considered to come the closest to all of the raw events in the romance exactly as they are, with no explanation or modifications. Therefore, Beroul's version is an archetype for later "common branch" editions.

After defeating the Irish knight Morholt, Tristan travels to Ireland to bring back the fair princess, Iseult for his uncle, King Marke of Cornwall, to marry. When Tristan brings Princess Isolde onto his ship to Cornwall, she becomes irritated by his apparent indifference to her. In fact, they are passionately in love, but their relationship is doomed. By substituting a love potion for poison that Isolde and Tristan intend to drink, the servant, Brangäne revives their love and it is in this ecstatic state that they arrive in Cornwall. Despite Isolde's marriage to Marke, the lovers' passion secretly unfolds, until one day they are discovered. Marke feels betrayed and becomes distraught at Tristan's behaviour. Mortally wounded by Melot, King Marke's vassal, who Kurwenal, Tristan's servant, kills in turn, Tristan dies in Isolde's arms. The princess collapses beside her deceased lover and they are reunited in their 'love death', the only possible outcome for their mystic union.

As with the Arthur–Lancelot–Guinevere love triangle in the medieval courtly love motif, Tristan, King Marke, and Iseult of Ireland all love each other. Tristan honours and respects King Marke as his mentor and adopted father; Iseult is grateful that Marke is kind to her; and Marke loves Tristan as his son and Iseult as a wife. But every night, each has horrible dreams about the future. Marke eventually learns of the affair and seeks to entrap his nephew and his bride.

In another version, Marke acquires what seems proof of their guilt and resolves to punish them: Tristan by hanging and Iseult by (partially) burning at the stake, later lodging her in a leper colony. Tristan escapes on his way to the gallows. He makes a miraculous leap from a chapel and rescues Iseult. The lovers escape into the forest of Morrois and take shelter there until discovered by Mark. They make peace with Mark after Tristan's agreement to return Iseult to Mark and leave the country. Tristan then travels to Brittany, where he marries (for her name and her beauty) Iseult of the White Hands, daughter of Hoel of Brittany and sister of Kahedin.

The earliest surviving versions already incorporate references to King Arthur and his court. The connection between Tristan and Iseult and the Arthurian legend was expanded over time, and sometime shortly after the completion of the Vulgate Cycle (the Lancelot-Grail) in the first quarter of the 13th century, two authors created the "Prose Tristan", which fully establishes Tristan as a Knight of the Round Table who even participates in the quest for the Holy Grail. The Prose Tristan became the common medieval tale of Tristan and Iseult that would provide the background for Thomas Malory, the English author who wrote *Le Morte d'Arthur* over two centuries later.

In the Prose version Tristan is mortally wounded by King Mark, who strikes Tristan with a lance from Morgan le Fay while Tristan is playing a harp for Iseult. The poetic versions of the Tristan legend offer a very different account of the hero's death. According to Thomas' version, Tristan was wounded by a poison lance while attempting to rescue a young woman from six knights. Tristan sends his friend Kahedin to find Iseult of Ireland, the only person who can heal him. Tristan tells Kahedin to sail back with white sails if he is bringing Iseult, and black sails if he is not. Iseult agrees to return to Tristan with Kahedin, but Tristan's jealous wife, Iseult of the White Hands, lies to Tristan about the colour of the sails. Tristan dies of grief, thinking that Iseult has betrayed him, and Iseult dies swooning over his corpse.

An English translation by Hilaire Belloc in 1903 tells that a thick bramble briar grows out of Tristan's grave, growing so much that it forms a bower and roots itself into Iseult's grave. It goes on to describe how King Mark tries to have the branches cut three separate times, and each time the branches grow back and intertwine. This behaviour of briars would have been very familiar to medieval people who worked on the land. Later versions heighten this aspect of the story, by having Tristan's grave grow a briar, but Iseult's grave grow a rose tree, which then intertwine with each other. Further versions hone this aspect even more, with the two plants being said to have been hazel and honeysuckle.

A few later stories record that the lovers had a number of children. In some stories they produced a son and a daughter whom they named after themselves; these children survived their parents and had adventures of their own. In the French romance *Ysaie le Triste* (Ysaie the Sad), the eponymous hero is the son of Tristan and Iseult; he becomes involved with the fairy king Oberon and marries a girl named Martha, who bears him a son named Mark. Spanish Tristan (*el Joven*) also dealt with Tristan's son, here named Tristan of Leonis.

There are references to "March ap Meichion" (Mark) and "Trystan" in the Welsh Triads, in some of the gnomic poetry, the *Mabinogion* stories, and in the 11th-century hagiography of Illtud. A character called Drystan appears as one of King Arthur's advisers at the end of *The Dream of Rhonabwy*, an early 13th-century tale in the Welsh prose collection known as *The Mabinogion*. Iseult is listed along with other great men and women of Arthur's court in another, much earlier Mabinogion tale, *Culhwch and Olwen*.

An ill-fated 'triantán an ghrá or love triangle features in a number of other Irish works, most notably in the text called *Tóraigheacht Dhiarmada agus Ghráinne* (The Pursuit of Diarmuid and Gráinne). In the story, the aging Fionn mac Cúmhaill takes the young princess, Gráinne, to be his wife. At the betrothal ceremony, however, she falls in love with Diarmuid, one of Fionn's most trusted warriors. Gráinne gives a sleeping potion to everyone but him, eventually convincing him to elope with her. The fugitive lovers are then pursued all over Ireland by the Fíanna.

It is suggested that the 11th-century Persian story *Vis and Rāmin* was the model for the Tristan legend because the similarities are too strong to be coincidental. But the evidence for this is circumstantial. Theories as to how this Persian story might have reached the West include the suggestion that it was through story-telling interactions during the crusades in Syrian courts and through minstrels who had free access to both Crusader and Saracen camps in the Holy Land.

Some believe the Roman poet, Ovid's *Pyramus and Thisbe*, as well as the story of *Ariadne at Naxos* might have also contributed to the development of the Tristan legend. The sequence in which Tristan and Iseult die and become interwoven trees also parallels Ovid's love story of *Baucis and Philemon*, husband and wife who are transformed as they die together into two different trees sprouting from the same trunk. However, this also occurs in the saga of *Deidre of the Sorrows* recorded in the Ulster Cycle of Irish mythology. It is a tale of beauty, lust, and death dating back to ancient Ireland.

The earliest representation of what scholars refer to as the "courtly version" of the Tristan legend is in the work of Thomas of Britain, dating from 1173. Only ten fragments of his Tristan poem, representing six manuscripts, have ever been located: the manuscripts in Turin and Strasburg are now lost, leaving two in Oxford, one in Cambridge and one in Carlisle. In his text, Thomas names another "trouvère" who also sang of Tristan, though no manuscripts of this earlier version have been discovered. There is also a passage telling how Iseult wrote a short tale out of grief that sheds light on the development of an unrelated legend concerning the death of a prominent troubadour.

In 1832, Italian composer, Gaetano Donizetti references this story in his opera *L'elisir d'amore* as the character of Adina sings the story to the ensemble, inspiring Nemorino to ask the charlatan Dulcamara for the magic elixir. Wagner's composition of *Tristan und Isolde* was inspired by the philosophy of Arthur Schopenhauer as well as by Wagner's affair with Mathilde Wesendonck. Widely acknowledged as one of the peaks of the operatic repertoire, *Tristan* was notable for Wagner's unprecedented use of chromaticism, tonal ambiguity, orchestral colour and harmonic suspension.

Premiered in 1865, Richard Wagner's *Tristan und Isolde* was composed between 1857 and 1859. Based largely on the 12th-century romance *Tristan* by Gottfried von Strassburg, depicts Tristan as a doomed romantic figure, while Isolde fulfils Wagner's quintessential feminine role as the redeeming woman. It premiered at the Königliches Hof-und Nationaltheater in Munich on the 10th of June 1865 with Hans von Bülow conducting. Wagner referred to the work not as an opera but called it "eine Handlung" (literally a drama, a plot or an action), which was the equivalent of the term used by the Spanish playwright Calderón for his dramas. The opera was enormously influential among Western classical composers and provided direct inspiration to composers such as Gustav Mahler, Richard Strauss, Karol Szymanowski, Alban Berg, Arnold Schoenberg and Benjamin Britten.

In Act 1 we are aboard a ship. Tristan, and his servant Kurwenal, are bringing the Irish princess Isolde to Cornwall, where she has been promised in marriage to King Marke. While the pair are passionately in love with each other, Isolde is annoyed by Tristan's feigned indifference to her. She explains to her maid, Brangäne, the hopeless state of their relationship and orders Brangäne to prepare a deadly brew for Tristan and her to drink. But the maid replaces the poison with a love potion which the lovers drink, convinced they will surely die, they are instead consumed with relentless love.

In Act 2, during a royal hunt, Tristan and Isolde secretly meet in the castle, while Brangäne keeps watch. Isolde is now married to

King Marke. A feverish duet ensues, during which the lovers revel in their passion and declare that only in the long night of death can they be eternally united. Brangäne warns Tristan and Isolde that the night is ending, but the lovers forget about the world around them. They are surprised by King Marke, who has suddenly returned. In a poignant monologue, Marke expresses his dismay at being betrayed by Tristan. Tristan is unable to explain his actions and asks Isolde to follow him into death. He accuses Melot of treachery and challenges him to fight. Tristan offers no defence and deliberately impales himself on Melot's sword.

In Act 3, Tristan lies unconscious, with his ever-faithful servant Kurwenal caring for him. An ominous shepherd's pipe can be heard in the distance. When the shepherd appears, Kurwenal asks him to play a more cheerful melody should Isolde's ship appear on the horizon. Gradually, Tristan regains consciousness. Delirious with pain, he thinks only of his reunion with Isolde. Kurwenal explains that he has sent for Isolde, and in a hallucination, Tristan sees her vessel coming towards him. Hearing the shepherd's pipe, Tristan recollects his parent's deaths when he was a young boy, and feels the melody now calling him. He laments the potion which he and Isolde brewed and the madness he now lives – ever-waiting for Isolde to arrive and escort him to death. He deliriously imagines Isolde coming to him across the water. Kurwenal sees nothing. However, a change in the shepherd's melody confirms that Isolde's ship has been sighted. Kurwenal goes to look for himself and sees that Isolde is indeed arriving. Tristan throws Kurwenal out to go and greet her and explodes with deadly passion for her. Tristan sees Isolde and rushes to her, only to die in her arms. Isolde tries to draw one last breath from Tristan but is only able to follow him into death herself.

Kurwenal's heart breaks when he sees dead master. The shepherd announces the arrival of a second ship: it contains King Marke, Melot and soldiers, as well as Brangäne. Thinking they have come in pursuit of Isolde, Kurwenal charges at Melot and kills him. As King Marke looks on in horror, Kurwenal rushes into death. Having learned from Brangäne about the love potion, King Marke has come to unite Isolde and Tristan and yield his own claim to her. All is dead. Isolde and Tristan transfigure through death.

The story has also been adapted into film many times. The earliest is probably the 1909 French film *Tristan et Yseult*, an early, silent version of the story. This was followed by another French film of the same name two years later, which offered a unique addition to the story. Here, it is Tristan's jealous slave Rosen who tricks the lovers into drinking the love potion, then denounces them to Mark. Mark has pity on the two lovers, but they commit double suicide anyway. A third silent French version appeared in 1920 and follows the legend fairly closely.

One of the most celebrated and controversial *Tristan* films was 1943's *L'Éternel Retour* (The Eternal Return), directed by Jean Delannoy (screenplay by Jean Cocteau). It is a modern retelling of the story with a man named Patrice in the Tristan role fetching a wife for his friend Marke. However, an evil dwarf tricks them into drinking a love potion, and the familiar plot ensues. The film was made in France during the Vichy regime, and elements in the movie reflect Nazi ideology, with the beautiful, blonde hero and heroine off-set by the 'Untermensch' dwarf. This was followed by the avant-garde French film *Tristan et Iseult* in 1972 and the Irish *Lovespell*, featuring Nicholas Clay as Tristan and Kate Mulgrew as Iseult. Clay went on to play Lancelot in John Boorman's epic *Excalibur* and Kate Mulgrew morphed into Captain Kathryn Janeway in the *Star Trek* franchise. Exploring strange new worlds as the captain of the Starfleet star ship USS Voyager, she was the lead character on the television series *Star Trek: Voyager*, and later a Starfleet admiral, as seen in the 2002 feature film *Star Trek: Nemesis*.

In the 2006 *Tristan & Isolde*, produced by Tony Scott and Ridley Scott, written by Dean Georgaris, directed by Kevin Reynolds,

Tristan is a Cornish warrior who was raised by Lord Marke after his parents were killed at a young age. In a fight Tristan defeats Morholt but is poisoned in the process. The poison dulls all his senses and his companions believe him dead. He is sent off alone in a boat to die. Isolde, regretting her unwilling betrothal to Morholt, leaves her home and finds Tristan on the Irish coast. She tells Tristan that she is called Brangäne, which is the name of her maidservant. She takes care of him and hides him from her father. They spend long days together and eventually they confess their feelings for one another and consummate their love. Tristan's boat is discovered, and Isolde's father begins a search for the Cornish warrior in Ireland. Isolde helps Tristan escape but cannot leave with him. Tristan returns to England and learns of a tournament between the Cornish tribes for the hand of the Irish princess named Isolde. He agrees to participate to win the princess as Marke's wife. After winning the tournament and discovering that the princess is the woman who had rescued him, Tristan is devastated but decides to bury his feelings, because her marriage to Marke would end decades of bloodshed. Eventually Tristan cannot stand to be apart from Isolde any longer and they start their adulterous relationship. Later, they are found out but Marke frees them after hearing their story. Tristan returns to defend Marke against a rebellion and dies a hero, with Isolde at his side.

I have read somewhere that the opera was performed for the first time in Dublin in 1901. It was performed here again in 1912 and was part of a Wagner concert here in 1913. The performance in Bayreuth was quite overwhelming. The singing overall was heroic. The orchestra, under the musical director, Christian Thielemann was marvellous. He had put the work aside for twelve years but was up for it. I was in Wagner Heaven, not for the first time I might add. Act I was musically excellent, although the production unremarkable. Act II musically beautiful, production amazing, lighting exquisite. Act III: by now I had been carried away. The hazed proscenium, the candles, hallucinations, triangles, all typical of a man dying from sepsis. The malevolence of King Marke shocked me – a new take on the story and more to the truth after all. Marke had Melot kill Tristan in Act II.

I was very affected emotionally by the entire performance. Afterwards, halfway down the Green Hill, an image of a 130-gram fillet steak and a buttered spud came into my mind's eye. I had recovered. I was glad to be alive, glad to have heard this marvellous performance – nay, privileged! I was happy to be in Wagner Heaven once more. I loved it! I thought, it was so beautiful, one could either die or cry. I chose life. Tears flowed.

# CHAPTER 15

# *Die Meistersinger von Nürnberg*

My first *Meistersinger* was in the Royal Opera House, Covent Garden on the 7th of August 1997. It was very hot in London that year, including the opera house. The opera was really good, and I came home full of the memory, the music still playing in my head. But deep wounds were soon to follow, one being the death of my mother. I had come to understand that we cannot progress as humans without experiencing existential crisis. We are deeply hurt at the time, but eventually we are stronger. A friend in Cork said, "It will take you ten years to really get over that, Chris." He was right. In the meantime, I continued to seek solace in music. My mother, a lover of classical music, would surely have approved.

*Die Meistersinger von Nürnberg*: (The Master-Singers of Nuremberg) is among the longest operas, usually taking around four and a half hours. It was first performed at the Kőnigliches Hog-und National Theater, today the home of the Bavarian State Opera, in Munich, on the 21st of June 1868. The conductor at the premiere was Hans von Bülow.

The story is set in Nuremberg in the mid-16th century. At the time, Nuremberg was a "Free Imperial City" and one of the centres of the Renaissance in Northern Europe. By this time the difference between Imperial Cities and Free Cities became indistinct, so that they became collectively known as Free Imperial Cities, and by the late 15th century many cities included both "Free" and "Imperial" in their name. Like the other Imperial Estates, they could wage war, make peace, and control their own trade, allowing little interference from outside. In the later Middle Ages, a number of Free Cities formed City Leagues (*Städtebünde*), such as the Hanseatic League or the Alsatian "Décapole" to promote and defend their interests.

The Renaissance was a cultural movement that emerged due to increased wealth, greater cultural exchange, and a renewed interest in classical works and philosophies. At the time. It initially began in Florence, Italy. Florence's position as a prosperous and wealthy centre of trade led to increased interest and investment in art, science, philosophy, and mathematics. By the 16th century, its influence was felt throughout Europe – in architecture, literature, music, politics and religion. The most widespread societal change during the Renaissance was the fall of feudalism and the rise of a capitalist market economy.

Renaissance scholars employed the humanist method in study, and searched for realism and human emotion in art. The *Meistersinger* story revolves around the city's Guild of Master Singers, an association of amateur poets and musicians who were primarily master craftsmen of various trades. The master singers had developed a craftsman-like approach to music-making, with an intricate system of rules for composing and performing songs. The work draws much of its atmosphere from its depiction of the Nuremberg of the era and the traditions of the Master-Singer Guild. One of the main characters, the cobbler-poet Hans Sachs, is based on a historical figure of that name (1494–1576), the most famous of the master singers. *Die Meistersinger von Nürnberg* is the only comedy among Wagner's mature operas, the first, *Das Liebesverbot* (The Ban on Love) an early comic opera in two acts with the libretto written by the composer. *Das Liebesverbot* was disowned by him in later life. Today, it is not recognised in Wagner circles – as if it never existed!

However, it is difficult not to recognise that undemonstrative sexuality versus eroticism, the central theme in *Das Liebesverbot* is repeated again and again throughout much of Wagner's work, most notably in *Tannhäuser*, *Die Walküre* and *Tristan und Isolde*. In each opera, the self-abandonment to love brings the lovers into conflict with the neighbouring social order. In *Das Liebesverbot*, because it is a comedy, the outcome is different: uninhibited sexuality triumphs as the wild, uncontrolled orgy of pleasure turns into a riot that carries on after the final curtain. Wagner conducted the premiere in 1836 at Magdeburg. It was as dramatic in real life as any opera. Poorly attended and with a lead singer who forgot the words and had to improvise, it was a huge flop. Its second performance had to be cancelled after a fistfight broke out backstage between the leading lady's husband and the lead tenor before the curtain had even risen. There were only three people in the audience, hardly worth the effort anyway. It was never performed again in Wagner's lifetime. It is also referred to as "the forgotten comedy". In the following hundred years, the opera was rarely performed, the first was in the United Kingdom in 1965. Later, the United States, Romania and Madrid, Spain. In 1994 *Das Liebesverbot* was performed at the Wexford Opera Festival. It was my first and only time to see it. The story did not appeal to me at all, but Wagner's music was, as always, superb.

*Die Meistersinger von Nürnberg. Meistersinger* has many signs of the earlier work and is also unusual among his works as it is set in a historically well-defined time and place rather than in a mythical or legendary setting. It is the only mature Wagner opera based on an entirely original story, devised by Wagner himself, and in which no supernatural or magical powers or events are in evidence. It incorporates many of the operatic principles that Wagner had railed against in his essays on the theory of opera: rhymed verse, arias, choruses, quintet and even ballet.

My first Bayreuther Festspiele *Meistersinger* was on the 2nd of August 1999, the wonderful Wolfgang Wagner production. And a

Berlin production in 2010 was my 10th *Meistersinger*. Five years later, at Staatsoper UDL im Schiller Theatre, on the 22nd of October 2015, my friend, Davy Byrne and I were in Row 5, to see it again. The curtain was open when we entered the house. The performers were assembling on stage, greeting each other, social kissing etc. One row had all the former great tenors on stage – Siegfried Jerusalem, Reiner Goldberg, Franz Mazura, Graham Clark and others. Daniel Barenboim joined the Meisters and there was hand shaking and warm greetings all round. He then sat down, and I wondered why he wasn't in the orchestra pit! I was starting to panic when the warning bell rang and up jumped Daniel and off stage to the pit. The baton was quickly in the air and we were in the Overture. It was very good, as were any overtures to the work I had the privilege to hear. Then into the chorale. The chorus turned their backs to the audience, a crucifix was lowered, and a Lutheran priest conducted the singing.

A woman in the audience had a coughing fit that couldn't stop. Davy was livid and after a few minutes, he got up and left the theatre. The chorus sang on, the unfortunate woman got another fit of coughing and began making her way out of the theatre, but on the way, she fell. She must have been mortified.

On stage, Walther, tall, long-haired and dressed in leather jacket and pants came from stage left and commenced wooing Eva (Julia Kletter). She was wearing a backless gown. He rubbed her back – very modern, very cheeky. Magdalene (Anna Lapkovskaja) brought a shawl which ended this indecorous behaviour from the knight.

The opera progressed with the moving of chairs here, there and everywhere by apprentices, who were all attired in dress suits with shining shoes. Stephen Rügamer sang the role of David and was wonderful, a really good singer. Graham Clarke was an outstanding 'David' in his day. Clarke sang the role of Kunz Vogelgesang. Then the entry of the Meisters and Beckmesser's lunatic behaviour started very early on. He worked and engaged with the audience. Hans

Sachs (Wolfgang Koch) sang beautifully. He has very impressive eyes, wild at times. Koch is a Wotan. Wotans can sing! Walther mounted a tall chair for his test and was off it immediately, to the annoyance of the Meisters. He was rule-breaking from the outset, treating all present with contempt, as young, impatient boys in love do. His singing was heavenly, sweet phrasing; unparalleled. He is the Walthe' of his generation. Eventually, he kicked over Beckmeisser's chalk board, chasing him off stage. The song motif was marvellous, leading to the conclusion of Act 1.

Act II commenced after a 40-minute interval. This act has some of the more beautiful music as Eva is losing hope of getting her man. Beckmeisser's act, Markus Werba was very funny, acting and singing, especially the serenade, leading to the rioting scene. The rioting scene was the best I've ever seen on stage.

Act III is where stamina is required. This one took two hours. The Wahn monologue, the construction of the Prize Lied to fit the new rules by Sachs. It's important to understand all scenes in Act III, so one knows where one is going. Then, the entry of David seeking forgiveness from Sachs for his part in the rioting the previous night. Walther sang his dream interpretation, helped by Sachs. Then exit Walther and enter Beckmesser, lots of fun here. Finally, Eva in a wedding dress with her shoe problem. In this production, Walther and indeed Sachs were very hands on – hands on Eva! Walther returned in his festive suit and saw Sachs and Eva in an embrace. He was not happy. Finally, Sachs capitulates with the *Tristan* melody and with Magdalena and David entering, the quintet commenced, Sachs first, then Eva in turn.

The scene was set in Sachs's library. The curtain was down for the new tableau. Berlin Cathedral is the backdrop, each group of gilds arriving by river on a barge, each with their banners. Trumpets and drums off-stage. Very impressive. The apprentices returned and laid down four tables. Sachs introduced the contest with the assistance of Veit Pogner (Kwanghul Young, a noted and impressive

Bayreuther, King Marke in the old production of *Tristan*). The competition commenced with Beckmeisser making an idiot of himself, eventually being laughed off the stage. At this point there were in excess of two hundred singers on stage. With Beckmesser gone, Sachs intervened to bend the rules for Walther to sing his Prize Lied. Vogt sang the piece beautifully. He is unequalled in this role. The choral conclusion was marvellous. The backdrop went from Berlin Cathedral to a meadow with balloons being released. Beautiful singing and playing by the orchestra, followed by at least fifteen curtain calls. This was a feast of music, never to be surpassed. The best performance of the work that I have attended.

Chris McQuaid (left) with Andrew Medlicott RW Verband
International and conductor Alexander Anissimov

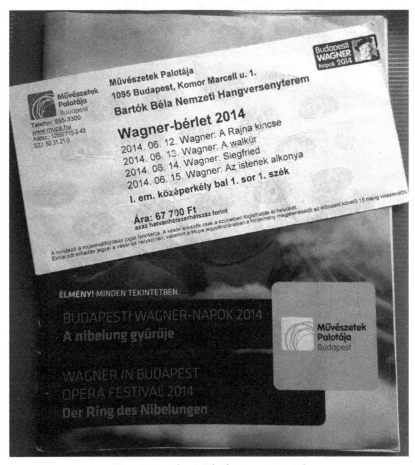

Der Ring des Nibelungen, 2014

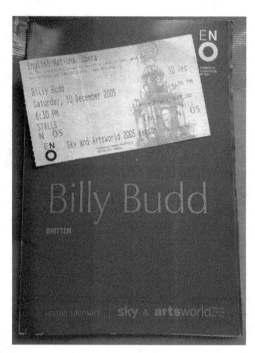

English National Opera, London, Billy Budd, 2005

Die Walküre, Bayreuth

2017, Die Walküre, Osterfestspiel

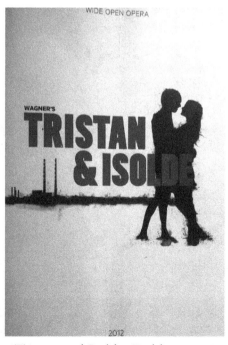

Tristan und Isolda, Dublin, 2012

November 2010, Der Freischutz, Staatstheater Gatnerplaz

'Born to sing Wagner', The late Miriam Murphy, Soprano

# CHAPTER 16

## *Changing Fortunes*

Wagner's experience of Paris was disastrous. He was unable to get work as a conductor, and the Opéra did not want to produce *Rienzi*. The Wagners were reduced to penury, relying on handouts from friends and from the little income that Wagner could make writing articles on music and copying scores. Although in terms of music and theatrical talent, there is no comparison to be made between Wagner and me, once I began studying his life, I did ponder on how my own circumstances sometimes mirrored his! I could well relate to some of his misfortunes.

In 2000, I had resigned from the Medical Council and been without work for almost eighteen months when a former colleague who now worked in in the Irish Air Corps at Baldonnel advised me that jobs for civilian employees had been advertised through FÁS, the then semi-state training and employment agency. I rang FÁS and was told that the competition was closed. But, after some persuasion I succeeded in having my name added to the list. I did a preliminary interview in the FÁS office in Clondalkin, followed by an interview conducted by an Air Corps officer and a civil servant in Irish Air Corps HQ in Baldonnel Aerodrome. The board of FÁS had reservations. Given that I was a former manager I was deemed to be overqualified. Could I step down to employee level? Would I get on with my new peers? Would I be happy with much less pay? I must have assured them that I could – and would – because I was offered the job and was happy to take it. I was more than grateful to have any job that would occupy my mind and provide me with an income at last.

But the ten years that I had spent in the main technical stores had been difficult. I tended to make life hard for myself. I was over-zealous and anxious – and quick to pull people up on anything that appeared to be off kilter. I had a row over LR6 batteries – of all things. A pack of four was the norm but one company supplied five in a pack. I accidentally came onto this when the man who looked after batteries was on sick leave. I researched it and took the batteries – four hundred and eighty in all – on charge by certified receipt voucher. There was holy blue murder. The supervisor sent for me and asked for an explanation. I told him that any surplus must be taken on charge. He wasn't happy. I was accused of bullying one of my colleagues. He was supported by the Union shop steward. A note from Personnel requested me to attend a meeting to answer the charge of bullying. My union, SIPTU took up the case and I was given a month's leave with pay and a transfer to Heli Wing. One of my friends, nicknamed 'The Professor" said "Oh, didn't Mister McQuaid get a severe punishment – a month off with pay and a transfer." It had been a close call and I tried my best to stay out of trouble from then on. And, as had been the case since I had taken up civilian employment, at the first sign of trouble, I hit the opera trail.

I first saw *The Flying Dutchman* in August 1999 at Bayreuth. The central theme of *The Flying Dutchman* (Der fliegende Holländer) is, yet again, redemption through love. Wagner conducted the premiere at the Königliches Hoftheater in Dresden in 1843. He claimed in his 1870 autobiography *Mein Leben* that he had been inspired to write the opera following a stormy sea crossing that he made from Riga to London in July and August 1839. At the beginning of 1839, the 26-year-old Richard Wagner was employed as a conductor at the Court Theatre in Riga. His extravagant lifestyle plus the retirement from the stage of his actress wife, Minna Planer, caused him to run up huge debts that he was unable to repay. Wagner was writing *Rienzi* and hatched a plan to flee his creditors in Riga, escape to Paris via London and make his fortune by putting *Rienzi* on to the stage of the Paris Opéra. However, this plan quickly turned to disaster: his passport having been seized by the authorities on behalf of his creditors, he and Minna had to make a dangerous and illegal crossing over the Prussian border, during which Minna suffered a miscarriage. Boarding the ship "Thetis", whose captain had agreed to take them without passports, their sea journey was hindered by storms and high seas. The ship at one point took refuge in the Norwegian fjords at Tvedestrand, and a trip that was expected to take eight days finally delivered Wagner and Mina to London three weeks after leaving Riga.

Wagner hit on the idea of a one-act opera on the theme of *The Flying Dutchman*, which he hoped might be performed before a ballet at the Opéra. He wrote:

*The voyage through the Norwegian reefs made a wonderful impression on my imagination; the legend of the Flying Dutchman, which the sailors verified, took on a distinctive, strange colouring that only my sea adventures could have given it.*

In his 1843 autobiographic sketch, Wagner acknowledged he had taken the story from Heinrich Heine's retelling of the legend in his 1833 satirical novel, *The Memoirs of Mister von Schnabelewopski* (Aus den Memoiren des Herrn von Schnabelewopski). Wagner originally wrote the work to be performed without intermission – an example of his efforts to break with tradition – and, while today's opera houses sometimes still follow this directive, it is also performed in a three-act version.

Act 1 – On the coast of Norway: On his homeward journey, the sea captain Daland is compelled by stormy weather to seek a port of refuge near Sandwike in southern Norway. He leaves the helmsman on watch and he and the sailors retire. (Song of the helmsman: "Mit Gewitter und Sturm aus fernem Meer" (With tempest and storm on distant seas.) The helmsman falls asleep. A ghostly vessel appearing astern, is dashed against Daland's vessel by the sea and the grappling irons hold the two ships together. Invisible hands furl the sails. A man of pale aspect, dressed in black, his face framed by a thick black beard, steps ashore. He laments his fate. (Aria: "Die Frist ist um, und abermals verstrichen sind sieben Jahr" (The time has come, and seven years have again elapsed). Because he once invoked Satan, the ghost captain is cursed to roam the sea forever without rest. An angel brought to him the terms of his redemption: "Every seven years the waves will cast him upon the shore. If he can find a wife who will be true to him, he will be released from his curse". Daland wakes up and meets the stranger. The stranger hears that Daland has an unmarried daughter named Senta, and he asks for her hand in marriage, offering a chest of treasure as a gift. Tempted by gold, Daland agrees to the marriage. The south wind blows, and both vessels set sail for Daland's home.

Act 2: A group of local girls are singing and spinning in Daland's house. There is the spinning song: "Summ und brumm, du gutes Rädchen" (Whir and whirl, good wheel). Senta, Daland's daughter, dreamily gazes upon a gorgeous picture of the legendary Dutchman that hangs from the wall and she desires to save him. Against the will of her nurse, she sings to her friends the story of the Dutchman (Ballad with the Leitmotiv), how Satan heard him swear and took him at his word. She vows to save him by her fidelity. The huntsman Erik, Senta's former boyfriend, arrives and hears her. The girls depart, and the huntsman, who loves the maiden, warns her, telling her of his dream, in which Daland returned with a mysterious stranger, who carried her off to sea. She listens with delight, and Erik leaves in despair.

Daland arrives with the stranger. He and Senta stand gazing at each other in silence. Daland is scarcely noticed by his daughter, even when he presents his guest as her betrothed. In the following duet, which closes the act, Senta swears to be true till death.

Act 3: Later in the evening, the local girls bring Daland's men food and drink. They invite the crew of the strange vessel to join in the merrymaking, but in vain. The girls retire in wonder. Ghostly forms appear at work upon the vessel "The Flying Dutchman", and Daland's men retreat in fear.

Senta arrives, followed by Erik, who reproves her for deserting him, as she had formerly loved him and vowed constancy. When the stranger, who has been listening, hears these words, he is overwhelmed with despair, as he thinks he is now forever lost. He summons his men, tells Senta of the curse, and to the consternation of Daland and his crew declares that he is The Flying Dutchman. As the Dutchman sets sail, Senta throws herself into the sea, claiming that she will be faithful to him unto death. This is his salvation. The spectral ship disappears, and Senta and the Dutchman are seen ascending to heaven. I returned to *The Dutchman* in Berlin and London. The conductor was Peter Schneider and it was simply brilliant.

Wagner was no slouch when it came to writing for chorus. His *Die Feen* is remarkable by any standards, for a twenty-year-old. Alas, the opera wasn't performed until 1888, in München, five years after his death. This is an opera in three acts, based on a story by Carlo Gozzi, about fairies and mortals. Arindal as loved by a fairy, Ada, who has him under a spell and torments him by making him perform some fiendish tasks. Meanwhile his sister Lora is defending Arindal's kingdom which is falling apart.

I attended *Die Feen* at Théâtre du Châtelet in Paris in 2009. The staging and décor by Spanish director Emilio Sagi were dazzling and the costumes by Daniel Blanco and Jésus Ruiz were spectacular. Ada appears in one scene from a huge rose, another scene has a towering chandelier that must have cost a fortune. Sometimes things were a bit over the top with male bare-chested fairies wearing gauzy skirts and the hero Arindal spends two acts wearing a green dress. The performance begins and ends in swirling pink satin, all dazzling.

The German singer Christiana Liber, who plays Ada, the fairy who falls in love with the mortal Arindal, was strong, pure and full of drama. Arindal's sister, Lora, as Lina Tetruashvili was first rate. Ensemble, chorus and orchestra were excellent under Marc Minkowski, In *Die Feen*, there is a musical sample of what was to come but also many of the themes that would be central to his later works, such as forbidden questions, weapons and objects with magical powers, fairy garden and concepts such as immortality and renunciation.

On the whole, it is a musical and dramatic treat. The extraordinary unaccompanied choral passage that starts off Act III, beautifully sung by the Choeur des Musiciens du Louvre Grenoble was absolutely magnificent, and Minkowski's direction of the Musiciens du Louvre was flawless. Whilst influences of Mozart's *Magic Flute*, Beethoven, Weber and Verdi were evident, the score is powerful and unique.

On this occasion, I also attended Mass at Notre Dame Cathedral. Notre-Dame de Paris has been a prominent part of Paris history and has overseen royal coronations and been a haven for believers during difficult times. It was damaged during the French Revolution in the 1790s and remained neglected until the 1840s when architects started to overhaul parts of the structure. In 2009 I never expected to see goods: candles and wall art being sold inside. I have no desire to return. On Monday, April the 15th 2019 a fire broke out and while the damage was devastating, most of the building and the relics were saved. As well as preserving France's tourism economy the rebuilding effort is about preserving an irreplaceable monument that has become a symbol of French national identity.

Towards the end of 2009, I realised retirement age was rapidly approaching. It had been twenty-three years since I'd left the army and ten years since I fell on my feet with a job in the Irish Air Corps. Fortunately, those years were a delight. The technicians were the best – good in their hearts and very skilled. The pilots too were very friendly. It was a privilege to work with them and Heli Wing was bliss. I have the highest respect for the technical people in the air corps. They are professionals who rate second only to my beloved 1st Motor Squadron in Fermoy. But by 2009, I was burned out – not from work but from a long and wearisome struggle with employers, with the Army Pensions Board, with unrecognisable and thus far, untreatable PTSD – all of which had robbed me of any ability to cope with retirement. I was not into DIY, I didn't play Bridge, or golf, I didn't gamble on dogs or horses and didn't take long holidays in the sun. I craved music and so, following retirement I planned to get to as many operas and other musical outings as possible, especially Wagner operas.

I had seen *Rienzi* in Leipzig in December 2007. The outstanding overture and a beautiful tenor aria remained with me for months. I had also visited St. Thomas's Church, because of its association with Wagner. St. Thomas's is a Lutheran church in Leipzig that was constructed in the early thirteenth century by the Augustinian monastic order. It was originally a monastery and then became the University of Leipzig in the fifteenth century and the St. Thomas school in the sixteenth century. In 1539 Martin Luther introduced religious reform to Leipzig while preaching at the church, which is also associated with the well-known composer Felix Mendelssohn Bartholdy. Johann Sebastian Bach worked here as a choir master from 1723 until his death in 1750. His remains are buried there.

*Rienzi, der letzte der Tribunen* (Rienzi, the last of the tribunes) is an early opera by Richard Wagner in five acts, with the libretto written by the composer after Edward Bulwer-Lytton's novel of the same name (1835). The title is generally shortened to *Rienzi*. Written between July 1838 and November 1840, it was first performed at Das Königliche Hoftheater, Dresden, on the 20th of October

1842, and was the Wagner's first success.

The opera is set in Rome and is based on the life of Cola di Rienzi (1313–1354), a late medieval Italian populist figure who succeeds in outwitting and then defeating the nobles and their followers and in raising the power of the people. Magnanimous at first, he is forced by events to crush the nobles' rebellion against the people's power, but popular opinion changes and even the Church, which had urged him to assert himself, turns against him. In the end the populace burns the Capitol, in which Rienzi and a few adherents have made a last stand.

Wagner had hoped for it to be premiered at the Paris Opéra. Several circumstances, including his lack of influence, prevented this. Moreover, Wagner's wife Minna, in a letter of the 28th of October 1840 to Wagner's friend Apel, who had likely first made the suggestion that Wagner compose *Rienzi*, mentions a plan to perform the overture to *Rienzi* "a fortnight hence", but her husband had just been committed to a debtors' prison. The full score of *Rienzi* was eventually completed on the 19th of November 1840.

In 1841 Wagner moved to Meudon, just outside Paris, where the debt laws could be more easily evaded, whilst awaiting developments for *Rienzi*, having already written to King Frederick Augustus II of Saxony, requesting that he order a production of the work in Dresden. With the support of German composer, Giacomo Meyerbeer, a staging of *Rienzi* was arranged in Dresden; Meyerbeer wrote to the Director of the Opera in Dresden, Baron von Lüttichau, that he found the opera "rich in fantasy and of great dramatic effect". Along with his successes in Paris, Meyerbeer, as a Prussian Court Kapellmeister (Director of Music) from 1832, and from 1843 as Prussian General Music Director, was also influential in opera in Berlin and throughout Germany. He was an early supporter of Wagner. His letter to Lüttichau, along with the proposed staging of *The Flying Dutchman* in Berlin, also supported by Meyerbeer persuaded Wagner to return to Germany in April 1842.

*Rienzi* premiered on the 20th of October 1842 in the new Dresden Opera House, designed by the architect Gottfried Semper and opened the previous year. Semper and Wagner were later to become friends in Dresden, a connection which eventually led to Semper providing designs which became a basis of Wagner's Festspielhaus in Bayreuth. The first performance of *Rienzi* was well received in Dresden despite running over six hours (including intermissions). One legend is that fearful of the audience departing, Wagner stopped the clock above the stage. In his later memoirs, *Mein Leben*, Wagner recalled:

> *No subsequent experience has given me feelings even remotely similar to those I had on this day of the first performance of Rienzi. The only too well-founded anxiety as to their success has so dominated my feelings at all subsequent first performances of my works that I could never really enjoy them or take much notice of the way the audience was behaving. The initial success of Rienzi was no doubt assured beforehand. But the uproarious way in which the public declared its partiality for me was extraordinary. The public had been forcibly predisposed to accept it, because everyone connected with the theatre had been spreading such favourable reports that the entire population was looking forward to what was heralded as a miracle. In trying to recall my condition that evening, I can remember it only as possessing all the features of a dream.*

Subsequently, Wagner experimented with staging the opera over two evenings and making cuts to enable a more reasonable performance in a single evening.

The opera opens with a substantial overture which begins with a trumpet call and features the melody of Rienzi's Prayer at the start of Act 5, which became the opera's best-known aria. The overture ends with a military march.

Act 1 – Outside Rienzi's house: The patrician Orsini and his cronies attempt to kidnap Rienzi's sister Irene. Stefano Colonna, also a patrician but inclined to support Rienzi, prevents them. Raimondo appeals to the parties in the name of the Church to stop their fighting; Rienzi's eventual appearance quells the riot. The Roman people support Rienzi's condemnation of the nobles. Irene and Adriano realise their mutual attraction. A gathering crowd of plebeians, inspired by Rienzi's speeches, offers Rienzi the crown; he demurs, insisting that he wishes only to be a Tribune of the Roman people.

Act 2 – A hall in the Capitol: The patricians plot the death of Rienzi; Adriano is horrified when he learns of this. Rienzi greets a group of ambassadors for whom an entertainment is laid on (a lengthy ballet). Orsini attempts to stab Rienzi, who however is protected by a vest of chain mail. Adriano pleads with Rienzi for mercy to the nobles, which Rienzi grants.

The Act 2 ballet is noteworthy as Wagner made a clear attempt to make it relevant to the action of the opera (whereas in most Grand Operas the ballet was simply an entertaining diversion). The Rienzi ballet was intended to tell the tale of "The Rape of Lucretia". This storyline (in which Tarquinius, the last king of Rome, attempts to rape the virtuous Lucretia), parallels both the action of Rienzi (Orsini's attempt on Irene) and its background (patricians versus the people). In its original form the ballet lasts for over half an hour – in modern performances and recordings it is generally drastically cut.

Act 3 – The Roman Forum: The patricians have recruited an army to march on Rome. The people are alarmed. Rienzi rouses the people and leads them to victory over the nobles, in the course of which Adriano's father, Stefano is killed. Adriano swears revenge, but Rienzi dismisses him.

Act 4 – Before the Lateran Church: Cecco and other citizens discuss the negotiations of the patricians with the Pope and with the Emperor of Germany. Adriano's intention to kill Rienzi wavers when Rienzi arrives together with Irene. Raimondo now announces that the Pope has laid a papal ban on Rienzi, and that his associates risk excommunication. Despite Adriano's urgings, Irene resolves to stay with Rienzi.

Act 5 – Scene 1: A room in the Capitol: Rienzi in his prayer "Allmächt'ger Vater" (Almighty Father, look down!) asserts his faith in the people of Rome. He suggests to Irene that she seek safety with Adriano, but she demurs. An apologetic Adriano enters and tells the pair that the Capitol is to be burnt and they are at risk. Scene 2: The Capitol is ablaze: Rienzi's attempts to speak are met with stones and insults from the fickle crowd. Adriano, in trying to rescue Rienzi and Irene, is killed with them as the building collapses.

In the original performances, Rienzi's final words are bitter and pessimistic: "May the town be accursed and destroyed! Disintegrate and wither, Rome! Your degenerate people wish it so." However, for the 1847 Berlin performance Wagner substituted a more upbeat rhetoric: "Ever while the seven hills of Rome remain, ever while the eternal city stands, you will see Rienzi's return!"

# CHAPTER 17

# *The Supreme Masterpiece*

*Tannhäuser* (Tannhäuser und der Sängerkrieg auf Wartburg / Tannhäuser and the Minnesingers' Contest at Wartburg) is an opera in three acts, music and text by Richard Wagner, based on two German legends: 'Tannhäuser", the mythologized medieval German Minnesänger and poet, and the tale of the Wartburg Song Contest. The story centres on the struggle between sacred and profane love, and redemption through love, a theme running through much of Wagner's mature work. Wagner made a number of revisions of the opera throughout his life and was still unsatisfied with its format when he died. The most significant revision was made for the opera's premiere in Paris in 1861; however, the production there was a failure, partly for political reasons.

The opera remains a staple of major opera house repertoire in the 21st century. The libretto of *Tannhäuser* combines mythological elements characteristic of German Romantic opera and the medieval setting typical of many French Grand Operas. Wagner brings these two together by constructing a plot involving the 14th century Minnesingers and the myth of Venus and her subterranean realm of Venusberg. Both the historical and the mythological are united in Tannhäuser's personality; although he is a historical poet composer, little is known about him other than myths that surround him.

The legend of Tannhäuser, the amorous crusading Franconian knight, and that of the song contest on the Wartburg came from quite separate traditions. Ludwig Bechstein laced together the two legends in the first volume of his collection of Thuringian legends, "Der Sagenschatz und die Sagenkreise des Thüringerlandes" which was probably the "Volksbuch" to which Wagner refers to in his autobiography. Wagner also knew of the work of another contemporary, Christian Theodor Ludwig Lucas, whose "Ueber den Krieg von Wartburg" of 1838 also combined the two. But the sources used by Wagner reflected a nineteenth century romantic view of the medieval period, with concerns about artistic freedom and the constraints of organised religion typical of the period of Romanticism.

During Wagner's first stay in Paris (1839–1842) he read a paper by Ludwig Lucas on the Sängerkrieg (minstrel contest) which sparked his imagination, and encouraged him to return to Germany, which he reached on the 7th of April 1842. Having crossed the Rhine, the Wagners drove towards Thuringia, and saw the early rays of sun striking the Wartburg; Wagner immediately began to sketch the scenery that would become the stage sets. Wagner wrote the prose draft of *Tannhäuser* between June and July 1842 and the libretto in April 1843.

The first performance was given in the Königliche Hoftheater (Royal Theater) in Dresden on the 19th of October 1845. The composer Ferdinand Hiller, at that time a friend of the Wagner's, assisted in the musical preparations for the production. The part of Elisabeth was sung by Wagner's niece Johanna Wagner. Wagner had intended to premiere the opera on the 13th of October, Johanna's 19th birthday, but she was ill, so it was postponed by six days. Venus was created by Wilhelmine Schröder-Devrient, and the title role was taken by Josef Aloys Tichatschek. The performance was conducted by the composer.

*Tannhäuser* was not the success that *Rienzi* had been, and Wagner almost immediately set to modifying the ending, adjusting the score through 1846 and 1847. For the first Dresden revival (1847) he clarified the representation of Venus's temptation of Tannhäuser in the final act and added vocal presentation of the pilgrims' chorus in this act (where it had previously been represented by orchestra alone). This version of the opera, as revised for publication in 1860, is generally known as the "Dresden version". After Franz Liszt produced the opera at Weimar Court Theatre in 1849, there were further performances between 1852 and 1856 in Schwerin, Kassel, Posen, Wiesbaden, Hanover, Munich and Berlin.

The Dresden version was also used for initial productions outside Germany, notably at Riga on the 18th of January 1853, at Tallinn in January 1854, at Prague in November 1854 at Theatre of the Estates, at New York City in April 1859 at the Stadt Theatre; and in London in May 1876 at the Royal Opera House, Covent Garden.

Wagner substantially amended the opera for a special 1861 performance by the Paris Opéra. This had been requested by Emperor Napoleon III at the suggestion of Princess Pauline von Metternich, wife of the Austrian ambassador to France. This revision forms the basis of what is now known as the "Paris version" of *Tannhäuser*. The venue meant that the composer had to insert a ballet into the score, according to the traditions of the house. Wagner agreed to this condition since he believed that a success at the Opéra represented his most significant opportunity to re-establish himself following his exile from Germany. However, rather than put the ballet in its traditional place in Act II, he chose to place it in Act I, in the form of an orgiastic musical composition (bacchanale), where it could make dramatic sense by representing the sensual world of Venus's realm. There were further extensive changes. The text was translated into French (by Charles-Louis-Étienne Nuitter and others). Venus, a role that in the Dresden version was considered a soprano, was rewritten as for mezzo-soprano. Venus's aria "Geliebter, komm!!" was moved down by a semitone, and its latter part was completely rewritten. A solo for Walther was removed from Act 2. Extra lines for Venus following Tannhäuser's "Hymn to Love" were added. The orchestral introduction to Act 3 was shortened. The end of the opera was reworked to include Venus on stage, where previously the audience only heard the Venus motif in an attempt to clarify the action.

*Tannhäuser's* first performance in Paris was on the 13th of March 1861 at the Salle Le Peletier of the Paris Opéra. The composer had been closely involved in its preparation over 164 rehearsals. There were disturbances including whistling and catcalls beginning to appear in Act II and becoming prominent by the end of the third act. For the second performance much of the new ballet music was removed, together with some actions that had specifically provoked mockery, such as the piping of the shepherd in Act I. At this performance however the audience disturbances were increased. This was partly due to members of the wealthy and aristocratic "Jockey Club", who objected to the ballet coming in Act I, since this meant they would have to be present from the beginning of the performance, thus disrupting their dining schedule. A further incentive to disruption was the unpopularity of Princess von Metternich and of her native country of Austria. At the third performance on the 24th of March (which Wagner did not attend) uproar caused several interruptions of up to fifteen minutes at a time. Wagner withdrew the opera after the third performance, marking the end to his hopes of establishing himself in Paris.

The first performance outside France of the Paris version was given in Bologna on the 7th of November 1872 at the Teatro Comunale, the first performance of the opera in Italy. The American and British premieres of this version were respectively in New York at the Metropolitan Opera on the 30th of January 1889, and at London's Royal Opera House on the 15th of July 1895. A few further changes to *Tannhäuser* were made for an 1875 performance of the opera in Vienna, the last production carried out under Wagner's own supervision. These included linking the end of the overture to the start of the opera proper. The "Vienna version" is that normally used in modern productions of the Paris version, often with the reinstatement of Walther's Act 2 solo. Wagner remained unsatisfied with the opera. His wife Cosima noted in her diary on the 23rd of January 1883 (three weeks before he died): *He says he still owes the world Tannhäuser.*

Wagner's *Ring des Nibelungen* completed in 1876 is a masterpiece without equal. Having completed the opera *Lohengrin* in April 1848, Richard Wagner chose as his next subject "Siegfried", the legendary hero of Germanic myth. Sigurd (Old Norse: Sigurðr) or Siegfried (Middle High German: Sîvrit) killed a dragon and was later murdered. It is possible he was inspired by one or more figures from the Frankish Merovingian dynasty and Sigebert I of Austrasia was the most popular contender. In October of that year he prepared a prose outline for "Siegfried's Death", which during the following months he developed into a full libretto. After his flight from Dresden and relocation in Switzerland, he continued to develop and expand his *Siegfried* project, having decided meantime that a single work would not suffice for his purposes; in his enlarged concept, "Siegfried's Death" would be the culmination of a series of musical dramas incorporating a network of myths from his sources and imagination, each telling a stage of the story. In 1851 he outlined his purpose in his essay "A Communication to My Friends":

*I propose to produce my myth in three complete dramas, preceded by a lengthy Prelude.* Each of these dramas would, he said, "constitute an independent whole, but would not be performed separately."

*At a specially appointed Festival, I propose, some future time, to produce those three Dramas with their Prelude, in the course of three days and a fore evening.*

In accordance with this scheme "Siegfried's Death", much revised from its original form, eventually became *Götterdämmerung* (The Twilight of the Gods). It was preceded by the story of Siegfried's youth, Young Siegfried, later renamed Siegfried, itself preceded by *Die Walküre* (The Valkyrie). Finally, to these three works Wagner added a prologue which he named *Das Rheingold*.

*Das Rheingold* (The Rhinegold) is the first of the four music dramas that constitute Richard Wagner's *Der Ring des Nibelungen*, (The Ring of the Nibelung). It was performed, as a single opera, at the National Theatre Munich on the 22nd of September 1869, and received its first performance as part of the *Ring* cycle at the Bayreuth Festspielhaus, on the 13th of August 1876.

Wagner wrote the *Ring* librettos in reverse order, so that *Das Rheingold* was the last of the texts to be written; it was, however, the first to be set to music. The score was completed in 1854, but Wagner was unwilling to sanction its performance until the whole cycle was complete. He worked intermittently on this music until 1874. The 1869 the Munich premiere of *Das Rheingold* was staged, much against Wagner's wishes, on the orders of his patron, King Ludwig II of Bavaria. Following its 1876 Bayreuth premiere, the *Ring* cycle was introduced into the worldwide repertory, with performances in all the main opera houses, in which it has remained a regular and popular fixture.

In his 1851 essay "Opera and Drama", Wagner had set out new principles as to how music dramas should be constructed, under which the conventional forms of opera (arias, ensembles, choruses) were rejected. Rather than providing word-settings, the music would interpret the text emotionally, reflecting the feelings and moods behind the work, by using a system of recurring leitmotifs to represent people, ideas and situations. *Das Rheingold* was Wagner's first work that adopted these principles, and his most rigid adherence to them, despite a few deviations – one being the Rhine maidens frequently singing in ensemble.

As the preliminary evening within the cycle, *Das Rheingold* gives the background to the events that drive the main dramas of the cycle. It recounts Alberich's theft of the Rhine gold after his renunciation of love, his fashioning of the all-powerful ring from the gold and his enslavement of the Nibelungs, Wotan's seizure of the gold and the ring, to pay his debt to the giants who have built his fortress Valhalla, Alberich's curse on the ring and its possessors, Erda's warning to Wotan to forsake the ring, the early manifestation of the curse's power after Wotan yields the ring to the giants and the gods' uneasy entry into Valhalla, under the shadow of their impending doom.

*Die Walküre* (The Valkyrie) is the second of the four music dramas that constitute Richard Wagner's *Der Ring des Nibelungen*, (The Ring of the Nibelung). It was performed, as a single opera, at the National Theatre Munich on the 26th of June 1870, and received its first performance as part of the *Ring* cycle at the Bayreuth Festspielhaus on the 14th of August 1876.

Wagner generally followed the principles related to the form of musical drama which he had set out in his 1851 essay "Opera and Drama" but showed flexibility in the application of these principles here, particularly in Act 3 when the Valkyries engage in frequent ensemble singing. As with *Das Rheingold*, Wagner wished to defer any performance of the new work until it could be shown in the context of the completed cycle, but the 1870 Munich premiere was arranged at the insistence of his patron, King Ludwig II of Bavaria. *Die Walküre* has achieved some popularity as a stand-alone work and continues to be performed independently from its role in the tetralogy.

The story of *Die Walküre* is based on the Norse mythology told in The Völsunga saga and the Poetic Edda. In this version the Volsung twins Sieglinde and Siegmund, separated in childhood, meet and fall in love. This union angers the gods who demand that Siegmund must die. Sieglinde and the couple's unborn child are saved by the defiant actions of Wotan's daughter, the title character, Valkyrie Brünnhilde, who as a result faces the gods' retribution.

*Siegfried* is the third of the four music dramas that constitute *Der*

*Ring des Nibelungen* (The Ring of the Nibelung). It premiered at the Bayreuth Festspielhaus on the 16th of August 1876, as part of the first complete performance of *The Ring cycle.* The libretto of *Siegfried* was drafted by Wagner in November–December 1852, based on an earlier version he had prepared in May–June 1851 and originally entitled "Jung Siegfried" (Young Siegfried), later changed to "Der Junge Siegfried". The musical composition was commenced in 1856, but not finally completed until 1871.

The libretto arose from Wagner's gradual re-conception of the project he had initiated with his libretto "Siegfried's Tod" (Siegfried's Death) which was eventually to be incarnated as *Götterdämmerung,* the final section of the *Ring* cycle. Having grappled with his text for Siegfried's Tod, and indeed having undertaken some musical sketches for it during 1851, he realised that it would need a preface. At this point he conceived that the prefatory opera, *Der Junge Siegfried,* could act as a comic foil to the tragedy of Siegfried's Tod. Preliminary musical sketches for *Der Junge Siegfried* in 1851 were however quickly abandoned, although Wagner had written to his friend Theodor Uhlig that "the musical phrases are making themselves for these stanzas and periods, without my even having to take pains for them. It's all growing out of the ground as if it were wild." Shortly afterwards he wrote to Uhlig that he was now planning to tell the Siegfried story in the form of "three dramas, plus a prologue in three acts" – a clear prefiguring of the *Ring* cycle.

Full work was finally commenced on the music of *Siegfried,* as the composer henceforth referred to it, in 1856, when Wagner prepared concurrently two drafts, a complete draft in pencil and a version in ink on up to three staves in which he worked out details of instrumentation and vocal line. The composition of Acts 1 and 2 was completed by August 1857. Wagner then left off work on *Siegfried* to write the operas *Tristan und Isolde* and *Die Meistersinger.* He did not resume work on Siegfried until 1869, when he composed the third act. The final revision of the score was undertaken in February 1871. Performance was withheld until the first complete production of the *Ring* cycle, at Bayreuth in August 1876.

In the story, Alberich's brother and fellow-Nibelung, Mime, has taken to live in the woods near Neidhole, where Fafner in the shape of a dragon guards the ring and the treasure. Here Mime found Sieglinde fleeing from Wotan's wrath and helped her give birth to Siegfried. Sieglinde died following the birth, leaving Mime with Siegfried and the broken pieces of Siegmund's sword.

As act I begins, seventeen years have passed. Mime is trying to work out how to make the sword, Nothung. He has raised Siegfried in the hope that he will one day kill Fafner and thus give Mime a chance to win the ring, but none of his own swords are strong enough for Siegfried's force and he cannot find out how to forge the pieces of Nothung together.

Mime is working at another sword when Siegfried returns home with a bear to frighten Mime. When the bear is gone, Mime presents Siegfried with the new sword, which Siegfried immediately smashes. They have a fight and Mime complains about Siegfried's ingratitude towards him. This leads Siegfried to inquire about his origins. He has never met another living person except for Mime, but by looking at the animals and his own reflection in the brook he has concluded that Mime is not "his father and mother in one", as he claims.

Siegfried forces Mime to tell him the whole story of his origins and when Siegfried demands proof, Mime presents him with the broken Nothung. Siegfried is overwhelmed with joy. He orders Mime to weld the pieces together at once and rushes off into the woods.

Mime is once again alone, unable to make the sword. The Wanderer enters his cave. The Wanderer is Wotan, who has now apparently decided to just watch the action, knowing that Siegfried can only succeed, if he is not under influence from Wotan, his grandfather. However, as Mime cannot work things out for himself,

Wotan/Wanderer enters his cave and forces him to answer a series of questions. Mime must accept and uses his three questions to inquire about things, he already knows: Who lives in the underworld? Answer: The Nibelungen (AKA Schwarzalben). Who lives on the earth? Answer: The Riesen (Giants). Who lives in the skies? Answer: The Gods (AKA Lichtalben).

Mime has missed his chance to inquire about things that could be of use such as how to make the sword, the Wanderer now has to force Mime to put his head at stake in a similar trial. Mime cannot but accept, and the Wanderer puts forward three questions: What family of humans is it that Wotan loves, but had to desert? Answer: The Wälsungen. With what sword will the Walsunge-child, Siegfried, be able to kill Fafner? Answer: Nothung. And finally, the crucial question: Who can make Nothung? Mime cannot answer and the Wanderer tells him that "only a man who does not know fear can forge Nothung." The Wanderer has won Mime's head, but he leaves it to the man who does not know fear.

When Siegfried returns home, he complains that Mime has not made Nothung. Mime asks Siegfried if he knows fear. Siegfried does not and Mime wants to teach him. Siegfried wants Mime to start working on Nothung but Mime remembers that only a fearless person can craft the sword. Siegfried makes Nothung, while Mime works out a plan to poison Siegfried after he has killed Fafner. Siegfried cuts Mime's anvil in two with his new sword.

Act II – Outside Neidhole: Alberich is sitting outside Neidhole, waiting for the moment when someone will kill the dragon, and planning to win the ring. The Wanderer approaches and Alberich recognizes his old enemy, Wotan. But Wotan claims that he has no desires for the ring anymore and he advises Alberich to look out for Mime instead: He will bring a hero, who will kill the dragon. The hero knows nothing of the ring, but Mime does.

Wotan suggests that Alberich warns the dragon of the impending danger. Wotan wakes Fafner and they try to persuade him to give away the ring. But Fafner is not interested: "Ich lieg' und besitz': lasst mich schlafen!" (I lie down. Let me sleep). Wotan leaves, confident that all is well: Siegfried is about to get the ring. Alberich hides in the woods to look out for Mime and Siegfried. As they enter, Mime tells Siegfried that this is the place where he is about to learn how to be afraid. Mime goes away to wait, and Siegfried enjoys the quiet woods. He wonders about his origins again: what did his mother and father look like? He hears a bird singing and tries to communicate with it by playing a flute that he has made. But he fails and instead plays a tune on his horn.

The music wakes Fafner and Siegfried demands that he teaches him fear. They engage in a battle and Siegfried kills Fafner. Before he dies, the giant warns Siegfried that his own death is being planned. When Fafner is dead, Siegfried takes his sword. But the dragon's blood burns on his skin and as he tastes it, he suddenly understands the bird talking. The bird tells him to go get the ring and the tarnhelm (magic helmet) in the dragon's nest. Alberich and Mime enter and fight over who is going to win the ring. They leave again as Siegfried comes out, carrying both the ring and helmet.

The woodbird now warns Siegfried: Mime wants the ring and plans his death. But thanks to the dragon's blood he can understand what Mime thinks. In the scene, where Mime sings his thoughts out loud instead of what he thinks he is saying, Siegfried finds out that Mime really does plan to poison him and cut his head off with Nothung, in order to get the ring.

Siegfried kills Mime instead and leaves him in the cave with Fafner. But now Siegfried feels lonely. He asks the bird how to get a companion and the bird advises him to go to the mountain where Brünnhilde lies sleeping. Siegfried asks the bird to show him the way and they rush off towards the mountain.

Act III – At the foot of the Valkyrie Rock: The Wanderer enters and calls for Erda to appear. She wakes up and appears and Wotan demands her to tell him how to stop things. Erda urges him to talk to Brünnhilde instead, but as she learns that Brünnhilde has been punished and is now sleeping, waiting for a man to wake her, she angrily refuses to help Wotan. Wotan insists, but Erda tells him, "You are not what you appear to be." He tells her that she is not what she appears to be either. Now her wisdom is not worth anything anymore, as his plan is going to succeed: Siegfried is to wake up Brünnhilde and they will inherit Wotan. Erda goes back to sleep.

Wotan sees Siegfried approaching. The woodbird disappears and Siegfried is left at the foot of the mountain. The Wanderer asks Siegfried where he is going and he tells him the story of Mime, Fafner, the woodbird's advice and how he is going to find Brünnhilde. But as the Wanderer continues to ask questions, Siegfried gets fed up and demands that he lets him pass. The Wanderer demands respect, but Siegfried refuses and threatens to move him by force. The Wanderer takes his spear and discloses that this is the spear that once shattered Nothung. Siegfried thus learns this is his father's murderer and splinters Wotan's spear, thus ending his powers. Siegfried continues towards the mountain and enters the fire that guards Brünnhilde.

At the mountain top Siegfried finds Brünnhilde. For the first time he is afraid. He wakes Brünnhilde with a kiss and she greets the light of the day. She learns it is Siegfried who has woken her up and tells him how she has loved him even before he was born. However, she cannot give herself to him and she tries to persuade him that they must love each other from a distance: If they engage in human love, they will destroy each other. Brünnhilde is afraid of the transformation from goddess to human woman. But in the end Siegfried conquers her and they engage in a triumphant love duet ending the scene in the words: "Leuchtende Liebe, lachender Tod" (shining love – laughing death).

# CHAPTER 18

# *My Second Favourite*

My hotel was only five minutes' walk from the tram and then a fifteen-minute taxi journey to the Finnish National Opera. I had been here before – for *Parsifal,* as part of the Richard Wagner Verband International. Now, I was here to see *Die tote Stadt* (The Dead City), an opera in three acts by Erich Wolfgang Korngold set to a libretto by Paul Schott, a collective pseudonym for the composer and his father, Julius Korngold. It is based on the 1892 novel *Bruges-la-Morte* by Georges Rodenbach.

Rodenbach's novel had already been adapted by the author into a play. The play was translated into German by Siegfried Trebitsch, an Austrian playwright, translator, novelist and poet under the title *Die stille Stadt* (The Silent City), which he later changed to *Das Trugbild* (The Mirage). Trebitsch was a friend of Korngold's father, Julius. The two met in the street one day and got into a conversation about a possible operatic adaptation. Trebitsch later met Erich, who was excited about the project. As soon as Erich read the play, he drafted a scenario for a one-act opera, but Hans Müller urged him to get away from one-act operas and he sketched the first of three acts in prose for Erich. However, his work on two of his own plays prevented him from getting much further.

Father and son decided to adapt the play themselves, and co-wrote the libretto, using the pseudonym Paul Schott. Julius decided to change the plot so that the murder occurs in a dream, rather than in real life, as in the original. Korngold started the composition in 1916. He left it for a year to take up military service before resuming and completing the score.

When *Die tote Stadt* had its premiere on December the 4th 1920, Korngold was just twenty-three years old with two short one-act operas, *Der Ring des Polykrates* and *Violanta*, already to his name. The success of these earlier works was so great that *Die tote Stadt* was subject to a fierce competition among German theatres for the right to the world premiere. In the end, an unusual double premiere was arranged, and the opera opened simultaneously at the Stadt-theater Hamburg and Cologne. In Cologne, the conductor was Otto Klemperer, and his wife Johanna Geisler sang Marietta. In Hamburg, Korngold himself was in the theatre, and the conductor was Egon Pollak. The opera's theme of overcoming the loss of a loved one resonated with contemporary audiences of the 1920s who had just come through the trauma and grief of World War I, and this undoubtedly increased the work's popularity.

*Die tote Stadt* was one of the greatest hits of the 1920s. Within two years of its premiere it had travelled around the globe, including several performances at the Metropolitan Opera in New York City. The Berlin première, conducted by George Szell was on the 12th of April 1924 with Lotte Lehmann as Marietta/Marie and the famous tenor and actor, Richard Tauber as Paul. But the work was banned by the Nazi regime because of Korngold's Jewish ancestry and after World War II it fell into obscurity. The main post-war revivals were at the Vienna Volksoper (1967) and the New York City Opera (1975). In recent years, however, the work has enjoyed notable revivals at the Theater Bonn Opera House, the Royal Opera House, the San Francisco Opera and at the Vienna State Opera.

The French premiere of the opera took place in a concert performance in 1982 at the Paris Théâtre des Champs-Élysées. The first French staged performance was in April 2001 in Strasbourg under the baton of Jan Latham-Koenig with Torsten Kerl (Paul) and Angela Denoke (Marietta).

The opera received its UK premiere on the 14th of January 1996 in a concert performance by the Kensington Symphony Orchestra conducted by Russell Keable at the Queen Elizabeth Hall, with Ian Caley (Paul) and Christine Teare (Marie/Marietta). The first UK staged performance was on the 27th of January 2009 at the Royal Opera House, Covent Garden.

The opera was first performed in Latin America at Teatro Colón in Buenos Aires, Argentina, on September the 19th, 1999, with Carlos Bengolea as Paul, Cynthia Makris as Marie/Marietta and David Pittman-Jennings as Frank; Stefan Lano was the conductor.

In Australia, the work was first premiered by Opera Australia on the 30h of June 2012 at the Sydney Opera House, with Cheryl Barker as Marie/Marietta, and Stefan Vinke as Paul, conducted by Christian Badea, directed by Bruce Beresford.

Act 1: When the opera opens, Paul, a younger middle-class man whose young wife, Marie, has recently died, cannot come to terms with the sad reality of her death. He keeps a "Temple of Memories" in her honour, including paintings, photographs and a lock of her hair. When his friend Frank pays him a visit at his house and urges him to honour Marie by moving on with his life, Paul flies into a rage and insists that Marie "still lives." He tells Frank that he has met a woman on the streets of Bruges who resembles Marie (indeed, Paul thinks that she is Marie) and invited her back to his home.

Soon the woman, Marietta, a young and beautiful dancer, appears for her rendezvous with Paul. They talk, she is put off by his odd behaviour, but persists in trying to interest him with her charms. She sings "Glück das mir verblieb" (Joy, that near to me remained) and dances seductively, but eventually gets bored and leaves. Paul meanwhile is driven into a state of extreme anxiety. Torn between his loyalty to Marie and his interest in Marietta he collapses into a chair and begins to hallucinate. He sees Marie's ghost step out of her portrait and urge him not to forget her, but then the vision of Marie changes and tells Paul to move on with his life.

Act 2: After a series of visions in which his pursuit of Marietta alienates him from all his remaining friends, the act ends with Marietta finally overcoming Paul's resistance and leading him off-stage locked in a passionate embrace. All this takes place in Paul's imagination.

Act 3: Paul's vision continues. Back in his house, living with Marietta, he quarrels with her. She gets fed up with his quirks and obsession with Marie and starts to taunt him by dancing seductively while stroking his dead wife's hair. In a rage, Paul grabs the lock of hair and strangles Marietta. Holding her dead body he exclaims, "Now she is exactly like Marie." Then he snaps out of his dream. Astonished that Marietta's body is nowhere to be found, he has barely had time to collect his thoughts when his maid informs him that Marietta has come back to pick up her umbrella which she left at the house when she departed a few minutes ago. With the shock of the traumatic dream still fresh in his mind, Paul is met by his friends Brigitta and Frank who note that although Paul's vision is there, his desire is dead. Frank begins to leave and asks if Paul will leave, to which he replies, "I will try". The opera ends with a repeat of "Glück, das mir verblieb" sung by Paul in what is apparently his last time in his Temple of Memories.

Its construction is based on the Leitmotif and is largely influenced by Richard Wagner and Richard Strauss. One can clearly hear Salome (Marietta, "I live to Dance") and *Parsifal* Act II (Kundry) within the work – the rage at Marie who has Paul's heart. But, like most men, lust takes over, temporarily, until after the sex act, when conscience and guilt return to plague them. Guilt is fearsome! The lock of hair is cut by Marietta from Marie's head with scissors and Marie leaves the stage in great distress. Marietta uses this lock of hair to taunt Paul and repeats "I live to dance". Despite his warnings that it is sacred, bringing about her death by strangulation.

As the work is set mainly in a dream, all is well and we, the audience can relax. Then we hear the concluding, amazingly beautiful poem and musical conclusion on the subject of leaving the dead to their rest, by not mourning them to extremes. Life is to be lived. For a twenty-three-year-old, it is beyond belief that such sensitive music could be written by someone so young.

Erich Wolfgang Korngold (May 29, 1897–November 29, 1957) was an Austrian-born composer and conductor. A child prodigy, he became one of the most important and influential composers in Hollywood history. He was a noted pianist and composer of classical music, along with music for Hollywood films, and the first composer of international stature to write Hollywood scores.

When he was eleven years old, his ballet *Der Schneemann* (The Snowman), became a sensation in Vienna, followed by his Second Piano Sonata which he wrote at age thirteen and which was played throughout Europe by Artur Schnabel. His one-act operas *Violanta* and *Der Ring des Polykrates* were premiered in Munich in 1916, conducted by Bruno Walter. At the age of twenty-three his opera *Die tote Stadt* (The Dead City) premiered in Hamburg and Cologne. In 1921 he conducted the Hamburg Opera. During the 1920s he re-orchestrated, re-arranged and nearly re-composed, for the theatre, operettas by Johann Strauss II. By 1931 he was a professor of music at Vienna State Academy.

At the request of director Max Reinhardt, and due to the rise of the Nazi regime, Korngold moved to the U.S. in 1934 to write music scores for films. His first was Reinhardt's *A Midsummer Night's Dream* (1935), which was well received by critics. He subsequently wrote scores for such films as *Captain Blood* (1935), which helped boost the career of its starring newcomer actor, Errol Flynn. His score for *Anthony Adverse* (1936) won an Oscar and was followed two years later with another Oscar for *The Adventures of Robin Hood* (1938).

Overall, he wrote the score for sixteen Hollywood films, receiving two more Oscar nominations. Along with Max Steiner and Alfred Newman, he is one of the founders of film music. Although his late classical Romantic compositions were no longer as popular when he died in 1957, his music underwent a resurgence of interest in the 1970s beginning with the release of the RCA Red Seal album *The Sea Hawk*: the Classic Film Scores of Erich Wolfgang Korngold (1972). This album was hugely popular and ignited interest in other film music of his (and other composers like Steiner) and in his concert music, which often incorporated popular themes from his film scores.

The Opera House in Helsinki is on the Töölönlahti bay in Töölö. It opened in 1993 and is state-owned through Senate Properties. The Finnish National Opera stages four to six premieres a year at the Opera House which features two auditoriums, the main auditorium with 1,350, seats and a smaller studio auditorium with 300–500 seats. The 2013 production of *Die tote Stadt* featured three sets of surtitles: Finnish, Swedish and English. The players were: Paul (Klaus, Florian Vogt), Marietta/Marie (voice), (Camilla Nylund), Actor – Marie – silent role (Kirsti Eiche), Frank/Fritz (Markus Eiche), Brigitta (Sari Nordqvist), Juliette (Hanna Rantala), Lucienne (Nina Keitel), Victorian (Per-Hakan Precht), Albert (Juha Rihimaki), Gaston (Antti Nieminen). The conductor was Mikko Franck. Outstanding. Regi Kasper Holten. The orchestra was the Finnish National Orchestra with choir and children.

The production had one large room as a setting with a very large bed – not out of context, for a change. Marie is on the bed and remains in the room for most of the opera. Paul interacts with her throughout the opera and in the final act, Marie is confronted by Marietta, who can see her from the beginning of the act.

The troubadours come up through the bed in Act II – very clever and indeed, funny. The Robert the Devil G. Meyerbeer part is very short-lived. Not a dead, resurrected nun in sight. I cannot imagine a sight uglier than a dead resurrected nun! So, we were spared these images. The procession scene was done tastefully with the end of the room, which had a large Venetian blind raised with little miniature houses etc., being used to display the heads of the choir. The children sang off-stage. Frank/Fritz (clown outfit) was dressed in a US Army uniform, a master sergeant with an iron cross pinned to his chest. He was a fine singer – not a Hermann Prey, but good. Brigitta was excellent, as were the Group. Camilla Nylund who sang Marietta and Marie off-stage was outstanding. Beautiful voice. Klaus Florian Vogt, who is not a natural Paul like Rene Kollo, sang beautifully (No high B Flat).

Act I was the most beautiful forty-five minutes I have ever heard in an opera house. Acts II and III were equally outstanding. The orchestra was brilliant, especially the Brass section and Timpani, with inspired reading by the conductor, Mikko Franck. I didn't want it to end. As the last notes faded, there was absolute silence, then thunderous applause. My only thought was of returning in December. *Die tote Stadt* is a beautiful opera, if performed by really good singers – and if the production isn't created by one of the modern lunatic producers.

The last time I saw this magnificent opera was in April 12th, 2019, this time at the National Concert Hall, Dublin – on my own doorstep. My good friend, Jarlath Jennings, from my Wagner Society of Ireland days had texted to say that he would be there. I did see him at a distance, chatting with a group. I didn't approach them, not wishing to intrude. The next day I received a text from him:

"Hope you enjoyed last night's performance as much as I did. Epic is the best word I can think of. Great work by NSO, great singing. Loved the organ and choirs. Was looking out for you upstairs but didn't see you".

Just over a month later, on the 14th of May Jarlath suddenly died, after a routine operation in St. Vincent's Hospital, Dublin.

Jarlath was Chief executive officer with McConnells, Ireland's largest advertising company. He also served on the Council of the Marketing Institute including a term as Chairman, ultimately receiving an MII Fellowship. In 2015 he wrote a very extensive and in-depth piece, *Bayreuth Diary 2014 – A Personal View*, including a review of *Der Ring des Nibelungen* in Bayreuth for the Wagner Society Newsletter. Like me, he enjoyed "the wonderful music and sublime acoustic of the Festspielhaus". We shared a great admiration and appreciation of the fantastic Klaus Florian Vogt and of course Wagner, Korngold and opera in general. He was one of a handful of people who had supported me during my latter dealings and ultimate parting of the ways with the Wagner Society. He was alone in Bayreuth for one of the productions in 2014 and afterwards wrote,

"The benefit from this solo experience is that it forced me to meet new people and engage in conversations which shed unique perspectives and insights regarding the productions." Unlike me, the "spy who creeps in and out of cities and venues under the radar".

His would have been one of the few whose company I would have enjoyed on such occasions. He was probably one of only two people with whom I could comfortably and happily waffle on interminably about all things opera and having many a good laugh along the way. The irony that the theme of our last opera: overcoming the loss of a loved one is not lost on me. I miss him terribly.

# CHAPTER 19

# *The Clarity of Hindsight*

I began the 15th Young Officers' Course in September 1983 at the Military College, the Curragh, County Kildare. Getting my teeth into projects would occupy my mind. The experience I had gained at the bicycle shop in Dublin, where I had worked in my youth now came to the fore. The Military College had a large storeroom that had about fifty unused bicycles, all in various stages of disrepair. I managed to extract thirty of them which I had restored, and I loaned them to the 1st Cavalry Squadron for a weekend cycling trip out into the hills. I was editor of the class magazine which I also enjoyed. I had a men's club constructed, including a bar. Years later, on my posting out in 1984, I was complimented by the College Commandant, Colonel Tom Waters on its operation. In a letter to me dated the 27th of July 1984 he said, "I fully appreciate the difficulties you may have encountered in getting the construction work completed and in the provision of barrack service equipment. You have done this in a most efficient manner without recourse to higher authority. You can be assured that the men whose morale has been boosted will fully appreciate your work on their behalf". His words were very gratifying and helped boost my own morale in no small measure.

But my time at the college was not without its problems I can now see that it was really about looking for shortcomings of any sort – problems that I could fix. I was beyond fixing. I had run-ins with some of the Cadet School officers about night observation devices (NODs) that hadn't been returned to the Third Battalion. The Third had complained to the Operations Commandant. I hadn't signed for them and told him that I had no responsibility for them.

All of this must have been overlooked by the course commander whose comments on my performance included, "a composed personality who related very well to his fellow students, a positive attitude to the course throughout, though of a quiet disposition, when called on to contribute to class discussion, he invariably had a pertinent comment to make. A dependable officer". Like my earlier class report, this one lay neatly in a file, unseen by me until many years later.

I had been headhunted for the Quartermaster's Branch, Infirmary Road, Dublin, in 1984. But soon, I was bored and besides, there were two civil servants with whom I met once a month to agree recruitment of civilian employees as per the Quartermaster General's priorities. I hated these two. While posted as duty officer in Defence Forces Headquarters, I had access to a storeroom stuffed with weapons and ammunition and I would fantasise about meeting them, armed with a pistol, and putting two neat holes in each of them! They were spared because I was busy selecting academic courses for staff, relevant to the logistician's job and I was involved in the sub-committee on computerisation of stores which took me away on a few 'swan trips': trips down the country. But this would be the twilight of my army career. I had no contact with troops. I was a civil servant in uniform, and I was missing the Military College.

Depression was a term that I had lately come to understand as the name for my state of mind. I had 'negative thoughts' and the incidences of urges to end my own life were increasing. I was working next door to the army psychologist who specialised in courses.

I liked him as a person, but I didn't speak to him about my issues. I didn't speak to anyone. I could never be at ease. I needed something else to fill the hours.

I went back to college to study psychology and mathematics – again at University College Dublin. I had always had an aptitude for mathematics but this time I failed. I was unable to concentrate, and I reverted to a single subject and a single course – a BA in Psychology. The study took me some way towards understanding human behaviour and while it helped me to see and deal with some of my own issues, it left many questions unanswered.

Albert Camus's book, *The Myth of Sisyphus* was a life saver. Like Sisyphus, a figure in Greek mythology who was condemned to repeat forever the same meaningless task of pushing a boulder up a mountain only to see it roll down again, I abandoned hope of ever making sense of, or overcoming my suffering, and tried to accept that I was a broken person, that I would remain broken – destroyed forever – and to get on with life as it was, to the best of my ability and embrace all that the unreasonable world had to offer.

The "Situations Vacant" pages of Friday's *Irish Times* became a must read. One Friday I spotted an advertisement for a Higher Executive Officer and an Executive Officer with the Medical Council. In mid-May 1986 I was HEO in the Medical Council, a statutory body whose roots went back to the General Medical Council, 44, Hallam Street, London. I was responsible for preparing briefs for quarterly Council meetings. Council meetings were held at Broc House on Nutley Lane. The food was excellent, and I considered it a privilege to be amongst these knowledgeable professors of medicine – even the grumpy ones. In the beginning, I got along well but interpersonal staff issues eventually caused problems.

As well as attending meetings and servicing Council meetings I looked after the registration committee, the education and training committee, the computer section and general administration. I had a row with my boss over the Annual Report in which I omitted the name of a pathologist. I made the error because he was giving me a hard time and because of this I was under pressure. Soon after that incident he reprimanded me because my signature on documents was 'too large'. This was the straw that broke the camel's back. A sudden, immense episode of depersonalisation hit me, the worst episode that I had since 1980 in Lebanon. As I was still an Army Reserve Officer, I could use the showers at Army HQ, I ran, choking for breath, trying not to fall flat on my face and I stood under a shower to give myself some time to come to. The episode took a long time to pass.

By now I was very sick, and I knew that I must leave the Council. I handed in my letter of resignation and I was given three months' salary in advance and my contributions to the pension fund were returned. My career was over. The clarity of hindsight is marvellous; I couldn't take correction, nor could I be challenged. I had moved from the 'frying pan' that was the army and into the fire and like a wounded animal, I was angry – and I was now unemployable.

To pass the time I began running again. I had been long-distance running for years and I had run three marathons. Now, the running filled a few hours each day and of course the exercise helped me feel better. My trips to opera and concert venues overseas soon took precedent. Live performances were becoming an addiction.

In recent times, I have come to understand more about how and why music has such a profound effect on me: why I cannot seem to get enough of it and why music has been my one and only interest. From the premise of the field of information in psychology and how music is acoustically different from all other stimuli, music therapists have to start with a description of music from an acoustic basis and how the brain perceives music and responds to music in its own unique way. But now there is a whole new field of neuroscience that is able to image the brain and actually watch the brain change in response to music. It is known that the brain responds to music with pleasure responses in all cultures and therefore a person's history with music, their familiarity with a particular type of music, their preference before a particular type of music makes it very powerful in terms of a therapeutic benefit.

For people who learn information while listening to music, that information it will be stored in a special part of the brain. Music can improve recall for people who have had neurologic disability or damage. The rhythm of music will help structure motor movement and recall can be improved by doing physical rehabilitation motor movement to music. Patients with Alzheimer's disease have music memory embedded very deeply in the centre part of the brain and music memory will last longer than memories about their family or relatives and that information can be used to help access communication with them as they go further into the Alzheimer's dementia process. It is only now that the imaging is helping to catch up and be able to explain how it works. As with other forms of therapy, clinicians and scientists can actually watch the brain change.

Music therapy procedures have been documented in the research on music and premature infants. In a neonatal intensive care unit in the United States staff are playing music to mask the aversive stimuli in the environment; helping the brain be nurtured and relaxed and not overly stimulated, thus allowing babies to be discharged sooner. Aversive stimuli in the environment refers to the harsh buzzing of lights and the churning of machines, the beeping of monitor alarms, the slamming of the door, turning on the water tap every time one of the medical personnel needs to wash their hands – a lot of auditory stimuli that create stress in the neonatal care unit. Research has shown that the babies' oxygen saturation increased while they were listening to music, they relaxed and breathed more deeply and there was more oxygen in the bloodstream.

But research has also been done even before birth. In one case, anything that the mother sang or books that she read out loud indicated that the baby was is listening and developing information and researchers have been able to document that on the first day of life the baby recognised the mother's voice, preferred women's voices to men's voices, could recognise a specific *Doctor Seuss* book that she read during the last month of pregnancy and could identify that book from all the other *Doctor Seuss* books.

Babies can detect grammar errors in their native language and can detect language sounds that are not native to its native language. So, for instance if an American baby is listening to the English language and all of a sudden there's a Japanese word in there the baby will react to that; its behaviour shows that it is responding to an unfamiliar stimulus. Babies come into the world with a great deal of information about language and music if it has been in their environment while they were in the womb. If the mother is listening to music in the room the baby is probably hearing it.

When I consider all of this I wonder if we have genetically inherited certain traits, certain tastes and preferences or if some of them are learned pre-birth. My mother loved music, especially classical music. I was her second child. With only one toddler to contend with, maybe she had more time to herself. Certainly, as a child, I remember that the radio was on a lot during the day. It is quite likely that my mother was relaxed and feeling contented – possibly uplifted – by much of what she was listening to. I was literally immersed in an atmosphere of music. Needless to say, this pleasurable atmosphere ended abruptly when I arrived into the clinical world of swishing, starched nurses' uniforms, swing doors, squeaking rubber soles on polished terrazzo floors, clattering surgical instruments on steel petri dishes, the air infused with ether and carbolic soap – that was the delivery room in Dublin's National Maternity Hospital.

As a teenager, I was never very far from home – until I joined the army, blissfully unaware of how a civil war on the other side of the world would change my life. Some of the older boys in our locality were my heroes, particularly those who had joined the army. Their status rose to dizzying heights when the first Irish UN peacekeepers went to the Congo in 1960. Every six months, the buzz of excitement grew as boys were coming home in uniform, looking grown up, sun-tanned and fit. I wanted to be like them. Filled with patriotic fervour and with the Congo in my sights, joining the army in 1963 seemed like the most natural direction in which to take myself. My previous part-time FCA training meant that I knew how to march and that I was an expert on the Mills-HE-hand and rifle grenade. The months between April and September 1963 seemed to fly. I was a Two-Star Private, trained on the FN rifle.

I was in No. 3 Platoon. My platoon officer was Lieutenant Johnny Martin and the platoon sergeants were Sergeant Michael Moore and Sergeant Dan Mannix DSM whom I would later learn had played a pivotal role in 'The Battle of the Tunnel' in Elizabethville in the Congo. Another Congo veteran was Corporal 'Manono' Lynch, who was Post Commander at Niemba following the death of Lieutenant Kevin Gleeson, of the ill-fated 33rd Battalion patrol ambushed by the Baluba on the 8th of November 1960. Corporal Lynch never mentioned the disaster that was Niemba and we didn't ask.

My mother was in shock. She saw the FCA as a pastime that she hoped I would outgrow. She hoped that joining the army might be a passing phase and that I would get over it. Like everyone else in the country, she had been distraught by events in the Congo – events that had come too close to home when her neighbour's son was killed in the infamous Niemba ambush. When his remains were finally found in 1962, they were repatriated and buried with military honours in Glasnevin Cemetery. She had wept for his family and felt deeply for them in their loss. She could not believe that his death had not altered my decision to go to "that awful place".

My mother's concerns, nor the tragic events in the Congo, had much effect on me. I was having fun with crowds of fellow teenage lads in Cathal Brugha Barracks where I spent much of mealtimes ducking as quarter loaves of bread were launched across a dining hall crammed with several hundred recruits. Punch-ups broke out regularly and were great fun. The barrack square reverberated with orders and the marching of the heavy leather hobnailed boots of four platoons. We could hear ourselves and each other marching – like a symphony orchestra, each soldier an instrument.

Excitement grew when preparations for the visit of President John F. Kennedy began. I was honoured to be selected as part of the military guard of honour lining the route for the Kennedy cavalcade procession through the centre of the city. Hours before 'Air Force One' touched down at Dublin Airport, the city of Dublin came to a standstill. Kennedy stood in the open-topped limousine, wearing a blue suit, his sandy hair copper highlighted by the summer sun and a permanent broad smile on his face as he waved to the crowds. At the Irish Leaders' graveside in Arbour Hill, the 36th Cadet Class performed the Funeral Drill. The drill made such an impression on the President that he spoke about it, ad nauseum on his return to the United States. We had practiced this Funeral Drill too, as part of our training.

The cheers of the crowds lining the route were still ringing in my ears as I presented myself at St. Bricin's Hospital in Arbour Hill to have a vaccination against smallpox and a troublesome tooth extracted. This necessitated forty-eight hours' excused duty (ED) and I found myself confined to nearby Collins Barracks while in recovery, itching to be on the move. Finally, I was summoned by the sergeant major, a kind, crusty old man. "Take off your shirt and turn right," he ordered. The marks on my arm, left by the smallpox vaccination were clearly visible. "Right," he said. "Pack your kit, you're going to the Congo." My whole body tingled with excitement and I floated out the door on a cloud.

The Congo campaign had claimed twenty-six young Irish lives. Their sacrifice and the bravery and competence of the thousands that had served over the past three years had left a quieter Congo for our 2nd Infantry Group now patrolling the Angolan border. Here we were living in tents, lulled to sleep at night by the sound of crickets – once we got used to it. The crickets and other insects played the evening symphony, a cacophony of sounds. Forked lighting danced across the sky at night, rainstorms flooded the drainage channels and we could soap and shower in the swollen rivers. Women with barrels on their heads and children in slings on their backs walked along the side of the road in single file for fear of being killed by a white man driving a car. We joked that the Congo was not a place to die; bodies would decompose very quickly.

My mother and I wrote letters to each other regularly. I was missing my mother and my siblings, but I could never speak of homesickness; it just wasn't the done thing. Besides, I was all grown up now. I was a soldier – an Irish soldier. I had an FN rifle and I was mandated by my country and by the United Nations to keep the peace in a country the size of Europe that had been hell bent on self-destruction. Thirty years later, on the day that my mother died I sat in my room and played the Largo from *Beethoven's 9th Symphony* on CD. I realise now, more than ever that we were deeply connected through music and perhaps I am still trying to reach out – from Bayreuth, Vienna, Munich, Berlin, London, Paris or the National Concert Hall in Dublin to connect with her in some way, trying to keep something of her inside. It's hard to know for sure the reasons for one's yearning. However, in the light of recent discoveries I do strongly suspect that even before I was born, music played a large part in the shaping of how I was going to be in later life.

# CHAPTER 20

# A Ramble Through Other Pastures

I am and will always be a passionate Wagnerian. But my love for Wagner does not preclude a taste for other great composers. Nevertheless, I sometimes feel a hint of guilt and betrayal when I slip away to attend a performance by someone other than Wagner. But I take comfort from no less a figure that his great-granddaughter who recently 'slipped away' to another 'shrine'. As a teenager growing up in Bavaria in the 1950s and '60s, Eva Wagner-Pasquier was swept up by an altogether different musical icon: Elvis Presley! In 2019 she joined her American-born son Antoine and went to Graceland to pay homage to the 'King'. "I've always wanted to go there," she said. "It was superb! We stayed at the Heartbreak Hotel, of course." It was a break from the business of directing the glittering Bayreuth Festival with her half-sister, Katharine. Both have directed the festival since 2008.

The Vienna Volksoper is another major opera house in Vienna, Austria. It produces three hundred performances of twenty-five German language productions during an annual season which runs from September through June. The Volksoper is a splendid, small by some standards, beautiful and intimate theatre. It was October 2013 and I was here for *The Marriage of Figaro*, an antidote *par excellence* for the past four weeks of my life – hospitalisation for a catheter ablation and a 'welding' of my colon to prevent post-ablation bleeding.

*The Marriage of Figaro* is a comic opera in four acts composed in 1786 by Wolfgang Amadeus Mozart, with an Italian libretto written by Lorenzo Da Ponte. It premiered at the Burgtheater in Vienna on the 1st of May 1786. It tells how two servants, Figaro and Susanna succeed in getting married, thwarting the efforts of their philandering employer Count Almaviva to seduce Susanna and at the same time, teaching him a lesson in fidelity.

Figaro, a barber turned valet to Count Almaviva, is engaged to be married to Susanna, the Countess's maid. Figaro is best known as the hero of *Le Barbier de Séville* ('The Barber of Seville' 1775) and *Le Mariage de Figaro* (The Marriage of Figaro 1784), two popular comedies of intrigue by the French dramatist Pierre-Augustin Caron de Beaumarchais. Beaumarchais' play was at first banned in Mozart's home city of Vienna because its anti-aristocratic overtones were considered dangerous in the decade before the French revolution. The opera was the first of three collaborations between Mozart and Da Ponte; their later collaborations were *Don Giovanni* and *Così fan tutte*. It was Mozart who originally selected Beaumarchais's play and brought it to Da Ponte, who turned it into a libretto in six weeks, rewriting it in poetic Italian and removing all of the original's political references. The libretto was approved by the Emperor before any music was written by Mozart. The Imperial Italian opera company paid Mozart 450 florins for the work; this was three times his yearly salary when he had worked as a court musician in Salzburg. Da Ponte was paid 200 florins.

Act 1 – A partly furnished room, with a chair in the centre: Figaro measures the space where the bridal bed will fit while Susanna tries on her wedding bonnet in front of a mirror (in the present day, a more traditional French floral wreath or a modern veil are often substituted, often in combination with a bonnet, so as to accommodate what Susanna happily describes as her wedding cappellino). Figaro is quite pleased with their new room, Susanna far less so as she is worried by its proximity to the Count's chambers. It seems he has been making advances toward her and plans on exercising his *droit du seigneur*, the purported feudal right of a lord to bed a servant girl on her wedding night before her husband can sleep with her. The Count had the right abolished when he married Rosina, but he now wants to reinstate it. The Countess rings for Susanna and she rushes off to answer. Figaro, confident in his own resourcefulness, resolves to outwit the Count.

Figaro departs, and Dr. Bartolo arrives with Marcellina, his old housekeeper. Figaro had previously borrowed a large sum of money from her, and, in lieu of collateral, had promised to marry her if unable to repay at the appointed time; she now intends to enforce that promise by suing him. Bartolo, seeking revenge against Figaro for having facilitated the union of the Count and Rosina (in *The Barber of Seville*), agrees to represent Marcellina pro bono, and assures her, in comical lawyer-speak, that he can win the case for her.

Bartolo departs, Susanna returns, and Marcellina and Susanna exchange very politely delivered sarcastic insults. Susanna triumphs in the exchange by congratulating her rival on her impressive age. The older woman departs in a fury.

The Countess asks for Susanna's aid with the Count. It seems the Count is angry with Cherubino's amorous ways, having discovered the page with the gardener's daughter, Barbarina, and plans to punish him. Cherubino wants Susanna to ask the Countess to intercede on his behalf. When the Count appears, Cherubino hides behind a chair, not wanting to be seen alone with Susanna. The Count uses the opportunity of finding Susanna alone to step up his demands for favours from her, including financial inducements to sell herself to him. As Basilio, the music teacher, arrives, the Count, not wanting to be caught alone with Susanna, hides behind the chair. Cherubino leaves that hiding place just in time and jumps onto the chair while Susanna scrambles to cover him with a dress.

When Basilio starts to gossip about Cherubino's obvious attraction to the Countess, the Count angrily leaps from his hiding place. He disparages the 'absent' page's incessant flirting and describes how he caught him with Barbarina under the kitchen table. As he lifts the dress from the chair to illustrate how he lifted the tablecloth to expose Cherubino, he finds Cherubino! The Count is furious but is reminded that the page overheard the Count's advances on Susanna, something that the Count wants to keep from the Countess. The young man is ultimately saved from punishment by the entrance of the peasants of the Count's estate, a pre-emptive attempt by Figaro to commit the Count to a formal gesture symbolising his promise that Susanna would enter into the marriage unsullied. The Count evades Figaro's plan by postponing the gesture. The Count says that he forgives Cherubino, but he dispatches him to his own regiment in Seville for army duty, effective immediately. Figaro gives Cherubino mocking advice about his new, harsh, military life from which all luxury, and especially women, will be totally excluded.

Act 2 – A handsome room with an alcove, a dressing room on the left, a door in the background (leading to the servants' quarters) and a window at the side: The Countess sings an aria lamenting her husband's infidelity. Susanna comes in to prepare the Countess for the day. She responds to the Countess's questions by telling her that the Count is not trying to seduce her; he is merely offering her a monetary contract in return for her affection. Figaro enters and explains his plan to distract the Count with anonymous letters warning him of adulterers. He has already sent one to the Count (via Basilio) that indicates that the Countess has a rendezvous of her own that evening. They hope that the Count will be too busy looking for imaginary adulterers to interfere with Figaro and Susanna's wedding. Figaro additionally advises the Countess to keep Cherubino around. She should dress him up as a girl and lure the Count into an illicit rendezvous where he can be caught red-handed.

Figaro leaves.

Cherubino arrives, sent in by Figaro and eager to co-operate. Susanna urges him to sing the song he wrote for the Countess "Voi che sapete che cosa è amor" (You ladies who know what love is, is it what I'm suffering from?). After the song, the Countess, seeing Cherubino's military commission, notices that the Count was in such a hurry that he forgot to seal it with his signet ring, which would be necessary to make it an official document. Susanna and the Countess then begin with their plan. Susanna takes off Cherubino's cloak, and she begins to comb his hair and teach him to behave and walk like a woman. Then she leaves the room through a door at the back to get the dress for Cherubino, taking his cloak with her.

While the Countess and Cherubino are waiting for Susanna to come back, they suddenly hear the Count arriving. Cherubino hides in the closet. The Count demands to be allowed into the room and the Countess reluctantly unlocks the door. The Count enters and hears a noise from the closet. He tries to open it, but it is locked. The Countess tells him it is only Susanna, trying on her wedding dress. At this moment, Susanna re-enters unobserved, quickly realises what is going on, and hides behind a couch. The Count shouts for her to identify herself by her voice, but the Countess orders her to be silent. Furious and suspicious, the Count leaves, with the Countess, in search of tools to force the closet door open. As they leave, he locks all the bedroom doors to prevent the intruder from escaping. Cherubino and Susanna emerge from their hiding places, and Cherubino escapes by jumping through the window into the garden. Susanna then takes Cherubino's former place in the closet, vowing to make the Count look foolish.

The Count and Countess return. The Countess, thinking herself trapped, desperately admits that Cherubino is hidden in the closet. The enraged Count draws his sword, promising to kill Cherubino on the spot, but when the door is opened, they both find to their astonishment only Susanna. The Count demands an explanation; the Countess tells him it is a practical joke, to test his trust in her. Shamed by his jealousy, the Count begs for forgiveness. When the Count presses about the anonymous letter, Susanna and the Countess reveal that the letter was written by Figaro, and then delivered by Basilio. Figaro then arrives and tries to start the wedding festivities, but the Count berates him with questions about the anonymous note. Just as the Count is starting to run out of questions, Antonio the gardener arrives, complaining that a man has jumped out of the window and damaged his carnations while running away. Antonio adds that he tentatively identified the running man as Cherubino, but Figaro claims it was he himself who jumped out of the window and pretends to have injured his foot while landing. Figaro, Susanna, and the Countess attempt to discredit Antonio as a chronic drunkard whose constant inebriation makes him unreliable and prone to fantasy, but Antonio brings forward a paper which, he says, was dropped by the escaping man. The Count orders Figaro to prove he was the jumper by identifying the paper, which is, in fact, Cherubino's appointment to the army. Figaro is at a loss, but Susanna and the Countess manage to signal the correct answers, and Figaro triumphantly identifies the document. His victory is, however, short-lived: Marcellina, Bartolo, and Basilio enter, bringing charges against Figaro and demanding that he honour his contract to marry Marcellina, since he cannot repay her loan. The Count happily postpones the wedding in order to investigate the charge.

Act 3 – A rich hall, with two thrones, prepared for the wedding ceremony: The Count mulls over the confusing situation. At the urging of the Countess, Susanna enters and gives a false promise to meet the Count later that night in the garden. As Susanna leaves, the Count overhears her telling Figaro that he has already won the case. Realising that he is being tricked, he resolves to punish Figaro by forcing him to marry Marcellina.

Figaro's hearing follows, and the Count's judgment is that Figaro must marry Marcellina. Figaro argues that he cannot get married without his parents' permission, and that he does not know who his parents are, because he was stolen from them when he was a baby. The ensuing discussion reveals that Figaro is Rafaello, the long-lost illegitimate son of Bartolo and Marcellina. A touching scene of reconciliation occurs. During the celebrations, Susanna enters with a payment to release Figaro from his debt to Marcellina. Seeing Figaro and Marcellina in celebration together, Susanna mistakenly believes that Figaro now prefers Marcellina to her. She has a tantrum and slaps Figaro's face. Marcellina explains, and Susanna, realising her mistake, joins the celebration. Bartolo, overcome with emotion, agrees to marry Marcellina that evening in a double wedding.

All leave, before Barbarina, Antonio's daughter, invites Cherubino back to her house so they can disguise him as a girl. The Countess, alone, ponders the loss of her happiness. Meanwhile, Antonio informs the Count that Cherubino is not in Seville, but in fact at his house. Susanna enters and updates her mistress regarding the plan to trap the Count. The Countess dictates a love letter for Susanna to send to the Count, which suggests that he meet her (Susanna) that night, under the pines. The letter instructs the Count to return the pin which fastens the letter.

A chorus of young peasants, among them Cherubino disguised as a girl, arrives to serenade the Countess. The Count arrives with Antonio and, discovering the page, is enraged. His anger is quickly dispelled by Barbarina, who publicly recalls that he had once offered to give her anything she wants in exchange for certain favours and asks for Cherubino's hand in marriage. Thoroughly embarrassed, the Count allows Cherubino to stay.

The act closes with the double wedding during the course of which Susanna delivers her letter to the Count, the Finale: "Ecco la marcia" (Here is the procession). Figaro watches the Count prick his finger on the pin, and laughs, unaware that the love-note is an invitation for the Count to tryst with Figaro's own bride Susanna. As the curtain drops, the two newlywed couples rejoice.

Act 4: Following the directions in the letter, the Count has sent the pin back to Susanna, giving it to Barbarina. However, Barbarina has lost it. Figaro and Marcellina see Barbarina, and Figaro asks her what she is doing. When he hears the pin is Susanna's, he is overcome with jealousy, especially as he recognises the pin to be the one that fastened the letter to the Count. Thinking that Susanna is meeting the Count behind his back, Figaro complains to his mother, and swears to be avenged on the Count and Susanna, and on all unfaithful wives. Marcellina urges caution, but Figaro will not listen. Figaro rushes off, and Marcellina resolves to inform Susanna of Figaro's intentions. Marcellina sings an aria lamenting that male and female wild beasts get along with each other, but rational humans cannot.

Motivated by jealousy, Figaro tells Bartolo and Basilio to come to his aid when he gives the signal. Basilio comments on Figaro's foolishness and claims he was once as frivolous as Figaro was. He tells a tale of how he was given common sense by Donna Flemma (Dame Prudence) and learned the importance of not crossing powerful people. They exit, leaving Figaro alone. Figaro muses bitterly on the inconstancy of women. Susanna and the Countess arrive, each dressed in the other's clothes. Marcellina is with them, having informed Susanna of Figaro's suspicions and plans. After they discuss the plan, Marcellina and the Countess leave, and Susanna teases Figaro by singing a love song to her beloved within Figaro's hearing. Figaro is hiding behind a bush and, thinking the song is for the Count, becomes increasingly jealous.

The Countess arrives in Susanna's dress. Cherubino shows up and starts teasing Susanna (really the Countess), endangering the plan. The Count gets rid of him by striking out in the dark. His punch actually ends up hitting Figaro, but the point is made and

Cherubino runs off.

The Count now begins making earnest love to Susanna (really the Countess) and gives her a jewelled ring. They go offstage together, where the Countess dodges him, hiding in the dark. Onstage, meanwhile, the real Susanna enters, wearing the Countess's clothes. Figaro mistakes her for the real Countess, and starts to tell her of the Count's intentions, but he suddenly recognizes his bride in disguise. He plays along with the joke by pretending to be in love with "my lady" and inviting her to make love right then and there. Susanna, fooled, loses her temper and slaps him many times. Figaro finally lets on that he has recognized Susanna's voice, and they make peace, resolving to conclude the comedy together.

The Count, unable to find Susanna, enters frustrated. Figaro gets his attention by loudly declaring his love for the Countess (really Susanna). The enraged Count calls for his people and for weapons: his servant is seducing his wife. Bartolo, Basilio and Antonio enter with torches as, one by one, the Count drags out Cherubino, Barbarina, Marcellina and the 'Countess' from behind the pavilion.

All beg him to forgive Figaro and the 'Countess', but he loudly refuses, repeating "No" at the top of his voice, until finally the real Countess re-enters and reveals her true identity. The Count, seeing the ring he had given her, realises that the supposed Susanna he was trying to seduce was actually his wife. Ashamed and remorseful, he kneels and pleads for forgiveness himself. The Countess, more kind than he, forgives her husband and all are contented.

The opera is a cornerstone of the repertoire and appears consistently among the top ten in the *Operabase* list of most frequently performed operas. The production was traditional and for once a bed in its rightful place. The scenery was perfect, as was the lighting. The singers, not big names, were outstanding. I was seated in Row 2, my ticket purchased online at Operabase.com cost €89, a bargain for such an expensive city. I had a lot of fun outside the Staatsoper – ticket-sellers, banter. Kaufman was singing "Dick

Johnson". Naturally, it was sold out, but no shortage of black-market tickets.

The Fandango was performed by the whole of the cast and while it worked and was very funny, although it failed to impart what this courting dance is about. It is about display – Spanish boys and girls dressed to kill, boys with tight pants, saying to the ladies, 'Look at my butt and see how fit I am; I could make passionate love all night!'.

The music was beautiful. *Die Hochzeit des Figaro*, Symphony No. 40 (love story), the clarinet concerto and the wonderful duet Papageno-Papagena from *The Magic Flute*. The bass from *Figaro* was on stage. He was brilliant! The soprano was superb. The encore was "An der schönen blauen Donau" (1866), Johann Strauss II. This was followed by *The Radetzky March* (1848) after Field Marshal Joseph Radetzky von Radetz. By Johann Strauss, (Vater). It is done every year at the Neujahrskonzert. So, I've been in the hall at the 'clapping piece' and now have no desire to attend the actual NYC. I had waited fifteen years. My appetite is satiated. Overall, it was a spiritual experience. My love of Wagner remains. He adored *Don Giovanni* as a youth. I love the *Serenade*. Mozart is balsam for the soul.

After the opera I took a taxi back to the Hilton Plaza and a bottle of dark (Dunkel) beer – my first beer since 2004. On Wednesday morning I purchased a ticket for the Mozart concert in Musikverein (Goldener Saal) from an official ticket agent, I'd been there before for Beethoven's *Third* with *Barenboim*, the Prelude and Liebestod to *Tristan und Isolde*, with the Wiener Philharmoniker, many years ago. These concerts are subscription concerts and tickets are re-sold at high prices. The ticket agency then was Travel for the Arts, a London based company. UK travel agents tend to add £500 pp to the trip, overall and one must book flights, hotel and tickets with them. I can generally do my own bookings, but Munich and the Staatsoper in Vienna are, in the main, impossible to book. I don't do waiting lists. The exception was Bayreuth when I waited for about seven years.

# CHAPTER 21

# *Beethoven Bach and Other Branches*

Wagner is like a 200-year-old oak tree: vast with deep roots and many branches. The roots comprise all great composers who preceded him – e.g. Mozart, Beethoven and Weber. The branches comprise all composers who were his contemporaries and all who succeeded him. Composers who opposed him are, nonetheless, affected by his work. These are in the branches – e.g. Richard Strauss, Eric Wolfgang Korngold, Mahler, Britten, Humperdinck, Berg, Shoenberg.

Giuseppe Verdi was a contemporary of Wagner but lived for a further eighteen years. Verdi was a great composer but not my cup of tea. I found the story of *Il Trovatore* quite boring, although the music was lovely. His *Nabucco* made him a national hero, especially "Va, pensiero", also known as the "Chorus of the Hebrew Slaves". It recollects the period of Babylonian captivity after the loss of the First Temple in Jerusalem in 586 BCE. The libretto is by Temistocle Solera, inspired by Psalm 137. There are some very nice pieces in *Luisa Miller* – e.g. "Quando le sere al placido". *Luisa Miller* is an opera in three acts by Verdi to an Italian libretto by Salvadore Cammarano, based on the play *Kabale und Liebe* by the German dramatist Friedrich von Schiller. *Rigoletto* is an opera in three acts, the Italian libretto written by Francesco Maria Piave based on the play *Le roi s'amuse* by Victor Hugo, a fine opera stuffed with fine music.

*La Traviata* tells the story of the tragic love between the Violetta Valery, a glamorous Parisian courtesan and the romantic Alfredo Germont, a young bourgeois from a provincial family When Alfredo's father directly appeals to Violetta to relinquish her one chance of happiness, Violetta submits, and her act of self-sacrifice leads to her paying the ultimate price. Perhaps this is the greatest theme of *La Traviata*. The opera is a touching story, not just because it is a story people can believe in, but because it is a story people want to believe in. It encourages the ideal that it is possible to experience the joy of a pure, redemptive love. I attended *La Traviata* on three occasions, in 2009 at the Staatsoper Unter den Linden, in September 2016 in Berlin and again Bayerischer Staatsoper München, the most beautiful opera house in Europe – apart from Russia.

Beethoven wrote only one opera. *Fidelio* was premiered on the 20th of November 1805 at the Theater auf der Wieden in Vienna. The overture was changed on four occasions. One aria "Komm, Hoffnung, lass den letzten Stern" by Leonore stands out. *Fidelio* is set in the eighteenth century, in a prison in Seville. Floristan is a Spanish noble dumped into prison by Pizarro, the prison Governor, for no good reason. Floristan's wife, Leonore dresses as a man and gets a job in the prison. She later sings a fantastic aria: "Abscheulicher, wo eilst du hin?". An attempt to stab Floristan by Pizarro fails due to the intervention of Leonore. There is a wonderful choral piece when the prisoners are allowed out into the air. This is a must-see opera.

I was at the English National Opera some twenty years ago, seated beside an elderly lady. Elderly ladies are filled to the brim with wisdom! The lady asked, "Have you attended Grimes?" I said, "No." "You must see Grimes," she said. I did finally attend my first *Peter Grimes* at Staatsoper and *Il Trovatore* at Volksoper on the 1st of December and the 30th of November, respectively. *Peter Grimes* is an opera by Benjamin Britten, with a libretto adapted by Montagu Slater from the narrative poem, "Peter Grimes", in George

Crabbe's book *The Borough*. Peter Grimes is a fisherman, living in a small Suffolk town. He is summoned to court after the death of his young apprentice at sea; the townspeople are convinced Grimes is to blame, but he is let off with a caution and warned not to take another apprentice. During a coroner's inquest at the town hall, the lawyer Swallow questions Grimes about the death of his apprentice during a storm at sea. Though the room is crowded with villagers who are hostile to Grimes, Swallow accepts the man's explanation of the event and rules that the boy died accidentally. He warns Grimes not to take on another apprentice unless he lives with a woman who can care for the boy. When the hall empties, Ellen Orford, the schoolmistress, asks Grimes to have courage and promises to help him find a better life.

The production of *Grimes* was brilliant. Beautiful opera with beautiful music. Interlude number five Pathos musically scored. One of six such interludes. In the Staatsoper, a blue inner screen dropped down for each interlude. We had a prologue followed by three acts with one pause for Act I, one hour of music. The diction was outstanding. Subtitles were on the backrest of the chair in front. English, German and French. The principals were Herbert Lippet as Peter Grimes, Gun-Brit Barkmin as Ellen Oxford, Ian Paterson as Balstrode, Antie-Monika as Bohinec, Wolfgang Bankel as Swallow, Christine Mielitz as Reggie and Graeme Jenkins as Ditigent. The chorus was outstanding with rowing scenes, assisted with the raising and lowering of the stage floor, large oars, all ebbing and flowing with contrary motion. The stage pictures were beautiful — blues, reds. Das Mond! The Prentice, a young boy (silent) was excellent, playing his role to perfection. Herbert Lippert is a fine singer, as were all others, with perfect English diction. The mob scene was as good as anything else I've seen on an opera stage, if not better. They were evil to the core. Evil is viral, a contagion. The mob after an "outsider", menacing. The scene was conducted most excellently. The interludes were beautiful with memories of Billy Budd, just before his execution by suspended strangulation, a slow and brutal death. The cruelty of man at his blood-lusting worst. Music wrought from pathos and empathy, scored from personal pain and suffering.

Johann Sebastian Bach was born in Eisenach in 1685. He could play organ and violin. He travelled a lot until finally settling in Leipzig, were in due course he was appointed Kantor of the Thomaskirche, in 1723. Bach was a towering genius. He designed the "Well -Tempered Clavier" comprising scales of Major and Minor keys. While frequency between keys wasn't perfect, it was almost so. He was a prolific composer unequalled; his output was enormous. He had composer sons: Carl Philipp, Emanuel and Wilhelm Friedemann. Bach wrote for the Lutheran Church. He wrote Oratorios such as The St John Passion, 1723 and the *St. Matthew Passion* 1729, and the Christmas Oratorio. He wrote a Mass and 198 Cantatas. My favourite are Cantatas are 140 and 147: "Wachet auf, ruft uns die Stimme" and "Herz und Mund und Tat und Leben".

I attended my first *Matthew Passion* in March 2008 in the Thomaskirche. Three hours of woundingly beautiful music. Solo voices, Chorus and orchestra. Bach's tomb is in the church. Next day I attended *Parsifal* at Oper Leipzig. Since then I have attended three *Matthew Passions*: 2011 in Concertgebouw Amsterdam, in 2013 at the National Concert Hall, Dublin and April 2015, again in Leipzig. Leipzig is one of my favourite cities for music. It has the Gewandhaus, Oper Leipzig and the Thomaskirche. Unlike Dresden it wasn't bombed to rubble during World War II. In Dresden, the Marienkirche was reduced to rubble but eventually rebuilt. I had the privilege of attending a concert there some years ago. In his later years Bach suffered from poor eyesight. He had an operation, the outcome of which was to make him blind. A sad end for a man who gave so much to the world and to Music.

*Faust* is based on the novel *Faust und Margarethe* by Johann Wolfgang von Goethe and the libretto was created by Jules Barbier and Michel Carré. It is the story of the old Doctor Faust who once again wants to be young and feel the passion of love. He completed a pact with the devil, Mephistopheles who helps him to seduce the beautiful Marguerite. The aria "Faites-lui mes aveux" (Flowersong) is sung in the third act by Siebel.

In Act I, Faust now old longs for youth. He plans to poison himself but sees in the street a beautiful girl. Mephistopheles suddenly appears and offers youth in return for Faust's Soul. There is a duet for both "A moi les plaisirs". In Act II, a crowd scene, chorus and dancing. Act III, we have two stunning duets for lovers, the highlight is "Air des Bijoux" (The Jewel Song). Faust sings "Faites-lui mes aveux". Act III, the lovers unite. Act IV, we have the "Soldiers' Chorus" a bright and lively number! Act V we find Marguerite in prison condemned to death for killing her child. A superb duet culminating with the angels bearing Marguerite to Heaven. Beautiful music. I attended *Faust* at the Gaiety Theatre in Dublin, in April 2006, remembering as always, my first opera *Turandot* there in 1986, twenty years older now and like Doctor Faust, wishing I could turn back the years.

In December 2014, I treated myself to *Hänsel und Gretel* in Munich at the historic Bavarian Staatsoper. *Hänsel und Gretel* was composed by nineteenth-century composer Engelbert Humperdinck, who described it as a fairy-tale opera. The libretto was written by Humperdinck's sister, Adelheid Wette, based on the Grimm brothers' fairy tale *Hansel and Gretel*. It is much admired for its folk music-inspired themes, one of the most famous being the "Abendsegen" (Evening Benediction) from act 2. Adelheid had written songs for her children for Christmas and after several revisions, the musical sketches and the songs were turned into a full-scale opera. Humperdinck composed *Hänsel und Gretel* in Frankfurt in 1891 and 1892. The opera was first performed in The Deutsche Nationaltheater and Staatskapelle Weimar on the 23rd of December 1893, conducted by Richard Strauss. It has been associated with

Christmas since its earliest performances and today it is still most often performed at Christmas time.

Engelbert Humperdinck met Wagner in Italy in 1980 while on a Mendelssohn travelling scholarship. They met in Naples and Wagner invited him to Bayreuth the following year to work as a copyist i.e. a colour grinder. Humperdinck arrived in Bayreuth and immediately engaged in work with Wagner, receiving first sheets of his *Parsifal* score. Wagner was working on the tricky Act I Transformation Scene, where a rolling cyclorama (a theatrical scenery invention in 1883) depicts the slow transformation of a gloomy forest into the Temple of the Holy Grail. Wagner could not get the scenery to roll fast enough, to fit the four-and-a-half minutes of music that he allotted for the scene change. Humperdinck was asked by the Meister himself to write an extension – three to five minutes of music – extending the tolling-bell theme of the Verwandlungsmusik, manipulating Wagner's thematic material to make the scenery synch properly to the moving image. The music was reportedly composed, added to the score, and used in rehearsals by conductor Hermann Levi. Before the premiere, Wagner's technical team fixed the uncooperative scenery, and Humperdinck's brief time of being heard at Bayreuth was over. The first performance was on the 25th of July, 1882. The work was received with prolonged applause, Wagner did not appear on the stage, but in the last performance, in the last Act, Wagner took the baton and conducted the act to its end. Humperdinck last met Wagner in Venice where Wagner died in 1883. There is a beautiful and moving account of the relationship between Humperdinck and Wagner, in Robert Hartford's Book *Bayreuth the Early Years* (ISBN 0 521 23822 6 1980).

Richard Strauss (1864-1949), composer of *Salome* (1905) and *Electra* (1909), *Der Rosenkavalier* and others was also a conductor, pianist, and violinist. Considered a leading composer of the late Romantic and early modern eras, he has been described as a successor of Richard Wagner and Franz Liszt. The soprano Pauline de

Ahna was the powerful presence behind Richard Strauss: his wife, his inspiration and a diva in every sense. Over his lifetime Strauss drew on many different forms of inspiration, but none more constantly than the soprano voice.

*Der Rosenkavalier*, (The Knight of the Rose) a comic opera in three acts premiered at the Dresden Royal Opera House the 26th of January1911. The opera is set in Vienna during the reign of Empress Maria Theresa. Strauss worked many waltzes into the score. The waltz, an early 19th-century creation, was unknown in 18th-century Vienna, but it was a staple in light opera at the beginning of the 20th century. Within a year of its Dresden premiere, *Der Rosenkavalier* had reached the stages of Vienna, Munich, Nürnberg, Cologne, Hamburg, Milan (in Italian), and Prague (in Czech), among many other European cities. In 1913, productions would be staged both in London and at the Metropolitan Opera House in New York City. At La Scala in Milan, purists booed the waltzes, which they viewed as suitable only for dance music. Nonetheless, *Der Rosenkavalier* was hugely popular and has remained the most often performed of Strauss's operas.

Act I: In the Marschallin's bedroom, the Marschallin Princess von Werdenberg and her young lover, Octavian, are awakening from a rapturous night. Octavian hides quickly as a servant comes in with breakfast. Soon after he returns to bed, there is a clamour in the outer room. The Marschallin recognizes the voice as that of her overbearing and crude cousin, Baron Ochs. She tells Octavian to hide behind the screen and find some clothes. Ochs storms in, demanding his cousin's attention. Although he is a nobleman, he has little money, so he intends to marry the young rich bourgeois Sophie. According to tradition, he must find a well-born messenger to present a perfumed silver rose to the woman as a marriage proposal.

The Marschallin mischievously recommends Count Rofrano (Octavian) for the job, and Ochs agrees. Octavian has reappeared, dressed in women's clothes as the housemaid Mariandel. Ochs flirts with her. Meanwhile, a number of visitors arrive in succession, demanding the Marschallin's attention. As an Italian tenor sings an aria, Ochs attempts to bully a lawyer into writing out a marriage contract that will favour him greatly. Mariandel slips away.

After everyone has left, the Marschallin reflects on her lost youth. Octavian returns, in his own clothing, and the Marschallin tells him that sometimes she gets up in the night and stops all the clocks hoping to hold time in its place. She declares that he will one day leave her for a younger woman, and he leaves in great distress. When she realizes that she has neglected to kiss him goodbye, she tries unsuccessfully to have him returned to her house.

Act II: In her father's reception hall, Sophie von Faninal awaits the arrival of the Knight of the Rose. Handsome and elegantly dressed, Octavian arrives bearing the silver rose in advance of the bridegroom's arrival. The two young people promptly fall for each other. Ochs comes in, accompanied by his loutish entourage, and he treats Sophie patronisingly. His extreme confidence turns Sophie off and she declares that she will not have him. When Ochs tries to force the issue, Octavian angrily draws his sword. The scene ends with chaos. Sophie's father threatens to send her back to the convent (where she has been at school) if she does not agree to the marriage.

Act III: In a private room at a seedy inn, the scene is set for a plan meant to humble the obnoxious Ochs. Mariandel has agreed to meet him, and they arrive together. His plans of seduction repeatedly run awry with continual interruptions by other conspirators; the ensuing pandemonium brings in the police. Ochs's mood is not improved by the arrival of Sophie and her father, who express shock. Mariandel hides and changes clothes and then returns as Count Rofrano. Then the Marschallin enters. Faced with all the people he most wished to impress Ochs marches off in a huff. After Baron Faninal leaves, only the Marschallin, Octavian, and Sophie remain. They reflect upon their different views on love. The Marschallin, with much sentimental feeling, surrenders her place in Octavian's life to the younger woman, and a duet is sung by Sophie and Octavian. "We are together," Octavian proclaims. "All else is like a dream."

I saw this wonderful opera for the first and only time at the Stralsund Theatre on the 12th of May 2010.

# CHAPTER 22

## *Changing Times*

*Tosca* is an opera in three acts by Giacomo Puccini to an Italian libretto by Luigi Illica and Giuseppe Giacosa. It premiered at the Teatro Costanzi in Rome on 14 January 1900. Tosca is a political thriller, set in Rome in June 1800, during the Napoleonic wars and a time of great political unrest. The plot centres around three main characters: Rome's diva Floria Tosca, her lover Mario Cavaradossi (a painter and republican) and the corrupt Chief of Police, Baron Scarpia. Scarpia has long lusted after Tosca, and when he suspects Cavaradossi of assisting an escaped political prisoner, seizes the opportunity to kill two birds with one stone. He will manipulate Tosca into revealing the prisoner's hiding place and Cavaradossi's involvement and have her for himself. When Cavaradossi is captured, Scarpia offers Tosca a horrific bargain – she must give herself to Scarpia, or her lover will be killed.

*Tosca* contains some of opera's most iconic music: The famous soprano aria "Vissi d'arte" (I lived for art), which is sung by Tosca during Act II of the opera. Finding both herself and her lover at the mercy of Scarpia, she prays, musing over her darkened fate and asking why God has seemingly abandoned her. Amazingly, this spellbinding moment of reverence and intense emotion was almost cut by Puccini, who believed the aria held up the action!

The heart-wrenching "E lucevan le stelle" (The stars were shining brightly), is Cavaradossi's farewell to life, sung as he awaits execution, and is one of the most popular arias in the Italian tenor repertoire.

The hugely impressive "Te deum" which closes Act I contrasts the sacred and the profane – the full chorus sing the "Te deum" hymn while Scarpia gloatingly anticipates his conquest of Tosca, accompanied by vast orchestral forces, organ, church bells, and cannon fire every four bars (which signals that the prisoner Angelotti has escaped).

I travelled to Staatsoper Wien in February 2019 to see *Tosca*. It was just after the launch of my first book, *Elegy for a Broken Soldier*. I was feeling a bit at sea, feeling under pressure from my publisher and others to publicise the book. But I backed away, quite at a loss as to how to deal with 'marketing' and all that goes with it – which I was learning for the first time. I had thought that everything would happen once the book had an ISBN and had gone into print; that it would automatically be found on Amazon and be snatched up by bookshops everywhere! I was in for a shock. I discovered that I would have to do a lot of legwork but talking to bookshop owners was too daunting. *Tosca* awaited. A 5.15 a.m. start from home on the 6th of February and an overnight in Vienna. *Tosca* had the Polish tenor, Piotr Beczala, now the world's greatest, and Thomas Hampson, baritone, the best. I loved the aria, "Recondita armonia", and "Vissi d'arte, vissi d'amore" was simply divine.

Handel was one of the most prolific composers ever. I loved his music, even as a child. In the recent past, I attended *Alcina* in Zurich opera house. The role of Ruggiero was sung by Philippe Jaroussky, Countertenor. He is a beautiful singer, the best Countertenor in the world. He can also play piano and violin to conservatory standard. He is French but his great-grandfather was Russian. I have attended Handel's *Messiah* on several occasions. *Messiah* is the New Testament converted into Music. Kenneth McKellar was an outstanding singer of the repertoire. Perfect diction. In the Sir

Adrian Bolt double CD of *Messiah*, there are additional tracks with McKellar singing pieces e.g. *Semele*. The work is comprised of 53 pieces composed in 1741 and premiered in Dublin on the 13th of April 1742. Piece no. 13 "PIFA" the "Pastoral Symphony" is used in the film *Manchester by the Sea*. The Oratorio opens with "Comfort ye my people".

It is beyond the scope of this book to list all the works I have attended; there are far too many. In thirty-three years, I have been to over three hundred performances across Europe. There have also been concerts and minor appearances by artistes at various venues in Ireland and overseas but although most of them were no doubt extremely enjoyable I have forgotten them. All in all, expenditure on performance tickets, flights, taxis, trains, accommodation and meals has amounted to a fortune – and cost me in other ways: on a number of occasions, a frantic phone call to my physician or a friend, or on one occasion an overnight in hospital, due to a panic attack. Yoga breathing learned late in life, as well as sheer force of will helped me through a very dodgy episode of a cardiac nature during a recent stay in Vienna. A visit to my cardiologist on my return home resulted in a change of medication. In March 2018, I had to have a second Cather ablation. For now, things have settled down again. Too often I have returned home exhausted, but I simply must go. I need the music. I need to be in the atmosphere of the theatre, watching the performers live on stage and listening to the orchestra in the proper acoustical setting.

In January 2020 I took myself to the National Concert Hall, Dublin to see *Fidelio* by Ludwig van Beethoven. It is Beethoven's only opera. The story is about how Leonore, disguised as a prison guard called 'Fidelio', rescues her husband Florestan from death in a political prison. *Fidelio* is an example of a "rescue opera", a type of opera in which the hero (or heroine) has to fight against cruel people in order to rescue a lover. It was written at the time of the French Revolution. At this time, ideas about freedom and peace were being talked about by everyone, and this led to wars all over Europe. The famous "Prisoners' Chorus" is a song for freedom, just like the last movement of Beethoven's *Ninth Symphony*.

The first time it was performed (in 1805) it was a three-act opera called *Leonore*. There were a lot of French military officers in the audience and they thought they were being criticised. In 1806 it was performed again with two acts and a new overture (now known as "Overture: Leonore No. 3"). But arguments between Beethoven and the theatre management meant there were no more performances. Eight years later Beethoven revised his opera again. This time it was called *Fidelio*, and it was a great success. It has remained a famous opera ever since.

I had tickets for *Lohengrin* in Barcelona in March, *Tristan und Isolde* in Berlin in November as well as *Parsifal* and *Elixir of Love* by Gaetano Donizetti. At the beginning of March, the now infamous 'Corona Virus' pandemic put paid to everything. The world went into lockdown. As I write, we have entered Phase 1 in an 'easing of restrictions' – perhaps a restaurant here and there reopening at reduced capacity, schools reopening gradually, with staggered timetables, hardware shops reopening and maybe the easing of travel restrictions. In this atmosphere of uncertainty, I am aware that although, the lockdown has not made much difference to my life in any way other than travel I suspect that my opera days are numbered.

The response to this pandemic has been much more rigorous and severe than to others. During the Hong Kong Flu in 1968 and 1969, after five years in the army, I was busy chancing my luck in the civilian workforce, ending with Aer Lingus at Dublin Airport where I joined a team of college students on the windy tarmac, loading and unloading baggage, sometimes amid the detritus of the aircraft toilets that was whipped about by the wind. Among the contents of the hold, steel coffins in transit, bound for repatriation and burial to other destinations were a grim reminder of the Vietnam War, still raging in South East Asia. But it was a tragic accident that brought a young Irish soldier home from Cyprus. Trooper Michael Kennedy died on July 1st, 1969 in a swimming pool accident and his remains were received with military honours at Dublin Airport. I met some of my old army friends who were in the guard of honour and as I watched the cortege move away, I suddenly felt adrift. I wanted to be back with my comrades in uniform. The 'Troubles' in Northern Ireland prompted me to re-enlist. In comparison to other pandemics, the Hong Kong flu yielded a low death rate. This pandemic struck in two waves with the second wave being deadlier than the first in most places. The same virus returned the following years: a year later, in late 1969 and early 1970, and in 1972. The total worldwide death toll is estimated to have been in the region of one million people. But unlike today, travel was unrestricted. Life in Ireland was about to change, but not because of flu.

Changes had been afoot in the echelons of power for almost a decade. Free secondary school education, introduced in 1966, would come too late for me but two significant factors contributed to the shift from the inward-looking Church and State policies of the 1940s and 1950s to the establishment of our country's role on the world stage. One was Ireland's admission to the United Nations and the other, the initiation of a programme for economic recovery. In 1951 I had just started school at Basin Lane in Dublin when Seán Lemass, veteran of the 1916 Easter Rising and the War of Independence, became Minister for Industry and Commerce. Lemass believed that a new economic policy was needed. But in the government mansion on Kildare Street T.K. (Ken) Whitaker, a thirty-five-year-old public servant from Rostrevor, north of the border was writing up a paper entitled, "Economic Development" out of which grew the Programme for Economic Expansion. The programme gave new hope to a country with a stagnant economy and mounting unemployment. Whitaker's programme was embraced by Seán Lemass and when Lemass became Taoiseach, tax breaks and grants were provided by his government to foreign firms wishing to set up operations in Ireland. Between them, Seán Lemass and T.K. Whitaker launched an integrated system of national development and the framework of the modern Irish economy.

Ireland's active participation at the United Nations would have an enormous impact on global issues. At home, its effects would run deep. Thousands of Irish families would offer sons, fathers and brothers to military service and for the first time since the foundation of the State, Irish soldiers would serve overseas under their country's flag – and under the blue flag of the United Nations. I would be among them.

I am still a soldier, doggedly holding my "station", plotting next year's schedule – Bayreuth, *Tannhäuser*, *Meistersinger*, maybe *Lohengrin*. Thirty-four years of exquisite music, the only respite from darkness will not be easy to relinquish. Watching an opera on DVD or listening to a CD is just not the same. I have a suitcase full of programmes – part of my library of books, DVDs and CDs that I hope will go to a music library in UCD or Trinity College. For now, this collection reminds me of the joy I have experienced through the music that became my saviour; my enduring comfort in the years that followed a terrifying incident in Jerusalem, when innocence, beauty and *joie de vivre* had been stripped away. Homeward bound, I carried a deep, dark secret. I could feel my stomach and chest tightening as the plane approached Dublin. At home, I could hardly speak to anyone.

I had immediately applied to return to overseas duty. I knew the drill in the army. I could hide from the world in the force and by working hard, I could keep the torment at bay. I had people there with whom I could relate, and I now knew how to be on my guard; for much of the time I would have a weapon and I would use it! I also knew that I would never sleep soundly overseas. Paradoxically, the only solution to my torment seemed to lie in getting away again. While I waited for my month's leave to be up, I stayed in my bedroom listening to Roy Orbison records. I played 'Only the Lonely' over and over, an apt accompaniment to my own loneliness as I sank deeper and deeper into morbidity. I had become addicted to overseas duty until a life-threatening incident in Lebanon in 1980 effectively ended my interest in progressing my career in the defence forces any further and I left in 1986. Then, overseas duty was replaced by overseas opera.

Whitaker's Programme for Economic Expansion grew and grew until the early 2000s when roads became motorways that shaved an hour or more off journeys across the country, when villages became towns and the skyline over Dublin bristled with cranes as glass boxes sprung up – and out – across the city and by 2010, the monster that was the "Celtic Tiger" had left new social classes and an increase in the population of nearly two million in its wake. Mass emigration followed, a replay of the 1930s, 1940s and 1950s – once again, a stagnant economy and another "brain drain": because of free secondary education which had opened up third level to the working classes, young graduates were joining the tradespeople to find work abroad. Now, just months into a new decade we face the unknown.

Like everyone else, I have taken change in my stride, but these strange times seem to have brought change to a new level: everyday things that I used to take for granted are no longer there – some family members and friends who have been mostly in 'isolation' have been out of reach, the travel restrictions also preventing visits to each other's homes or even to a café for a coffee and a chat. Freedom of movement as we have known it has been suspended for months and life is changing again – for everyone. A sense of security that, even if illusory at the best of times, we still cling to and no matter how uncertain, holds us in a world that appears familiar is fading fast. As I reflect on these things, the opening line from a monologue by the character, Jacques, in Shakespeare's play, *As You Like It* comes to mind:

*All the world's a stage, and all the men and women merely players:*
*they have their exits and their entrances; and one man in his time plays*
*many parts, his acts being seven ages.*

Shakespeare saw life as a drama acted out on a stage and each
phase of life as an act in the drama. He understood a lot about the
lives of monarchs, about low life in the inns and taverns of London,
and he knew about the lives of country people as well as about
warfare and diplomacy and he used the theatre to hold the mirror
up to nature. This monologue is a way of presenting a man's journey from birth to the grave. And again, in *Macbeth*, the king says:

*Life's but a walking shadow, a poor player,*
*That struts and frets his hour upon the stage,*
*And then is heard no more.*
*It is a tale*
*Told by an idiot, full of sound and fury,*
*Signifying nothing.*

There are about two hundred operas based on Shakespeare's
plays, among them, Verdi's *Otello*, Berlioz's *Beatrice and Benedict*,
Britten's *Midsummer Night's Dream*. Richard Strauss was an avid
fan of Shakespeare. *Macbeth, Op. 23*, is a symphonic poem written by Strauss between 1886 and 1888. It was his first tone poem,
which he described as 'a completely new path' for him in terms of
composition.

Opera – like Shakespeare's dramas – involves hatred and cruelty, the pain of loss as well as love – the gamut of emotion sung
rather than spoken, the orchestral music soaring and falling, taking the audience with it; music that has been my haven from the
everyday world. In this sole pursuit, I may have cut myself off
from other possibilities. With the recent changes wrought by the
Corona Virus – or "Covid19", as it is called – comes the realisation that our world is a stage, and life as fragile and ephemeral as
any made-up story.

Of course, one of the major casualties of the Corona pandemic is the cancellation of the Bayreuth Festival. Every year the faithful ascend the city's famed Green Hill to the orange, brick-clad Festspielhaus built by Wagner himself to present his revolutionary works, among them his four-part *Ring* cycle in the innovative setting he felt it required. The Bayreuth Festival became the first music festival of modern times, except that at Bayreuth, only Wagner's works are presented. After his death in 1883, the festival and the theatre became a hallowed shrine for his followers. This year, the Bayreuth Festival has been suspended and the new production of the *Ring* planned for this year will probably not be able to celebrate its premiere until 2022. Bavaria's Minister of Art, Bernd Sibler is just one of many who regret that we will not be able to enjoy the performances on the Green Hill this year. "For cultural life, the cancellation is a bitter loss," he said.

Yet, through all the disasters of modern German history, the festival has endured. In the same week Eva Wagner was born in a neighbouring village in April 1945, Allied warplanes levelled two-thirds of Bayreuth. Wahnfried the stately home and gravesite was forty-five percent destroyed in the first of four bombing raids. But somehow the Festspielhaus was spared. By 1951, the festival was up and running again under the direction of Wieland Wagner, the composer's grandson. Yet Wagner devotees have not wavered, queuing up for a decade and more to attend. The reward is a direct encounter with the sublime. This is enthralling music and elemental drama to touch the soul.

Today thousands of books are listed in the Library of Congress catalogue under Wagner's name. Still more have been published in his bicentennial year, more are being currently written and twenty-two new and revived *Ring* productions are being launched across the world.

In my pursuit of healing, I found music and was ultimately so drawn to the music of Richard Wagner that I felt compelled to try to bring his music to a wider audience. For this reason, I founded the Wagner Society of Ireland in 2002. Despite my subsequent troubled association with the society, it still exists, and I have treasured memories of the activities that my role as founder afforded me, not least the privilege of meeting members of the Wagner family.

If you have ever been roused by the wedding march "Here Comes the Bride" (from Wagner's *Lohengrin*) or seen the film *Apocalypse Now* (The Ride of the Valkyries helicopter assault), you have already tasted the nectar. Those of us who have immersed ourselves in Wagner's full operas, some of which are lengthy and demanding yet flowing and turbulent like a great river, have experienced a sense of awe.

# CHAPTER 23

# *The Young Friends*

Each generation comes to Wagner anew. Since 1949, The Society of Friends of Bayreuth has ensured the longevity of the Bayreuth Festival, thanks to the support of its 5,300 Friends and numerous sponsors. Without the Society of Friends of Bayreuth, there would be no Festival. The Society gathers enthusiasts of Wagner and his heritage from around the world – people and companies who are keen to perpetuate and constantly reinvent his grand tradition. The Friends' mission is to maintain Wagner's work and ideals through the maintenance and restoration of the Festspielhaus: the ultimate venue for Wagner's operas, designed by the composer himself and the financing of annual productions of the Festival.

The Young Friends of Bayreuth is an initiative to give young Wagnerians an opportunity to gain interesting insights into festival events, the activities behind the scenes, the artistic work, including joint opera and rehearsal visits at Bayreuth Festival and other opera houses, as well as workshops and discussions to bring them closer to the world of Richard Wagner. I had the good fortune to meet two of the young friends – twin brothers, Paul and Johannes Marsovszky in 2018.

While I was studying Psychology at UCD, our lecturer, the late Dr Delaney introduced us to Sir Cyril Burt's thesis on "Nurture and Nature", as regards twins – i.e. Diazygotic and Monozygotic. Burt was an English educational psychologist and geneticist who also made contributions to statistics. He is known for his studies on the heritability of IQ. Now, I had met two young men who not only looked identical, but who shared the same interests and possessed the same genius.

I met Paul Marsovszky and his brother Johannes during the first interval after Act I, of Lohengrin on the 6th of August 2018, at the Bayreuther Festspiele. Afterwards we maintained contact by way of social media, and I met them again the following year in MUPA (Palace of the Arts) in Budapest at the *Ring*, a four-day, back-to-back version. Both Paul and Johannes have honours masters' degrees in music, both are graduates of conducting at the Franz Liszt Academy of Music, Budapest. Meeting people like these young geniuses makes me glad that, despite everything, I founded the Wagner Society of Ireland and through the society I have been able to contribute to The Young Friends of Bayreuth, thus supporting future generations in bringing the music to even wider audiences around the world. I asked Paul to write a paper on the art of conducting, to which he kindly agreed. I wish to devote the final chapter to his very insightful piece, through which his enthusiasm and expertise shines.

# ABOUT CONDUCTING

## *Paul Marsovszky*

### Introduction

I have been in regular contact with Christopher McQuaid since August 2018, when we first met in the first intermission of *Lohengrin* by Richard Wagner during the Bayreuth Festival. This prestigieous festival is held annually at the very festival theatre that Wagner designed and constructed for his operas. By a sheer miracle it was not bombarded during the second world war, and its original wooden structure of stage and audience room, which gives it its unique sound, remained intact.

If I had been told a year prior, that I would witness three performances of the operas of my most favourite composer in this very place, I would have had trouble believing it. Ticket prices are high, hotel prices even higher, and not too long ago several-year-long waiting lists were in place. The very first Wagner Society was founded by Richard Wagner himself to let people, especially the youth, get to know his music. I was fortunate to receive the Bayreuth Scholarship, offered by the Budapest Wagner Society, to which I owe utmost gratitude. This granted my trip to Bayreuth.

During this intermission I stood by the entrance, and Christopher (whom I did not know) stepped out of the door with the words "That was fun!". We started a conversation, and (as with Wagner enthusiasts) immediately built a true connection and a lasting friendhip, for which I am truly thankful.

Since my graduation from the Franz Liszt Music Academy Budapest a few months prior, this has been truly the coronation and biggest reward of my years as a conducting student. A year later I started working as an assistant conductor with Ivan Fischer and the Budapest Festival Orchestra, with whom working is fascinating and inspiring. It is from these experiences that I took the courage to accept Christopher's kind offer to write this article about the profession I love most. It is based on my observations and experiences and I hope it helps you in understanding this métier, and being more able to judge a conductor on stage. The examples of conducting technique are my own. These and similar ones are in every detailed professional literature.

My sincere thanks go to Christopher, for his kind idea of including my article into his book.

    I.    Historical overview – how to become a conductor?
    II.   Technical approach – how to study scores?
    III.  The position of the conductor
    IV.  Beyond the score – when is conducting art?

## I. Historical overview

The famous composer Richard Wagner recalls in his book on conducting, *Über das Dirigieren*,[1] that in his childhood orchestras were mostly led by the concertmaster,[2] without a conductor, and orchestras would play through the major works every winter, resulting in solid performances. In the early 18th century, when operas were performed, conductors were not in front of the ensemble, but rather directly in front of the stage instructing, giving cues only to the singers on stage (which was usually at chest height), while the

---

[1] Wagner, Richard. On Conducting (Über das Dirigieren): a Treatise on Style in the Execution of Classical Music. English translation by Edward Dannreuther
[2] The first player of the first violin, who is not only section leader, but also leader of the entire orchestra

concertmaster held the orchestra together. Later, conductors worked from the harpsichord or fortepiano,[3] like

W. A. Mozart did. J. S. Bach led his cantatas often from the violin.

Early portraits show conductors using rolled up music sheets to enhance their gestures, making them more visible. The next step would be the familiar white conductor's baton; a painted, straight stick, it is no more than that. The handle varies in length, shape (ball, pear, stick), material (wood, plastic), some have weights inside etc. A lot of these are irrelevant to the purpose, which is to provide a good grip, so the baton does not fly away (which still happens sometimes). Wagner and Bruckner are portrayed with shorter batons, Toscanini often had a longer one, each to their own liking. Although the popular association of the baton is what distinguishes him (or her), it is not the baton itself that makes a conductor.

In Richard Wagner's times composers often conducted their own works, conducting was therefore a consequence of composing. But since the popularity of some works extended beyond their composers' lifespan, more and more musicians and composers performed works of others (i.e. Wagner conducting Beethoven's 9th symphony in Bayreuth, 1872 at the ceremony to mark the laying of the foundation stone for the Festival Theatre).

Carl Maria von Weber is one of the first conductors in the modern sense, meaning a person who rehearses (new compositions were previously played mostly prima vista)[4] and conducts a given piece. It was certainly in the late classical / early romantic period that the need arose for a leading role to be played by someone who was not limited by having to play an instrument simultaneously, during rehearsals and concerts.

However, people living solely off of their conducting activities

---

[3] Early version of today's piano
[4] First sight

came much later, the best example being Gustav Mahler, who was a conductor by profession during the opera season. He had time to compose only during the summer when the theatre and orchestra season was over. Therefore the type of conductor we know today is a phenomenon of the modern era.

### How to become a conductor?

If somebody wishes to acquire the skill of a conductor, we can trace the history of conducting schools for guidance. Many didn't appear until the second half of the 20th century, the most famous being Hans Swarowsky's conducting class in Vienna. Before that, conductors like Toscanini, Mahler, Furtwängler etc studied an instrument and composition. The combination of an instrument (piano being the most practical for this profession) and theoretical studies has remained the norm today for becoming a conductor.

Learning to express yourself on an instrument is the first step. Later, harmonic studies, composition techniques, building up knowledge about the various instruments, learning about singing, all contribute to the overall skills of the conductor.

Naturally there are quite a number of conductors who were soloists or orchestral musicians before, and later discovered their interest in leading an ensemble.

For those who chose to study conducting, there are three main ways to become a working conductor after the studies:

By starting as a repetitor at an opera house or theatre. This is a long way of getting to know the repertoire, working with singers and establish a well built up knowledge.

Sometimes a repetitor is asked to conduct a rehearsal, or in cases a performance for a colleague who has fallen ill. A good performance can give rise to more and more opportunities.

By assisting a conductor with their orchestra. Conductors usually work with assistants (in the opera other conductors or repetitors assist with rehearsals) who listen during rehearsals, correct balance issues or situations in which musicians are not playing together, etc.

Similar to being a repetitor, one can learn the repertoire and get useful experience on rehearsal technique this way.

Conducting competitions are a way of achieving quick success and getting assignments with different orchestras.

When asked for advice by a conducting student, Carlos Kleiber described the ways of becoming a conductor as follows[5]:

*"Try as coach [assistant] in some opera company [...].*

*When the conductor gets sick, there's a chance to take over the performance. If you don't blow it, you're in. ,Symphonies' can wait. Symphonic music means, mainly, rehearsal. Opera means technique, in the broader sence of the word. With a good technique you can forget technique. It's like with manners. If you know how to behave, you can missbehave. That's fun! (At least that's my theory.)"*

## II. Technical approach
### What does a conductor do?

A conductor "beats" the rhythmic structure of the music, which is written in a specific "time signature". These are bars or measures. They do not change over a longer period (as modern composers experiment with the known boundaries of music, this naturally has also undergone change, notably in the late romantic, early modern era), therefore one "pattern" remains fairly consistent. These patterns consist of beats that correlate to the music's basic rhythm:

a $\frac{4}{4}$ bar has four beats. So four points have to be reached and connected: down, left, right, up. This resembles the pattern of a cross:

---

[5] Letter to Ms Wright

in execution it looks like this:

In a $\frac{3}{4}$ bar we have a triangle (left, right, up):

in practice:

A $\frac{2}{4}$ Bar in practice (down, up):

Naturally, more complicated bars have more complicated patterns:

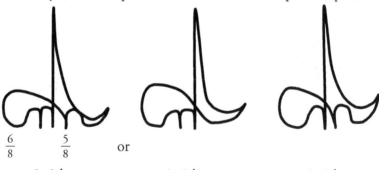

$\frac{6}{8}$     $\frac{5}{8}$     or

3+3 beats      3+2 beats      2+3 beats

But what happens, if the composer writes an accelerando?[6] The

---

[6] Getting faster

conductor beats the pattern faster and faster, until it gets too fast: then the pattern is divided, a simpler pattern is applied:

$\frac{4}{4}$ (four beats) → $\frac{2}{2}$ (two beats).

The music still has four beats, but the conductor shows two. This ensures that the musicians can follow, and that it does not appear hectic (an important aspect when dealing with the coordination of 60+ musicians – it is not an aesthetic consideration). But how to divide a $\frac{5}{8}$ bar? The solution is rather pragmatic: in two, but one beat is longer (3+2 or 2+3).

These patterns are similar in any school of conducting. Variations may occur:

and are used for $\frac{3}{4}$ bars

I prefer the first, this way nobody mistakes it for a $\frac{4}{4}$ bar (the first beat is the key here, it goes to the left, not straight down). This is important, as sometimes an instrumentalist has to wait more than 100 bars, and any changes to the bar must be as clear as possible.

Using the hands for different tasks is not easy for everyone. The dominant hand keeps showing the time, while the other can give cues, or show the more linear characteristics of the music. (These were just a few examples, and serve for a basic illustration of the first time signatures a student may learn.)

No musician in the professional world needs to watch every move of the conductor. Of greater importance is the peripheral view, in which one can see the conductor's gestures while looking at the score. Here the baton has an important role: the white stick is far more visible in the distance than the hand. Different shapes and colours maintain or lose contour when far away. Skin colour (any skin colour) and the form of the hand blur in the distance, while a baton is more visible, especially in poorly lit orchestra pits.

When observing a conductor, one can see these patterns – since each conductor's body language is different, so is the execution of these patterns. Naturally the tempo, character and dynamic alter the conducting.

When accompanying a singer or soloist, a conductor must pay attention to the singer/soloist's needs, for example when he or she needs to take a breath. Therefore the conductor must study the solo part, or the opera's text thoroughly and at the given moment delay the next beat, which signals to the orchestra that they should wait.

Conducting may differ when performing opera or a symphonic concert. Apart from festivals or special events, opera performances involve little to no rehearsals. There, a conductor has to be as clear as possible to ensure a smooth performance. Mistakes occur when information is not clear enough. At a concert performance (or at festivals), the conducting tends to be the result of one week's work with the ensemble. The musicians already know what to expect. Still, being clear is very important, but apart from transitional spots (tempo changes, structural key points), there should be no surprises. Nevertheless, the best concerts still maintain spontaneity. There are things that can be rehearsed in a certain way and still be different in concert.

**How to study scores:**
Studying scores is a long, time-consuming process. Each composition is different in orchestration, every composer uses instruments differently, creating new combinations of sound and balance. Every concert hall has its unique resonance, working on the same musical piece at a different location changes the balance, creating new challenges.

To extract the essence of an œvre, to "translate" it to the audience is the number one task.

It is vital that a conductor not only knows the score, but prepares in order to be able to think ahead of the music. One must conduct in the *present*, react to the *past* (what the orchestra plays), if needed modify the conducting, and to think in the *future*, what comes next. It is reassuring for the musicians to see a conductor making eye-contact a few bars prior to their entrance – it builds up trust. Even for the best prepared orchestra small details like these help the performance. This is why (though many ensembles exist without a conductor) a conductor is needed, even for the best orchestras. Therefore, when studying a musical piece one has first too look at the instruments that play the least to remember their entrance.

Studying scores should start by analysing the overall structure and then moving to smaller details – from big to small. The musical themes must be established. With classical symphonies this means the 1st and 2nd theme, harmonic structure and development of that, with symphonic poems or romantic operas Leitmotifs/themes. After that one should work on phrasing. A theme or motive can have different characteristics: is it leading somewhere? Is it closing a chapter? Is it new, or reminiscent of an earlier theme? All attributes like heroic, sorrowful, joyful, romantic, etc have an impact on articulation. Relations between notes, even one note at a time. Just like trying to learn a classical drama: Structure, scenes, dialogs, lines, words, single letters. from big to small.

Then the next phase can begin – putting it back together. This process must be repeated when rehearsing: taking the piece apart, rehearsing sometimes with one section alone on a melody, adding the accompaniment, then a longer passage, etc.

The result is playing the piece with an eye for the longer terms, drawing a big arch from beginning to end – with attention to local happenings.

### III. The position of a conductor

First we must look establish the different types of orchestras. There are the big symphonic orchestras, opera orchestras, chamber orchestras, self-managing ensembles, baroque orchestras, etc. Some play entirely without a conductor, so for our topic the bigger orchestras are relevant. In some, the musicians vote on which conductors to invite (not all orchestras, by far, have votes or preferences, but a lot do).

Usually musicians decide on whom to invite to audition, and finally vote on them. The programme is decided by a team consisting of the director, manager, and the chief conductor. Aspects like a soloist's request regarding a concert piece, festivals, thematic program of the season, all weigh in on the decision.

The orchestra is built up in sections, winds, brass, percussion (timpani is mostly a section of its own), strings. each section can have sections of their own (Strings: double bass, cello, viola, 2nd violin, 1st violin), each of which has a section leader. The section leaders decide on bowing, fingering, articulation, etc and also hold the section rehearsals (one section alone, for examply only the violas). This way the section is well-prepared and mistakes are corrected during these smaller rehearsals.

The concertmaster leads the 1st violins, and also the orchestra. If there is a difference between the 1st and 2nd violines over a specific bowing or fingering, usually the leaders come to an agreement, but the concertmaster can decide on the outcome. Naturally if a conductor prefers a certain bowing, he can ask this of the orchestra.

The section leaders also represent the section in front of the orchestra and the conductor.

The concertmaster represents the orchestra in front of the audience and the conductor. If there are personal issues between a player and the conductor, the concertmaster has to find a way to negotiate. This hierarchy has a double role: it ensures preparatory work and discipline but also protects the musicians from personal attacks. Unfortunately, since music making is a profession involving highly differing views, opinions can grow into personal dislikes.

## IV. Beyond the score – what type of conducting is art?

This section could offer a way of judging a conductor, with or without musical education or knowledge of the given piece.

The ideal is that a conductor has syncronized his intentions with his gestures, meaning he is able to show what he wants to hear. A good conductor has tools to achieve his interpretation, he can react quickly and have an impact on the outcome.

My observation is that if the audience has trouble understanding what a conductor wants, likely the orchestra has trouble as well. The difference is that the musicians know the piece and the conductor, so they have adapted and learnt to interpret the gestures.

Sometimes people in the audience are too timid to develop an opinion, simply because they have not been trained in understanding this non-verbal communication. A good conductor will show a stable way of communication. It is best to watch when a familiar piece is played.

Looking for already-known changes in the music will help to judge – is the conductor preparing the next section? Do the movements, the gestures correspond to the music? Is it confusing or does it give clarity? In short, is it true to the music?

Hectic waving or an overexaggerated cue will seem hectic or exaggerated to the musicians too. When observing a conductor, try to focus on bars that are "not important": for example, a classical symphony will most of the time have units of eight bars, that can be further divided in two sub-units (four bars). A good conductor will emphasize the first beat of these larger units or sub-units.

The other bars and beats within these will have less intensity. It is best to show what has significance. This again is not a "cosmetic" consideration, but a way of structuring the piece. If every beat or bar is conducted the same way, they lose importance. One must build a hierarchy of bars, phrases, and these bigger steps.

When giving a cue or a soloist enters, does the conductor show the flow of the music into this, helping the soloist?

The main problem is that we play and conduct music that has been composed a long time ago and since then has been played numerous times. Each performance or recording shows a new way of interpreting it, while most stay true to the composer's intention. The difficulty (and matter of argument) is to find out what that is.

Some try to imitate the original sound to be closer to the kind of instruments and therefore sounds which were in the composer's mind. But this can only partially enlighten us, as we only reproduce the outside appearance, not the inner expression. A lot of times this results in strangely fast tempos, accentuation of bowings, notes, etc.

So, if we use periodic instruments, we must know, that it is only the first step.

Every conductor today has the dilemma of trying to find new ways of playing what we have been playing for centuries. We must determine, what is abstract in the music, that stays throughout any interpretation or recording, and what is a 'zeitgeist' phenomenon, that will disappear.

What will not work, is trying to reinvent the music. Take any opera by Mozart, whose music is perfectly clear and understandable. A good conductor will take in account the tempo relations between arias, which have a clear relation to each other, throughout the entire pieces.

### How to determine the right tempo?
Richard Wagner writes:

*"The right comprehension of the melos is the sole guide to the right tempo."*[7]

This is short for understanding how the melos / melodic line works, which can be a number of tempos, but within a certain limit.

In conclusion, after our brief historical overview, we discussed the different stages of acquiring the knowledge and skill of a con-

---

[7] "On Conducting", see footnote 1

ductor and arrived to the part that is a never-ending process of selfreflection, questions to oneself and learning through experience. This last section is also one that is not constant (although with time, one can get a more objective view), because with the change in personality comes change in view and interpretation.

Conducting is not only keeping an ensemble together, it is also the result of a vision for the given piece, a reflection of the preparatory work and one of the few art forms that is concentrated around one person. The conductor is the initial beginner of the concert, and it ends with the last beat of the baton. He must guide not only the musicians, but also the audience through the music, telling the story, showing the depth of the piece and achieve the goal of true music making. It is the one profession, where you have influence on the outcome while the performance.

I sincerely hope that I was able to supply you with some information that you can use the next time you visit a performance.

For closing, I include one last quote by H. Berlioz in his book about conducting:

*"Music appears to be the most exacting of all the Arts, the cultivation of which presents the greatest difficulties, for a consummate interpretation of a musical work so as to permit an appreciation of its real value, a clear view of its physiognomy, or discernment of its real meaning and true character, is only achieved in relatively few cases."* [8]

Paul Marsovszky

May 2020

---

8

# APPENDIX 1

# *The Elements of Opera*

**Music:**

Music moves the action of a story, expresses emotions and moods, and deepens our understanding of the characters.

**Orchestra:**

In most cases, operas are accompanied by a group of musicians. Led by a conductor, an orchestra is an ensemble that is comprised of string, woodwind, brass, and percussion instruments.

**Score:**

Musicians read from a score which is a notated piece of music showing each voice or instrumental part on its own staff.

**Overture:**

An overture is an orchestral piece that may be played at the very beginning of the opera before any action takes place on stage (not all operas have overtures).

**Themes:**

Musical themes are complete ideas that are crafted to be memorable to the listener. They are heard throughout operas and are associated with a particular character or characters, a situation, an idea, object, or emotion.

There are four types of musical forms that composers use to help them describe how characters are feeling during the course of an opera:

*Recitative:* Composed to sound like natural patterns of speech, a recitative is singing that has the rhythm of talking. It is used for conversation between characters or to move the plot of the story.

*Aria:* A vocal solo expressing personal emotion or reflection.

*Ensemble:* A piece that is sung by two or more characters at the same time (duet for two characters, trio for three characters, quartet for four characters, etc). Different melodies are sung simultaneously by each character involved in the ensemble.

*Chorus:* Often providing background music for the above, a chorus is a group of people singing together in parts or in unison. Each musical form is sung by singers in one of the six basic vocal categories which are listed below:

**Vocal Types**
All classical singers fall into one of the categories listed below. A singer cannot choose his/her voice-type – it is something they are born with. Composers usually assign a voice type to a character based on his/her personality or age.

### *Soprano*
This is the highest female voice and has a range similar to a violin. In opera, the soprano most often plays the young girl or the heroine (sometimes called the Prima Donna), since a high bright voice traditionally suggests femininity, virtue and innocence. The normal range of a soprano is two octaves up from middle C, sometimes with extra top notes. Most women are sopranos.

### Mezzo-Soprano

Also called a mezzo, this is the middle female voice and has a range similar to an oboe. A mezzo's sound is often darker and warmer than a soprano's. In opera, composers generally use a mezzo to portray older women, villainesses, seductive heroines, and sometimes even young boys (like Hansel). This is a special operatic convention called a 'trouser role' or a 'pants role'.

### Contralto

This is the lowest female voice and has a range similar to a clarinet. Contraltos usually sing the roles of older females or special character parts such as witches and old gypsies. The range is two octaves from F below middle C to the top line of the treble clef. A true contralto is very rare.

### Countertenor

This is the highest male voice, which was mainly used in very early opera and oratorio (a genre of classical vocal music similar to opera but generally based on a religious topic and accompanied by a choir). The voice of a countertenor sounds very much like a mezzo-soprano's voice and they often sing the same repertoire. Like the contralto, true countertenors are very rare.

### Tenor

This is usually the highest male voice in an opera. It is similar to a trumpet in range, tone, colour, and acoustical ring. The tenor typically plays the hero or the love interest in an opera.

### Baritone

This is the middle male voice and is close to a French horn in range and tone colour. In opera buffa (comedic opera), the baritone is often the ringleader of the comedy, but in opera seria (serious or tragic opera), he is usually the villain.

## Bass

This is the lowest male voice and is similar to a trombone or bassoon in range and colour. Low voices usually suggest age and wisdom in serious opera. In comic opera they are generally used for old characters who are foolish or laughable.

## Scale and Keys

A scale is any set of musical notes arranged by basic frequency or pitch. A scale arranged by increasing pitch is an ascending scale, and a scale arranged by decreasing pitch is a descending scale. A scale can be likened to climbing the rungs of a ladder which is represented by a stave.

### Common types of scale:

*Chromatic* – Taking in all 12 notes found within an octave, the chromatic scale isn't generally used a great deal other than as a collection of every note you can possibly play on the keyboard, so it's more useful as a teaching and practice aid rather than a practical scale to be used in your tracks.

*Major* – The major scale is usually the first one we learn, chiefly because it has a cheerful, happy demeanour and is one of the easiest scales to memorise and play. If you start on a C and play the seven white keys to the right in sequence, you'll get a C major scale – C D E F G A B.

*Natural minor* – If a major scale is played from the sixth note in the sequence, the interval pattern produces the natural minor scale, which sounds darker and moodier than its major cousin. So with the 6th degree of C major being A, we get A B C D E F G – A natural minor. C natural minor would therefore be C D Eb F G Ab Bb.

*Major pentatonic* – While major and minor scales have seven notes, pentatonic scales have only five. Essentially a major scale minus the 4th and 7th – C D E G A – the major pentatonic is a staple of folk, blues, rock and country, as it uses the five notes from a major scale that work over the largest number of underlying chords.

*Minor pentatonic* – The minor version of the pentatonic scale is formed in a similar way to its major cousin, but by omitting two notes from the natural minor scale. The missing two notes in a minor pentatonic are the second and sixth degrees, so C minor pentatonic would be spelled C Eb F G Bb.

*Heptatonic* – A heptatonic scale is a musical scale that has seven pitches (tones) per octave. Examples include the major scale or minor scale; e.g., in C major: C D E F G A B C and in the relative minor, A minor, natural minor: A B C D E F G A; the melodic minor scale, A B C D E F# G# A ascending, A G F E D C B A descending; the harmonic minor scale, A B C D E F G# A.

*Diatonic* – A diatonic scale is a heptatonic scale that includes five whole steps (whole tones) and two half steps (semitones) in each octave, in which the two half steps are separated from each other by either two or three whole steps, depending on their position in the scale.

*Octave* – An octave is the interval between the first and eighth notes of Diatonic Scale.

**Libretto:**

The words of an opera are known as the libretto (literally, 'small book'). Some composers, notably Richard Wagner, have written their own libretti; others have worked in close collaboration with their librettists – e.g., Mozart with Lorenzo Da Ponte. Traditional opera, often referred to as 'number opera', consists of two modes of singing: recitative, the plot-driving passages sung in a style designed to imitate and emphasise the inflections of speech, and aria (an 'air' or formal song) in which the characters express their emotions in a more structured melodic style.

Duets, trios and other ensembles often occur, and choruses are used to comment on the action. In some forms of opera, such as Singspiel, opéra comique, operetta, and semi-opera, the recitative is mostly replaced by spoken dialogue. Melodic or semi-melodic passages occurring in the midst of, or instead of, recitative, are also referred to as arioso. During the baroque and classical periods, recitative could appear in two basic forms: secco (dry) recitative, sung with a free rhythm dictated by the accent of the words, accompanied only by continuo, which was usually a harpsichord and a cello; or accompagnato (also known as strumentato) in which the orchestra provided accompaniment. By the nineteenth century, accompagnato had gained the upper hand, the orchestra played a much bigger role, and Richard Wagner revolutionised opera by abolishing almost all distinction between aria and recitative in his quest for what he termed 'endless melody'. Subsequent composers have tended to follow Wagner's example.

**Drama:**
Operas are the telling of a dramatic or comic story involving a protagonist, antagonist, and/or a hero/heroine. Actors that portray these roles must be very good at both singing and acting. Certain character tendencies often exist for each vocal category. They include the following:

*Soprano:* most often the heroine of the opera.
*Mezzo-Soprano:* mothers, older women, villains, servants, women playing men.
*Contralto:* old women, witches, comic roles.
*Tenor:* most often the hero of the opera.
*Baritone:* helpful companions, villains, sometimes heroes.

*Bass:* kings, villains, priests.

Operas usually feature primary and secondary characters who figure in the dramatic flow of the story:

*Principals:* The primary roles of an opera. These may be heroes/ heroines, villains or other strong characters. Principal roles are sung by the more experienced artists who have already made a name for themselves in smaller roles.

*Comprimarios:* The secondary roles of an opera. Comprimario roles are often confidantes, maids, servants, messengers, or medical personnel. They are usually sung by younger or lesser known artists. Similar to a play, opera tells a story that is divided into acts and scenes.

Each scene is further divided into numbers, each representing a different musical form (i.e. aria, recitative., chorus number, or ensemble). In contrast to plays, the text is written with the intention of being accompanied by music.

**Spectacle:**
The spectacle of an opera encompasses sets, costumes, special effects, props and staging. These elements are combined to tell the story in a multi-dimensional manner.

*Set:* The place where the action will occur on stage. Operas often have large, spectacular sets that reflect the time and place of the story being told.

*Costumes:* The outfits worn by each actor to reflect the time and place of an opera as well as the personality of each character.

*Props:* Items that may be carried onstage in an actor's hands or that 'dress' the set (such as furniture or decorative accessories).

During the course of an opera, it is not uncommon to have a large number of people on stage. Many of these people will be chorus while the others will appear as supernumeraries or extras.

*Super/Supernumerary:* A performer who appears in a non-singing role; a 'super' might have a solo walk-on to deliver a message or might be included as part of a large procession, for example. The stage director impacts how the action is conveyed by assigning various blocking.

*Blocking:* The patterns of movement of the people onstage as the opera progresses.

*Stage Right/Stage Left:* The division of the stage from the performer's point of view, thus when a singer goes stage right, he moves to his/her right but to the audience's left.

*Upstage/Downstage:* The position on stage farthest or nearest the audience; because of the raked stage which was so prevalent in early opera houses, the farther 'back' a singer went on the stage, the higher he seemed to become in stature, thus the distinction of being 'upstage'. 'Downstage' would be lower and closer to the audience.

## The Different Styles of Opera
### Bel Canto
This Italian phrase means 'beautiful singing'. These operas grew from a style of singing emphasizing long phrases, breath control, and flexibility in singing both loudly and softly. Because the voice is considered the most expressive instrument, the words are often secondary. Gaetano Donizetti composed in this style.

### Opera Buffa
Comic opera, always sung in Italian. The jokesters in these operas

are usually the working class, such as maids, peasants, or servants, who are preoccupied with getting the better of their employers. Gioachino Rossini composed in this style.

### Opera Seria

Serious opera. These stories are often tragic, and typically involve heroes and kings or ancient myths and gods. Some of Handel's operas are in this style. Singspiel 'Songplay' evolved in German speaking countries out of the comic opera tradition. It includes elements of comic opera, spoken dialogue interjected among the sung phrases, and, often, an exotic or fanciful theme. Mozart's *The Magic Flute* is an example of this style.

### Grand Opera

Spectacular opera. It is performed with elaborate sets and costumes. Many people are needed to make it happen. Grand opera involves royalty, heroism, an elaborate ballet scene, and is often long. Composer Giacomo Meyerbeer wrote opera in this style.

### Music Drama

A style of opera that is created by a single artist who writes both the text and the music to advance the drama. This style combines many art forms and makes each one as important as the others. Composer Richard Wagner defined this style.

### How an Opera is Staged

Each production is led by a director, and a conductor. The director is in charge of the staging for the production and directs the acting of the singers.

### Leaders

The conductor works closely with the singers and coach in rehearsals, and also prepares the orchestra. He or she conducts the orchestra in the pit and soloists and chorus on stage during performances.

The coach and chorus master prepare and rehearse with the singers before they sing with the whole orchestra. The chorus begins rehearsing several months before the production.

## Rehearsals

The conductor begins orchestra rehearsals about a week and half before opening night. They have four rehearsals with the conductor, and then the singers are added into the mix. The size of the orchestra will vary with each production, depending on what the composer has written for.

## Sets & Costumes

Some opera companies own some sets, but many of the sets are rented from other opera companies. Many of the costumes are also rented from other opera companies.

Sometimes costumes have to be altered or made specially if there aren't enough, or if there is nothing that fits.

The Opera production staff works with staff at the theatre to get all of the lighting and technical aspects of the production together.

The orchestra comes together with the singers in a special rehearsal called sitzprobe. There are no costumes during the sitzprobe, this is mainly to hear the voices with the orchestra. There is a piano dress rehearsal, when the singers rehearse in full costume for the first time so they can get used to wearing and moving in them. Finally, singers and orchestra come together for two full dress rehearsals leading up to opening night.

# APPENDIX 2

# *Wagner's Voices from His Operas 1833-1882*

| | | |
|---|---|---|
| Orchestra | Hermann Landgrave | Erda |
| King of the Fairies | of Thuringia | Woodbird |
| Ada | Tannhäuser | Gunther |
| Zemina | Wolfram von Eschenbach | Hagen |
| Forzana | Walter von der Vogelweide | Gutrune |
| Antonio | Biterolf | First Norn |
| Arindal | Heinrich der Schreiber | Second Norn |
| Lora | Reinmar von Zweter | Third Norn |
| Morald | Elizabeth | Vassals |
| Gernot | Venus | Women |
| Dralla | Shepherd | Tristan |
| Gunther | Four Pages | King Marke |
| Harald | King Henry | Isolde |
| Voice (Groma) | Lohengrin | Kurwenal |
| Fairies | Elsa of Brabant | Melot |
| People | (silent) Gottfried | Brangäne |
| Invisible Spirits | Friedrich von Telramund | Shepherd |
| Friedrich | Ortrud | Steersman |
| Luzio | Herald | Young sailor |
| Claudia | Four Noblemen | Sailors |

| Women | Four Pages. Counts | Knights and Esquires |
|---|---|---|
| Angelo | Nobles | Hans Sachs |
| Isabella | Pages | Veit Pogner |
| Mariana | Vassals | Kunz Vogelgesang |
| Brighella | Serfs | Konrad Nachtigal |
| Danieli | Wotan | Sixtus Beckmesser |
| Dorella | Donner | Fritz Kathner |
| Ponto Pilato | Froh | Balthasar Zorn |
| Nuns | Loge | Ulrich Eisslinger |
| Judges | Alberich | Augustin Moser |
| Policemen | Mime | Hermann Ortel |
| Citizens | Fasolt | Hans Schwarz |
| Country Folk | Fafner | Hans Folz |
| Band of Musicians | Fricka | Walther von Stolzing |
| | | |
| Cola Rienzi | Freia | David |
| Irene | Erda | Eva |
| Steffano Colonna | Woglinde | Magdalene |
| Adriano | Wellgunde | Night Watchman |
| Paolo Orsini | Flasshilde | Citizens |
| Raimondo | Siegmund | Guilds |
| Baroncelli | Hunding | Journeymen |
| Cecco del Vecchio | Sieglinde | Apprentices |
| Messenger of Peace | Brünnhilde | Women |
| Herald, Ambassadors | Waltraute | Boys |
| Priests | Gerhilde | Amfortas |
| Nobles | Ortlinde | Titurel |
| Citizens | Schwertleite | Gurnemanz |
| Senators | Helmwige | Parsifal |

| | | |
|---|---|---|
| Daland | Siegrune | Klingsor |
| Senta | Gromgerde | Kundry |
| Erik | Rossweisse | First and Second Knights of the Grail |
| | | |
| Mary | Siegfried | Four Esquires |
| Steersman | Wanderer | Voice from Above |
| Dutchman | | Flowermaidens |
| Norwegian Sailors | | Knights of the Grail |
| Dutchman's Crew | | Youths and Boys |
| Women | | |

# APPENDIX 3

# *Performances Attended*

## 1986 – 1999

1986: *Turandot* – Gaiety Theatre, Dublin.

1987: *Don Pasquale* – Dublin Grand Opera Society/Opera Ireland.

4th May 1989: Stars of the Kirov & Bolshoi Opera – Wexford Opera.

27th September1989: *Die Walküre* – Royal Opera House, London.

1st December1989: Bach, Beethoven, Schubert, Mozart, Chamber Orchestra of Europe – Barbican Centre London.

9th January 1990: *Othello* – The Royal Opera House, London

25th August 1990: *Aspects of Love* – Prince of Wales Theatre, London.

12th October 1990: *Der Ring des Nibelungen* – Royal Opera House, London:

8th April 1994: Mozart Symphony No. 40 in G Minor. Mahler Das Lied von der Erde – National Concert Hall, Dublin

26th November 1994: *The Magic Flute* – English National Opera, London.

2nd March 1996: *Götterdämmerung* -The Royal Opera House, London

12th August 1996: *Parsifal* – Bayreuth.

19th October 1996: *Götterdämmerung* – The Royal Opera House, London

22nd February 1997: *Lohengrin* – Royal Opera House, London.

31st May 1997: *Elektra* – Royal Opera House, London

7th July 1997: *Die Meistersinger von Nürnberg* – The Royal Opera House, London.

5th August 1998: *Parsifal* – Bayreuth

17th August 1998: *Parsifal* – Bayreuth

6th August 1998: *Das Rheingold* – Bayreuth

7th August 1998: *Die Walküre* – Bayreuth

9th August 1998: *Siegfried* – Bayreuth

12th August, 1998: *Götterdämmerung* – Bayreuth

17th August, 1998: *Parsifal* – Bayreuth

23rd January 1999: Bayerische Staatsoper

31st July 1999: *Lohengrin* – Bayreuth

1st August 1999: *The Flying Dutchman* – Bayreuth

2nd August 1999: *Die Meistersinger von Nürnberg* – Bayreuth

3rd August 1999: *Parsifal* – *Bayreuth*

4th August 1999: *Tristan und Isolde* – Bayreuth

## 2000 – 2009

14th January 2000: Beethoven Symphony. No. 4 in B Flat, *Die Walküre* (Wagner) – Royal Albert Hall, London.

21st January 2000: Beethoven Symphony No. 7 in A – National Concert Hall, Dublin.

4th February 2000: Beethoven Symphony No.3 in E Flat – National Concert Hall, Dublin.

26th March 2000: *Tannhäuser*, Wiener Staatsoper

26th May 2000: Beethoven Symphony No.1 in C minor. *Wesendonck*. (Wagner) – National Concert Hall, Dublin.

17th August 2000: *Die Meistersinger von Nürnberg* – Bayreuth

18th August 2000: *Parsifal* – Bayreuth

20th August 2000: *Lohengrin* Bayreuth

21st October 2000: *Tristan und Isolde* – The Royal Opera House, London

3rd December 2000: *Tannhäuser* – Bayerische Staatsoper

1st January 2001: Concert: Di Capodanno – New Year's Concert, Teatro La Fenice

25th February 2001: *Götterdämmerung* – Staatsoper Unter den Linden Berlin:

5th April 2001: *The Flying Dutchman* – Gaiety Theatre Dublin.

22nd April 2001: *Lohengrin* – Staatsoper Dresden

4th August 2001: *Lohengrin* – Bayreuth

3rd August 2001: *Parsifal* – Bayreuth

11th November 2001: *Parsifal* – Staatsoper unter den Linden Berlin

8th February 2002: *Tannhäuser*, Overture: Mahler *Kindertotenlieder*: Brahms, Symphony in E Minor – National Concert Hall, Dublin.

13th April 2002: *The Flying Dutchman* – Staatsoper unter den Linden, Berlin.

14th April 2002: *Der Ring des Nibelungen* – Staatsoper unter den Linden: Berlin,

15th April 2002: *Lohengrin*.

14th June 2002: Beethoven Night; Markson, Egmont, Piano Concerto N0.5 in E – National Concert Hall, Dublin

16th August 2002: *Tannhäuser* – Bayreuth

18th October 2002: Travel for the Arts – Munchen.

19th October 2002: *Le nozze de Figaro* – Bayerische Staatsoper

5th December 2002: Concert Musikverein – Wiener Philharmonic

15th December 2002: *Tristan und Isolde*, Wiener Philharmoniker, Musikverein,

Beethoven Concert No. 3 C fur Klavier und Orchester

18th April 2003: *Parsifal* – Deutsche Oper Berlin

20th April 2003: *Der Rosenkavalier* – Amsterdam

15th August 2003: *Lohengrin* – Bayreuth

16th August 2003: *The Flying Dutchman* – Bayreuth

17th August 2003: *Götterdämmerung* – Bayreuth

18th August 2003: *Tannhäuser* – Bayreuth

19th September 2003: Concert: Rimsky-Korsakov – National Concert Hall, Dublin.

20th September 2003: BBC Proms – Royal Albert Hall, London.

15th October 2003: Wexford Festival Opera.

16th October 2003: *Die Drei Pintos* – Wexford Festival Opera

17th December 2003: *Messiah* – National Concert Hall, Dublin.

11th March 2004: Mozart Requiem/Stravinsky. K. 626. National Concert Hall, Dublin.

19th March 2004: Concert: Beethoven Piano Concert No. 5 in E flat, National Concert Hall, Dublin.

21st March,2004: Concert: Stefhan Mickish Piano – Richard Wagner Kongress, Augsburg.

7th April 2004: *Tosca* – Opera Ireland

20th May 2004: Highlights from *Tristan und Isolde* – Augsberg.

22nd May 2004: *Tannhäuser* – Augsberg:

18th August 2004: *Parsifal* – Bayreuth

19th August 2004: *Tannhäuser* – Bayreuth

10th September 2004: Concert: *Overture to Der Freischutz*, Piano Concerto No.1 in B Flat Minor, Tchaikovsky; *Symphony No. 7 in A Major*, Ludwig Van Beethoven – National Concert Hall, Dublin.

October 2004: National Symphony Orchestra: Borodin, Tchaikovsky, Stravinsky – National Concert Hall, Dublin.

27th November 2004: International Piano Competition – National Concert Hall, Dublin.

27th November 2004: *Orfeo ed Euridice* Opera Ireland – Gaiety theatre, Dublin

21st December 2004: *Hänsel und Gretel* – Staatsoper, Bayerische.

4th February 2005: *Die Zauberflöte* (Mozart), Schubert 6, Mahler Das Laurent – National Concert Hall, Dublin

13th May 2005: Beethoven festival – National Concert Hall, Dublin

18th July 2005: *Die Walküre*, Act I – Royal Albert Hall, London

16th August 2005: Tristan un Isolde – Bayreuth

17th August 2005: *Parsifal* – Bayreuth

18th August 2005: *Tristan und Isolde* – Bayreuth

19th August 2005: *Lohengrin* – Bayreuth

29th October 2005: *Die Walküre* – Karlsruhe

25th November 2005: *Die tote Stadt* – Staatsoper Hamburg

26th November 2005: Wagner in Concert: – Royal Concert Hall Glasgow

10th December 2005: *Billy Budd*. English National Opera, London

2nd. January 2006: *Die Walküre*

2nd February 2006: *Die Walküre* – RWVI Congress, Teatro la Fenice

10th February 2006: Beethoven Piano Concerto No. 5 in E Flat Major. Shostakovich SymphonyNo.7 in C – National Concert Hall, Dublin

3rd March 2006: Violin concerto in D Major- Tchaikovsky Symphony No. 9 in E Flat Major – National Concert Hall, Dublin

29th April,2006: *Faust* – Gaiety Theatre, Dublin

27th May 2006: *Parsifal* – Operhaus Helsinki

22nd August,2006: *Das Rheingold* – Bayreuth

23rd August 2006: *Die Walküre* – Bayreuth

25th August 2006: *Siegfried* – Bayreuth

27th August 2006: *Götterdämmerung* – Bayreuth

28th August 2006; *Tristan und Isolde* – Bayreuth

30th September 2006: *Siegfried* – Staatstheater Karlsruhe

25th November 2006: Mozart 250 Years. Raymond Gubbay, Piano, Clarinet – National Concert Hall, Dublin

25th January 2007: 5th Veronica Dunne, International Singing Competition – National Concert Hall, Dublin

3rd March,2007: *The Creation*, Dun Laoghaire Choral Society – National Concert Hall, Dublin.

19th May 2007: *Die Walkur* – Staatskap Weimer

7th June 2007: Schumann Op15, Bach Goldberg Variations. National Concert Hall, Dublin.

17th June 2007: *Siegfried* -Teatro La Fenice

12th August 2007: Prom 39 *Götterdämmerung* – Royal Albert Hall, London.

20th August 2007: Piano Concert: Haydn PC in C Minor, Beethoven Sonata

No.31 in A Flat Major, Schubert Impromptu No. 1 in F Minor No.3 in B Flat Major, Mozart PC in C Minor. Pianist: Alfred Brendel – National Concert Hall, Dublin.

26th August 2007: *Parsifal* – Bayreuth.

27th August 2007: *Tannhäuser* – Bayreuth

28th August 2007: *Die Meistersinger von Nuernberg* – Bayreuth

19th October 2007: Wagner, Beethoven, Strauss: Soprano, Miriam Murphy – National Concert Hall, Dublin.

21st October 2007: Thais – Venice.

20th March 2008: *Matthew Passion* – Thomaskirche Leipzig.

21st March 2008: *Parsifal* – Oper Leipzig.

18th April 2008: Berlioz, Overture Le Carnaval Romain, Mozart Piano Concerto No. 21. Puccini Capriccio, Pini Di Roma, Cascioli Piano – National Concert Hall, Dublin.

2nd May 2008: *Lohengrin* – Grand Theatre de Geneve.

18th May 2008: *Swan Lake* by Petr Iljic Cajkovskij Statni – Opera Prague.

20th August 2008: *Das Rheingold* – Bayreuth

21st August 2008: *Die Walküre* – Bayreuth

23rd August 2008: *Siegfried* – Bayreuth

25th August 2008: *Götterdämmerung* – Bayreuth

5th November 2008: RTE Symphony Orchestra: Verdi, Gluck, Gounod, Massenet, Puccini; Alagna, Manfrino – National Concert Hall, Dublin

20th April 2009: UNESCO Concert for Peace -Theatre La Fenice

1st May 2009: Mozart Piano Concerto No.23 in A Major,

Beethoven Symphony No. 9 in D Minor – National Concert Hall, Dublin

14th August,2009: *Die Meistersinger von Nürnberg* – Bayreuth

15th August 2009: *Parsifal* – Bayreuth

27th September 2009: *La Traviata* – Giuseppe Verdi. Berlin Staatsoper

1st November 2009: *Fidelio*, Wiener Staatsoper

28th November 2009: *Tristan und Isolde* – Deutsche Oper Berlin

## 2010 – 2020

14th February 2010: *Die Meistersinger von Nürnberg* – Deutsche Oper Berlin

12th February: *Tannhäuser* – Deutsche Oper Berlin

13th February2010: *Lohengrin* – Deutsche Oper Berlin

19th March 2010: *Billy Budd* – Danish National Opera

27th March 2010: *Tannhäuser* – den Norske Opera & Ballet

10th April 2010: *Mette,* Peter Konwitschny, Michael Schonwandt, Det – Kongelige Teater

13th to 16th May: International Richard Wagner Congress, Stralsund

26th May 2010: International Piano Competition – The National Concert Hall, Dublin

27th June 2010: *Die tote Stadt* – Teatro Real, Madrid

17th August 2010: *Lohengrin* – Teatro Real, Madrid

18th August 2010: *Parsifal* – Teatro Real, Madrid

19th August 2010: *Die Meistersinger von Nürnberg* – Teatro Real, Madrid

16th October 2010: Romeo et Juliette – Muziektheatr Amsterdam.

17th November 2010: *Der Freischutz* – Staatsthearer Gatnerplaz

17th December 2010: *Fidelio* – Het Muziektheater, Amsterdam.

1st January 2011: New Years' Day Concerto Di Capodanno – Teatro La Fenice

15th January 2011: Johann Strauss Konzert Wiener Gala. Alte –

Oper Frankfurt

28th January 2011: Bruckner Symphony N.8 in C Minor. Markson NCH, NSO.

4th February 2011: Concert: Conductor Mariss Jansons – Het Concertgebouw, Amsterdam

12th March 2011: Ballet Capricen/Nocturnes/ Variations Serieuses – Staatstheater, Karlsruhe

8th April 2011: *The Matthaus Passion* – Concertgebouw Amsterdam

20th April 2011: *Das Reingold* – Staatsoper Karlsruhe

24th April 2011: Ballet Romantick – Staatsoper Karlsruhe

25th April 2011: *Götterdämmerung* – Bayreuth

1st May 2011: Parsifal – Staatsoper Hamburg.

20th May 2011: Der Rosenkankavalier – Het Muziektheater, Armsterdam

19th June 2011: *Die tote Stadt* – Stadt Theatre Bern

19th July 2011 – 23rd July 2011: Act 1- Venusberg from *Tannhäuser* – Het Concertgebouw, Amsterdam

13th August 2011: *Tannhäuser* – Bayreuth

14th August 2011: *Lohengrin* – Bayreuth

15th August 2011: *Parsifal* – Bayreuth

16th August 2011: *Tristan und Isolde* – Bayreuth

31st August 2011: *Die Walküre* – Bayreuth

9th December 2011: Wagner, Rouse, Brahms: Buribayev, Piano – National Concert Hall, Dublin

1st January 2012: Concerto Di Capodanno – Teatro La Fenice

27th April 2012: *Die tote Stadt* – Bilbao Opera

12th,13th, 14th, 15th June 2012: *Der Ring des Nibelungen* – Budapest, Bela Bartok National Concert Hall

17th June 2012: *Rameau-Hippolyte Et Aricie*, Opera National De Paris Palais Garnier

18th August,2012: *The Flying Dutchman* – Bayreuth

19th August,2012: *Lohengrin* – Bayreuth

20th August 2012: *Tristan und Isolde* – Bayreuth

5th & 6th September 2012: Festival Bayreuth *Lohengrin /Tristan und Isolde* – Bayreuth

30th September to 6th October 2012: Wide Open Opera: *Tristan und Isolde* – Bord Gáis Energy Theatre, Dublin

12th October 2012: *Tannhäuser* – Staatstheater Karlsruhe

21st October 2012: *Parsifal* – Deutsche Oper Berlin

4th January 2013: Wagner 200th Birthday Celebrations National Concert Hall, Dublin

25th January 2013: Berg Violin Concerto, Beethoven Symphony No. 9 – National Concert Hall, Dublin

23rd March 2013: *Tristan und Isolde* – Deutsche Oper, Berlin

19th May 2013: *Die Meistersinger Von Nürnberg* – Oper Leipzig

20th May 2013: *Parsifal* – Oper Leipzig

22nd May 2013: Geburtsag Concert – 200 years – Bayreuth

29th June 2013: *Götterdämmerung* – La Scala Theatre, Milan

1st July2013: *Tristan und Isolde* – Opernhaus Bonn

14th August 2013: *Das Rheingold* – Bayreuth

15th August 2013: *Die Walküre* – Bayreuth

17th August,2013: *Siegfried* – Bayreuth

19th August 2013: *Götterdämmerung* – Bayreuth

20th August 2013: *The Flying Dutchman* – Bayreuth

25th August 2013: Concert – Prom 57. *Parsifal* – Royal Albert Hall

8th October 2013: *The Marriage of Figaro* – Volksoper Wien

12th October 2013: *The St Matthew Passion* – Leipzig

23rd October 2013 -3rd November 2013: *Il cappello di paglia di Firenze* (Nino Rota) – Wexford Festival Opera

16th November 2013: *Die tote Stadt* – Helsinki

30th November 2013: *Il Travatore* Volksoper Wien

1st December 2013: *Peter Grimes* – Wiener Staatsoer Staatsoper

11th December 2013: *Messiah* – National Concert Hall, Dublin.

31st December 2013: *La Boheme* – Stattsoper Unter den Linden, Berlin

1st January 2014. Pablo Heras-Casado, Samuil, Lepkousky –

Staatskapple Berlin

11th January 2014: *Beethoven 9* – Staatskepple, Berlin

29th January 2014: Sinfonietta – National Concert Hall, Dublin

2nd February 2014: *Cavalleria Rusticana/Pagliacci* – Wiener Staatsoper

26th April 2014: *Messiah* – Theater an der Wien

28th April 2014: *Lohengrin* – Wiener Staatsoper

27th June 2014: Beethoven Piano Concerto No. 5 Symphony No.5 in C Minor 0 National Concert Hall, Dublin

16th August 2014: *The Flying Dutchman* – Bayreuth

17th August 2014: *Lohengrin* – Bayreuth

18th August 2014: *Tannhäuser* – Bayreuth

21st September 2014: Dr Veronica Dunne Lifetime Achievement Award – National Concert Hall, Dublin

6th October 2014: *Swan Lake* – Wiener Staatsballett

15th December 2014: *Stagione Di Musica Da Camera* – Teatro la Fenice

25th January 2015: Piano Pieces; Rameau, Franck, Chopin, Grandos Benjamin Grosvenor – National Concert Hall, Dublin

25th January 2015: *Tristan und Isolde* – Opernhaus Zurich

24th February 2015: *The Flying Dutchman* – Royal Opera House, London

7th March 2015: *Die Meistersinger von Nuremberg* – English National Opera, London

3rd April 2015: *The St. Matthew Passion* -Thomaskirche,in Leipziz

12th April 2015: *Parsifal* – Staatsoper im Schiller, Berlin

15th May 2015: Concert: Mozart Piano Concerto No.21 in C. – National Concert Hall, Dublin

17th May 2015: *Parsifal* – Birmingham

18th August 2015: *Tristan und Isolde* – Bayreuth

20th August 2015: *Das Rheingold* – Bayreuth

27th August 2015: *Lohengrin* – Bayreuth

22nd October 2015: *Die Meistersinger* – Staatsoper Schiller Berlin

14th December 2015: *Peter Grimes* – Theater an der Wien

18th March 2016: Rachmaninov Piano Concerto No.2 in C Shostakovich, Symphony No.8 in C Minor – National Concert Hall, Dublin

25th March 2016: *Parsifal* National Theatre Mannheim

5th May 2016: *Lohengrin* – Deutsche Oper, Berlin

27th May 2016: Concert: Glinka, Prokofiev.Violin Cncerto Tchsikovsky – National Concert Hall, Dublin

6th June 2016: *Der Ring des Nibelungen: Rheingold, Die Walküre, Siegfried, Götterdämmerung* – Budapest

21st August 2016: *Die Walküre* – Bayreuth

22nd August 2016: *Tristan und Isolde* – Bayreuth

23rd August 2016: *Siegfried* – Bayreuth

24th August 2016: *Parsifal* – Bayreuth

25th August 2016: *Götterdämmerung* Bayreuth

21st September 2016: *La Traviata* Bayerischer Staatsoper

17th October 2016: – Swan Lake Wiener Staats Ballet

4th November 2016: *The Marriage of Figaro* – Volksoper Wien

5th November 2016: Musikverein: Das Concerto Chamber Orchestra. Maciasz., Barenboim

18th November 2016: Wagner, Strauss, Bruckner – National Concert Hall, Dublin

31st December 2016: *Alcina* – Opernhaus Zurich

2nd January 2017: *Hansel und Gretel* – Wiener Staatsoper

20th January 2017: *Die tote Stadt* – Wiener Staatsoper

25th January 2017: Bach: Sacred Cantatas. Philippe Jaroussky, Countertenor – Concergebouw Amsterdam

10th March 2017: *Die Lustige* – Volksoper Wien

12th March 2017: *Tristan und Isolde* – Wiener Staatsoper

19th March 2017: *Barenboim* – Staatsoper im Schiller Berlin

24th March 2017: Concert: *Saint-Saëns*, Symphony No. 3 in C Minor – National Concert Hall, Dublin

16th April 2017: *Parsifal* – Wiener Staatsoper

17th April 2017: *Die Walküre* – Osterfestspiel

19th May 2017: *The Dream of Gerontius* – National Concert Hall, Dublin

14th August 2017: *Parsifal* – Bayreuth

15th August 2017: *Die Meistersinger von Nürnberg* – Bayreuth

16th August 2017: *Tristan und Isolde* – Bayreuth

8th October, *The Importance of Being Ernest* Wide Open Opera – Gaiety Theatre, Dublin

13th December 2017: *Der Rosenkavalier* – Wienerstaatsoper

15th December 2017: *Romeo et Juliette* – Wiener Staats Ballet

1st January 2019: Pablo Heras-Casado – Staatskapple Berlin.

9th January 2018: Concert: Wagner, Korngold, Verdi, Saint-Saens, Gluck, Wallace, Gounod, Tchaikovsky, Giordano, Rossini – National Concert Hall, Dublin

10th February 2018: *The Sound of Music* – Volksoper Wien

15th April 2018: *Tristan und Isolde* – Mainfranken, Theatre, Wurzburg

15th April 2018: *Götterdämmerung* – Wiener Staatsoper

21st April: Karlsruhe. *Ring Des Nibelungen*: *Walküre*:

16th May 2018: *Don Pasquale* – Wienerstaatsoper

25th May 2018: *Peter Grimes* – Theatre Wein

25th May 2018: Brahms Opus 82, *Tannhäuser* – National Concert Hall, Dublin

25th May2018: *Peter Grimes* – Theatre Wein

2nd June 2018: *Die Feen* – Paris

6th August 2018: *Lohengrin* – Bayreuth

21st August 2019: *Tannhäuser* – Bayreuth

10th September 2018: *Retour a la vie* Lelio ou le Hector Berlioz, Symphonie – Wiener Musikvereinssaal

2nd November 2018: Piotr Beczala: Verdi, Bizet, Berlio, Berlioz, Giordana.- National Concert Hall, Dublin

31st December 2018: *Alcina* – Zurich

7th February 2019: *Tosca* – Wiener Staatsoper

6th December 2019: Tchaikovsky Violin concerto; Berlioz Symphony – National Concert Hall, Dublin

Also: October 2011: London: Wagner News: Review of the performance of *Tannhäuser* on the 13th of August 2011 at Bayreuth by Cristopher McQuaid

# APPENDIX 4

# *Library – Books, CDs, DVDs*

**Books:**

| | |
|---|---|
| Erick Wolfgang Korngold | Phadion 1996 |
| Wagner and the Art of the Theatre | Yale 2006 |
| Kobbe's Complete Opera Book | Earl of Harwood 1922, 1976, 1987. |
| My Life with Wagner | Thielemann 2005 |
| Gustaf Mahler | Deryck |
| Cooke1980 – Faber | |
| Wexford's 50th Celebrations | Gus Smith 2001 – Atlantic |
| Ludwig II of Bavaria | Gregg King 1996 – Aurum |
| The Sorcerer of Bayreuth | Barry Millington 2012 |
| Siena Cathedral & Museum | Enzo Carli 1990 |
| The Master Musicians: Wagner | Barry Millington – Dent |
| Opera Guides: Die Meistersinger von Nürnberg English | National Opera. |
| A History of Opera-the Last 400 Years | Abbate /Parker |
| Wagner and Die Meistersinger von Nuernberg Rayer | 1940 – Oxford |
| My Life in Opera | Birgit Nilsson – North Eastern University Press |
| Wagner Nights | Ernest Nemwan – Putnam |

| | |
|---|---|
| Visions of Valhalla – a Poetic Tribute to Richard Wagner | John Davidson Poet |
| Wagner's Ring of the Nibelung- A Companion with full German/English | Text Spencer & Millington |
| Wagner on Music and Drama | Goldmann & Sprincher 1964 NYC – Decapo, |
| Wagner and the Volsungs- Icelandic Sources of Der Ring Des Niblelungen | Arni Bjornsson 2003 – Viking Society London |
| The AB Guide to Music Theory Part I | Eric Taylor 1989 – ABRSM |
| Winifred Wagner | Brigitte Harmann 2005 – Granta |
| Herbert Von Karajan -A Life in Music | Richard Osborne – Chatto & Windus |
| The Bluffer's Guide to Music | Peter Grammond 2008 |
| The Fischer -Dieskau Book of Lieder 750 lieder in German & English, 1991 | Gollonez |
| Vivaldi | Michael Talbot 1978 – Dent |
| Text Book – Die tote Stadt | Eric Wolfgang Korngold – Schott, |
| Wagner and the Romantic Hero | 2004 |
| Aspects of Wagner | Bryan Magee 1988 Oxford |
| Tenor -History of a Voice | John Potter 2009 |
| Mozart's Operas-A Critical Study | Edward J. Dent 1947 – Claredon |
| The Perfect Wagnerite | George Bernard Shaw 1967 -Dover |
| Introducing Music to Beginers | Otto Karoly 1965 – Penguin |

The Cambridge Wagner Encyclopedia    Nicholas Vazsonyi 2013 – Cambridge

Wagner Rehearsing the Ring    Heinrich Porges 1983 – Cambridge

The AB Guide to Music Theory Part II    Eric Taylor 1991 – ABRSM

Daniel Baremboim – A Life in Music    Weiderfeld & Nicolson

The ABC Directory of Music - 3 Books    David Bouman,Rheingold

Ronnie Dunne Authorised Biography    Alison Maxwell 2016 – Asfield

Eduard Hanslick – On The Musically Beautiful    Translated by Geoffery Payzank 1986

The Opera Lovers Guide to Europe    Carl Plentamjura Robson

Wolfgang Wagner -An Appreciation    Hongkong

Wagner's Parsifal – the Journey of a Soul-    Peter Bassett 2000 Wakefield

The Diary of Richard Wagner- the Brown Book 1865-1882    Translation by George Bird 1980 – Camelot

The Wagner Tuba – A History    William Melton 2008 – Ebenos

Overture Opera Guides - Der fliegende Holländer    English National Opera 1982

Liszt    Derek Watson 1989 – Schirmer

The Swan King-Ludwig II of Bavaria    McIntosh 2003 Tauris

Solti on Solti- A Memoir    Solti 1998 – Vintage

Johann Sebastian Bach    Christopher Wolff 2001 – Oxford

Wagner and Philosphy    Bryan Magee 2000 – Penguin

Classical Music    Burrows 2005 – DK

Acts – the Authobiography of
Wolfgang Wagner
Swastikas on Stage Opera
Trends in Production of Wagner
operas on Stage in Germany
Wagner Opera and Drama

John Brown 1994,
-Weidenfeld & Nicholson

Bernd Weifl 2015 –
Probusiness
Translated by W. Ashton
Ellis 1995
(1893) – Bison

Bayreuth -A History of the
Wagner Festival Fredrick
Bayreuth -The Early Years
1876-1914
Hans Hotter-Memoirs

Spotts 1994 – Yale

Robert Hartford –
Cambridge
Donald Artlu – New
England

Wagner in Russia, Poland and
the Czeck Lands
The Tragic and the Ecstatic
Tristan und Isolde
Cosima Wagner – The Lady
of Bayreuth
Gottfried Von Strassburg Tristan
Sibelius

Richard Taruskin 2013 –
Routledge
Eric Chaffe 2005 – Oxford

Oliver Aimes 2010 -Yale

1960 – Penguin
Robert Loyfol 1965 –
Dent,

Tristan und Isolde

Arthur Groos 2011
Cambridge

The Wagner Clan
Nietzsche -a Philosophical
Biography
My Life -Richard Wagner
Wagner Remembered

Jonathon Carr 2007 – Faber
Rudiger Saffanski 2002

Echo
Steward Spencer 2000 –
Faber

Beethoven

Denis Matthews 1985 –
Dent

| | |
|---|---|
| Wagner's Ring and its Symbols | Robert Donnington 1963 Faber |
| Richard Strauss | Michael Kenneddy 1976 – Dent |
| Reggie the Life of Reginald Goodall | John Luca 1993 – JM |
| The Phadon Ring, A Companion Rheingold, Die Walküre, Siegfried, Götterdämmerung. | Rudolf Sabor |
| Wagner Pocket Guide | Michael Tanner 2010 – Faber |

The Life of Richard Wagner:
A set of four volumes
-Volume I, (1813-1848)
-Volume II (1848-1860)
-Volume III (1859-1866)
-Volume IV ( 1866-1885)                    Ernest Newman 1966 –
                                          Cambridge

University Press
Being Wagner                              Simon Callow 2017 –
                                          Harper Collins

The Real Wagner                           Rudolf Sabor 1987
The World as will and Representation Arthur Schopenhour
-Volume I & Volume II
   EFJ Payne 1958
The Ring                                  Richard Wagner – Porter
                                          1976 – Dawson

An Illustrated Encyclopaedia              Flamethree
   of Opera
-Music and Drama in Classical Antiquity
-Music in Medieval Drama
-Music and Drama in the Renaissance
-Early & Middle Baroque
-Classical

-Early Romantic

-High Romantic

-Turn of the Century

-Twentieth Century

| The Concise Oxford History of Music | Gerard Abraham – Oxford |
| Collins Encyclopaedia of Music | 1959/1976 – Collins, |
| John McCormack -The Great Irish Tenor Gordon | T. Ledbetter 2003 – Tourhouse |

## CDs

| Der Ring Des Nibelungen – 8 CD Set 1976 | |
| -Director Patrice Chereau, | |
| -Bayreuther Festspiele. | Centenary Production |
| Parsifal Domingo Document with some extracts | DG Arthaus, |
| Great Composers- Series Bach | BBC |
| Death in Venice | Britten,Dynamic, |
| The Essential Pavarotti – 13th April 1982 | RAH Decca |
| Orpheus und Eurydice | Belar |
| The Richard Wagner Story live. | |
| The Meistersinger – Klaus Florian Vogt | Sony |
| Europakonzert Aus Bayreuth | Euroarts |
| Great Composers -Wagner | BBC |
| Peace and Conflict | Britten, NTSC |
| Erich Wolfgang Korngold | Arthaus |
| Lohengrin Metropolitan Opera | DG |
| Die tote Stadt -Korngold | Opus Arte |
| La Boheme Sanfrancisco Opera 1980 | Kultur |
| Lohengrin Dresden 2016 | DG |
| Wagner A Genius in Exile | Belar |

Beethoven Symphony No. 9

- Berlin Karajan1977                              Unitel

New Year's Day Concert Venice 2012   Arthuus

Lohingrin Bayreuther Festspiele 1980 –

Herzog Scheinder                                  DG

Barenboim on Beethoven                       EMI

Baremboim -Tristan und Isolde – Bayreuth 1983

Der fliegende Holländer Bayreuth 1985 –

Kupfer                                                  DG

Tannhäuser -Sinopoli 1989 –                  Euro Arts
    Wolfgang Wagner

Great Composers Tchaikovsky               BBC

Jaroussky – Great Concerts                   Virgin

Fritz Wunderlich -Life and Legend         DG

Die Meistersinger Von Nürnberg Wagner

Bayreuth – Stein 1994                           DG

Fidelio – Beethoven -Zubin                    United
    Mehata 2006

Carreras – The 50 Tracks                      Decca

Giulio Cesare – Handel                         Apex

Colours of My Life – Judith Durham      Decca

Fritz Wunderlich – The 50 Tracks         DG

L'enfance du Christ                              Ultima

Tristan und Isolde -Introduction           Naxos

Juan Diego Florez –                             Decca
    'Una Furtiva Lagrima'.

Kenneth McKeller Sings Handel           Decca

Hansel und Gretel – Humperdinck         Decca

Die tote Stadt – Korngold                     Sony

Tenor Arias – Joseph Calleja               Decca

Symphonie Fantastique – Berlioz          Naxos

Die Grossen Opern Chore Bayreuth      Philips

Wagner Chore Pitz                              DG

| | |
|---|---|
| Essential Bach 36. | Decca |
| Grosse Stimmen – Wunderlich | DG |
| Der Letzte Liederabend Wunderlich | DG |
| Jacqueline Du Pre | EMI |
| Sir Thomas Beecham -Wagner | Sony |
| J. S. Bach Glen Gould | Sony |
| J. S. Bach Andras Schiff | Decca |
| La Traviata Complete | DG |
| The Well-Tempered Clavier – Angela Hewitt Hyperon | |
| Wagner Preludes & Overtures | Virgin |
| Jaroussky -The Voice | Erato |
| Jaroussky – Carestini | Erato |
| Jaroussky -The Handel Album | Erato |
| Jaroussky – Farinelli | Erato |
| Jaroussky – Bach la dolce fiamma | Erato |
| Jaroussky – Opera Arias | Erato |
| Jaroussky -La storia di Orfeo | Erato |
| Jaroussky -Orfeo ed Euridice | Erato |
| Jaroussky -Bach Sacred Cantatas | Erato |
| Kaufmann -Wagner | Decca |
| Tchaikovsky – Lang Lang | DG |
| Waltraud Meier -Wagner | RCA |
| Rossini -Stabat Mater | Decca |
| Anne Evans BBC Proms 1994 | BBC |
| Rachmaninov Historical | Naxos |
| Vier Letzie – Lieder Jessie Norman | Philips |
| Der Rosenkavalier | DG |
| The Magic Flute | Decca |
| Finghin Collins Impromptu | RTE Lyric |
| Schubert Symphony 5 & 6 | DG |
| Gounod -Faust | EMI |
| Gounod- Romeo et Juliette | EMI |
| Parsifal Historical | Naxos |

| | |
|---|---|
| Robert Dean Smith -Wagner | Artenova |
| Monologues – Bass Clarinet | RICO |
| Peter Hofmann – Rock Classics | Sony |
| Thielemann -Wagner | DG |
| Sinopoli -Wagner | DG |
| Elizabeth Woods Soprano | Self |
| Florez – Tenor Arias | Decca |
| Tannhäuser Without Words | Sony |
| Gasdia -Vivaldi | Monoo, |
| Die Wunderharfe | DG |
| Flagstad Great Voices | Memoir |
| Sacred Arias | EMI |
| Don Giovanni – Mozart | DG |
| Smetana – Mavlast | DG |
| Scholl –'Ombra mai fu' | Harmonia |
| Der Ring Des Nibelungn – Sir Georg Solti | |
| -14 CDs in a Box Set | Decca |
| Kaufmann – the Verdi Album | Sony |
| Sibelius- Finlandia | Naxos |
| Fisher-Dieskau – Mahler | DG |
| Messiah – Bolt | Decca |
| Abbado – Berg | DG |
| Klemperer -Das Lied von der Erde | EMI |
| Semele – Handel | Regis |
| Mendelssohn – Fingal's Cave EMI | |
| Renee Fleming – Strauss | Decca |
| Musik Stadt – Leipzig | Philips |
| Musik Stadt – Leipzig | Philips |
| Titanic – Horner | Horner |
| Violinkoncert – Abbado | DG |
| Handel – Opera Duets | Veritas |
| Wagner Classics | MCPS |
| Bach Cantatas BWV 58-61 | Hanssled |

| | |
|---|---|
| La Forza Del Destino | Decca |
| Saint-Saens – Le Carnaval des Animaux | DG |
| Wunderlich – Arias | BMG |
| Tristan und Isolde Duet Scenes | OEHMS |
| Mendelssohon – Elijaih | Classics |
| Klemperer PC # 5 | EMI |
| Lortzing -Hans Sachs | Line |
| Matthew Polenzani | VAI |
| Bach J.S. Easter Oratorio | Ardiv |
| Mendelssohn Bruch | ENI |
| Perahia – Goldberg Variations | CB811 |
| Die Zauberflote -Bohm | DG |
| Elmning-Wagner Gala | DACDD |
| Dvorak-Rusalka | Line |
| Verdi Gala | DECCA |
| Elgar – The Dream of Gerontius – Britten Decca | |
| Eisinger Paraphrasen – Piano | Camus |
| Sounds of Finland -The Tapiola Childrens' Choir | BIS |
| Farinelli iL Castrato – Sound Track | Naive |
| Der Ring Ohne Worte – Maazel | Telarc |
| Stephen Gately -Bright Eyes | SC |
| Schumann – Dichterliebe -Wunderlich | DO |
| Bayreuth 1936 | Telodec |
| Renee Fleming BY Request | Decca |
| Previn- Rosenkavalier Suite | DG |
| Great Scenes From The Ring-Solti (CD)/Cassette Decca | |
| Peter Hofmann -Wagner | CB811 |
| Matthäus-Passion BMV 244 Rondeall | |
| The Best of Wagner | Naxos |
| Bach J.S. -Karl Richter – Matthaus Passion Arehiv | |

| | |
|---|---|
| Parsifal – Kegel | Berlin Classics |
| Parsifal Bayreuther Festspiele 1962 | |
|   -Hans Knappertbusch | Philips |
| Konzert Fur Flote & Harf | DG |
| Lohengrin – Berlin 1943 | MONO 90043 |
| Korngold – Midsummer | CPO |
|   Night's Dream | |
| Beethoven Piano Sonatas | BELART |
| Kaufmann -Romantic Arias | Decca |
| O'Riada sa Gaiety | GAEL LINN |
| Wiener Musik | Eurodrak |
| Sibelius – Finlanda | DG |
| Hummel Piano Sonatas | Hyperion |
| Der Rosenkavalier -Solti | Decca |
| Hayden -Die Schopfung | DG |
| Parsifal 1954 NYC | ADOMS |
| Beethoven -Fidelio – Haitink | Decca |
| Das Liebesmahl der Apostel. Coviello | |
| Exploring Classical Music -Lyric fm Lyric fm | |
| BBC Mahler Symphony No. 10 BBC | |
| Beethoven's Violin Concertos | Philips |
| Wagner Orchestral Music | Hodre |
| Wagner Festival 2002 -NYOI NYOI | |
| Schubert Choral Works | Philips |
| John O'Conor Piano | TELRC |
| Napola Sound Track | ZYX |
| Mozart Piano Sonatas | Philips |
| Mozert – Die Entfuhrung aus | DG |
|   dem Serial Bohm | |
| Bach Christmas Cantata 63 | Linn |
| Rachmaninov Piano 1 & 2 | HMV |
| Lohengrin – Berlin 1943 | MONO 900432 |
| Handel Nine German \| Arias | Wigmore, |

| | |
|---|---|
| Joshua Bell -Bruch Mendelsohn | DECCA. |
| Liebestraum | ZYX Mine, |
| Vivaldi -Four Seasons | Philips |
| Hermann Prey – Schubert | Philips |
| Homage to Horst Stein | OSR |
| Bach – St. John Passion | DG |
| Lully – Armide | Harmonic |
| Vivaldi Sacred Music | Hyperion |
| Mozart – Great Mass in C minor -Solti | Decca |
| Perahia Concertos | Sony |
| Last Night of the Proms 1996 | OS |
| Beethoven Symphony No.9 | EMI |
| Brendal at Salzburg | ORF |
| Rachmaninov – Rhapdo | |
| Rachmaninov – Rhapsody on -a Theme of Paganni | HMV |
| Handel – Nathalie Stutzmann | Eralo |
| Alanga -Christmas Albumn | DG |
| Tristan und Isolde 1953- Furtwangler | EMI |
| Bach -Famous Cantatas | |
| Die Entfulthring | DG |
| Horowitz-Schubert /Beethoven | Sony |
| Mozart- Piano Concertos | DG |
| Valkyrie-Sound Track | Ottman |
| Beethoven-Fidelio 1978 | DJ |
| Wagner – Lohengrin - Kempe-Bayreuther Festisplele – 1967 | Orfeo |
| Hindesmith -Das Marienleben 1998 | Koch |
| Glen Gould -Goldberg Variations 1955 & 1981 | Sony |
| Humperdinck – Hänsel und Gretel | EMI |

| | |
|---|---|
| Lohengrin – Jarowski | Pentatone |
| Bach -Goldberg Variations | Stemra |
| Parsifal- Hans Knapperbush | Arkadio |
| Mozart -Le Nozze Di Figaro 1977 Orfeo | |
| Die tote Stadt -Korngold | RCA |
| Wagner-Other Works | EMI |
| Wagner -Parsifal -Goodall | EMI |
| Parsifal -Netherland's Radio | Surrand |
| Wagner -Parsifal Archive | ARTS |
| Beethoven | WTFK |
| Lohengrin -Leinsdorf – Koyna | RCA |
| Bach -Goldberg Variations | Stemra |
| Tristan und Isolde | Decca |
| Kaufmann-50 Arias | Decca |
| Wagner – Das Liebesverbot | Orfeo |
| Stefan Mickish – Der Ring | Ondine |
| 261 Leitmotives | |
| Pekka Kuusisto | Ondine |
| Puccini -La Boheme -Pavarotti/Freni | Decca |
| Parsifal -Jordan | Erato |
| Wagner-Lohengrin | |
| -Sawallisch -Bayreuther Festspiele | Philips |
| Mozart – Cosi Fan Tutte | DG |
| Der fliegende Holländer | Berlin |
| Britten – War Requiem | Decca |
| Wagner – Tannhäuser-Bayreuther | Philips |
| Festspiele | |
| Puccini -Tosca | DG |
| Der Evangelimann | EMI |
| Wagner -Parsifal Solti | Decca |
| Vogtwagner | Sony |
| Handel- Messiah | Newton |
| Tristan und Isolde -Bohm -Bayreuther Festspiele Philips | |

Parsifal -Wiener Phil                        Decca
Die Meistersinger Von Nürnberg Philips
Aida – Pavarotti/Maazel-Verdi                Decca
Rienzi – Hollreiser                          EMI
Der fliegende Holländer -Bayreuther Festspiele Philips
Vogt-Helden Heroes                           Sony
Britten- Billy Budd-Hickox                   Chandos
Humperdinck - Hänsel und                     Decca
   Gretel – Sir Coln Davis
Mozart-Le Nozzi Di Figaro                    Decca
Handel- Messiah -Bolt                        LSO
Der Ring – 13 CD Set –
Knappertsbush 1956 Bayreuth                  Music & Arts
Meistersinger-Goodall-Live Sadler Wells
   -in Englsh                                BBC
Lohengrin – Bayreuth 1958 –
A. Clutens                                   MYTO
Wagner -Tannhäuser -Franz                    EMI
   Konwhschny
Korngold -Das Wunder der Heliane   Decca
Peter Grimes -Vickers/Davis                  Decca
Parsifal Historic 1951 Bayreuth Knappertsbush Teldec
Die Meistersinger Von                        EMI
   Nürnberg-Karajan
Bach -Weihnachtsoratorium –                  BWV 248
   Karl Richter
-1965 Fritz Wunderlich                       Archive
Wagner -Die Feen -Sawallisch                 Orfeo
Der Freischütz – Kleiber                     DG
Handel – Acis and Galatea                    Erato
Der Ring – Hongkong- Jaap Van Zweden
14 CD Set                                    Naxos
Der Ring -Furtwangler -13 CDS Set Intense

Lohengrin- Bayreuth – A. Clutens 1958

## DVDs

| | |
|---|---|
| Wagner Epic Story 3 DVDs | Dolby. |
| Great Composers Mozart (1756-1791) | BBC |
| Pagliacci Leoncavallo /Cavalleria Rusticana | |
| Short operas | |
| Wahnfried -Peter Patzak | Lighthouse |
| Hans Neuenfels, Andris | Nelsons |
| Lohengrin – Bayreuth 2010 | |
| Rienzi 2010 – Berlin,Kerl, Nylund, Lang | Arthaus |
| Andrea Chenier – Alla Scalla 1985 -Carreras, Marton – NVC Arts | |
| Le Corsaire – American Ballet Theatre. | Arthaus |
| The Golden Ring 1965 Film | BBC |
| Lohengrin 2018 Bayreuth | |
| Thielamann, Pitor Beczala | DG |
| Tristan und Isolde -Thielamann | DG |
| The Dream of Gerontius 1968 – Elgar | BBC |
| Peter Grimes – Britten – Zurich 2005 | EMI |
| Beethoven 7,8,9 -Thielemann -Wiener Phil Musikverian – 2010 | Unitel |
| Tristan und Isolde – Bayreuth -Muller, Baremboin | DG |
| Winifred Wagner -Wahnfried 1914-1975 | Syberberg 2006 |
| Great Composers Beethoven | BBC |
| Faust | |

-Gounod, Pappano Terfel
-ROH 2010

Hänsel und Gretel – Humperdinck

Solti, Wiener Phil.                          United

Wagner Dresden – 21st May 2013     United

Alcina Handel Philippe Jaroussky

Mi lusinga il dolce affetto                  Erato

Orlando Furioso 2011 – Vivaldi

Jaroussky, Lemieux

Theatre Des Champs -Elysees

Handel -Theodora 2015                    Erato

Die Thomaner Leipzig
    -800 Year Anniversary

Georg Christoph Biller

Peter Grimes – Britten – 1981- ROH

Parsifal Schiller Berlin – 2015

Tcherniakov, Kamp, Pape, Koch, Tomasson.

Alcina Handel

Wiener Staatsoper – 2010

Harteroids, Kasarova

Hitler's Siegfried – Max                   Medici
    Lorence 1938

Only the Sound Remains –

Philippe Jaroussky 2016 Amsterdam,

Parsifal Bayreuth Wolfgang Wagner 1998

Sinopoli, Elming, Watson,                United
    Struckmann

Osterfestspiele Salzburg 2017

Die Walküre – Staatskepple Dresden

Thielemann, Seiffert, Zeppenfeld, Hartelos,

Kampe, Mayer                             United

Tannhäuser (Paris Version) – 2008

Gambill, Nylund, Meier, Trekel,         Arthaus

Milling, Jordan.
Dvorak Rusalka 2014 NYC
Fleming, Beczala, Magee, The Met      Decca,
Der Freischütz Carl Maria Von Weber 1999
Hamburger Staatsoper.          Arthouse
Venice New Year's Concert 2011 Daniel Hardy

# References and
# Source Material

**Books:**

| | |
|---|---|
| Mozart's Operas-A Critical Study | Edward J. Dent 1947 – Claredon |
| The Diary of Richard Wagner-the Brown Book 1865-1882 | Translation by George Bird 1980 – Camelot |
| The World as Will and Representation | Arthur Schopenhauer |
| -Volume I & Volume II EFJ Payne 1958 | |
| The Real Wagner | Rudolf Sabor 1987 |
| The Life of Richard Wagner: Volume I, (1813-1848), Volume II (1848-1860) Volume III (1859-1866), Volume IV (1866-1885) | Ernest Newman 1966 – Cambridge University Press |
| The Phadon Ring, A Companion Rheingold, Die Walküre, Siegfried, Götterdämmerung. | Rudolf Sabor |
| The Swan King-Ludwig II of Bavaria | McIntosh 2003Tauris |
| The Wagner Clan | Jonathon Carr 2007 – Faber |
| Wagner on Music and Drama | Goldmann & Sprincher 1964 NYC – Decapo, |

| | |
|---|---|
| Wagner's Parsifal – the Journey of a Soul | Peter Bassett 2000 -Wakefield |
| Wagner Pocket Guide | Michael Tanner 2010 – Faber |

Personal diaries and notes, concert programmes.

Personal reviews and reports as Chairman of the Wagner Society of Ireland

Wikipedia

Review Requested:
We'd like to know if you enjoyed the book. Please consider leaving a review on the platform from which you purchased the book.

CPSIA information can be obtained
at www.ICGtesting.com
Printed in the USA
LVHW051312100121
675854LV00007B/293